IMMERSED IN THE LIFE OF GOD

William J. Abraham

IMMERSED IN THE LIFE OF GOD

The Healing Resources of the Christian Faith

Essays in Honor of William J. Abraham

Edited by

Paul L. Gavrilyuk, Douglas M. Koskela, & Jason E. Vickers

WILLIAM B. EERDMANS PUBLISHING COMPANY
GRAND RAPIDS, MICHIGAN / CAMBRIDGE, U.K.

Published 2008 by
Wm. B. Eerdmans Publishing Co.
2140 Oak Industrial Drive N.E., Grand Rapids, Michigan 49505 /
P.O. Box 163, Cambridge CB3 9PU U.K.

Printed in the United States of America

13 12 11 10 09 08   7 6 5 4 3 2 1

Library of Congress Cataloging-in-Publication Data

Immersed in the life of God: the healing resources of the Christian faith:
    essays in honor of William J. Abraham / edited by Paul L. Gavrilyuk,
    Douglas M. Koskela & Jason E. Vickers.
        p.   cm.
    Includes bibliographical references.
    ISBN 978-0-8028-6396-6 (cloth: alk. paper)
    1. Theology. 2. Healing — Religious aspects — Christianity.
    I. Abraham, William J. (William James), 1947-   II. Gavrilyuk, Paul L.
    III. Koskela, Douglas M., 1972-   IV. Vickers, Jason E.

    BR50.I456   2008
    230 — dc22
                                                    2008021260

www.eerdmans.com

Contents

Contents

Introduction

"[Canonical traditions] are not only gifts of the Spirit to be received in humility and joy; they also involve the reception of the Giver of the gifts, the life-giving Holy Spirit who comes to baptize and immerse us into the life of God."[1] Perhaps more than any other, these words represent William Abraham's mature theological vision. They also inspire this volume. It is fitting, therefore, to say a few words at the outset about their author.

An Oxford-educated Irish Methodist, William Abraham is the embodiment of the ecclesial practice historically associated with Methodism itself, namely, itinerancy. Constantly on the move, he is by turns a philosopher, a pastor, an evangelist, a missionary, a catechist, a systematic theologian, a keen observer of politics, a preacher, a Sunday school teacher, a spiritual and theological mentor to students, a distinguished university teaching professor at Southern Methodist University, and a close personal friend to many clergy and professional academics. Those who know him best marvel at his passionate commitment to his vocation. Indeed, it would not be too much to say that William Abraham is a modern-day John Wesley, the primary difference between the two having to do with the mode of transportation: Wesley had his horses; Abraham has his airplanes.[2]

---

1. William J. Abraham, *Canon and Criterion in Christian Theology* (Oxford: Oxford University Press, 1998), p. 54.

2. Wesley was legendary for reading on horseback. Abraham is notorious for devouring entire books on trans-Atlantic flights.

Like his travel schedule, Abraham's mind is at once well-organized and constantly on the move. He is in many respects a polymath, moving effortlessly among a range of intellectual disciplines, including analytic philosophy, philosophy of religion, epistemology, systematic theology, history of Christianity, patristics, evangelism, mission, biblical studies, Wesley studies, politics, and, more recently, international terrorism.

Abraham's theological vision is the fruit of three decades' work. Through the first two decades, Abraham's scholarship ran along two distinct trajectories. The first trajectory reflects his philosophical interests, as indicated by such titles as *Divine Revelation and the Limits of Historical Criticism* (1982, republished in 2000 as an Oxford Scholarly Classic), *An Introduction to the Philosophy of Religion* (1985, still in print), and, most recently, *Crossing the Threshold of Divine Revelation* (2006). Perhaps more than any other Christian philosopher of our time, Abraham has contributed to restoring the epistemological credentials of divine revelation in contemporary theological discourse.

The second trajectory represents his engagement with the life of the church, as evidenced by such titles as *The Coming Great Revival: Recovering the Full Evangelical Tradition* (1984), *The Logic of Evangelism* (1989, still in print), *The Art of Evangelism: Evangelism Carefully Crafted into the Life of the Local Church* (1993), *Waking from Doctrinal Amnesia* (1995), and *The Logic of Renewal* (2003). Abraham conceives of evangelism as a major part of the process of initiation into the church and God's kingdom. This process is a discovery of the means of grace and immersion into the life of God. Discovering the means of grace and discerning the presence and work of the Holy Spirit therein requires prolonged catechesis, a practical task that Abraham undertakes weekly in his local Methodist parish in Dallas, and periodically around the world, in countries as distant as Kazakhstan, Nepal, Malaysia, and Costa Rica.

Over the past decade, Abraham has integrated these two streams into a wide-ranging theological proposal. In his magnum opus, *Canon and Criterion in Christian Theology: From the Fathers to Feminism* (1998), Abraham gives a complex and ground-breaking account of intellectual history in order to show how, during the second millennium A D, the enterprise of theology in the West came to be dominated and undermined by various epistemological strategies. Abraham proposes an expanded and enriched understanding of the notion of canon that includes not only Scripture, but also the creeds, councils, sacraments, sacred images, ministerial orders, and saints. He further developed this understanding of canon in his latest book, *Canonical Theism: A Proposal for Theology and the Church* (2008).

Professor Abraham's enduring interest in mining the riches of the Christian tradition to uncover resources for healing gives this volume its particular shape. While the essays reflect the diversity of his scholarly interests, they are all driven by the concern to highlight the therapeutic import of knowing and loving God. Some contributors explore practices that foster healing, while others examine primarily intellectual resources to be used in addressing various cognitive maladies. Each aims to begin drawing out the possibilities envisioned by Abraham in the following suggestive passage:

> Within her bosom the church possesses the medicine for her many illnesses, and there is no reason to think that someone someday will not find the recipe we need to cure us of our current waywardness. Once the medicine begins to take effect, the grace of God now resisted will be the source of boundless healing; it is the gospel of our Lord and Saviour, Jesus Christ, which alone can save us from our corruption and idolatry.[3]

Addressing a contemporary gap in theological reflection on conversion, Jason E. Vickers offers a fresh treatment that aims to situate conversion within its proper ecclesial setting. He explores the reasons for the neglect of this crucial concept, including a theological reductionism that often accompanies the concept of conversion in many Protestant evangelical subcultures. By reworking the framework in which conversion is understood and attending to the full range of the church's canonical heritage, Vickers suggests that this vital work of the Spirit can be restored to its rightful place on the theological landscape.

Acknowledging the widespread ignorance of basic beliefs and practices among contemporary Christians, Paul L. Gavrilyuk turns to the rich catechetical patterns of the patristic era. Out of the great variety of catechetical practices in the early church, he traces the common elements of the five-stage process of initiation. Gavrilyuk suggests that the ancient catechumenate was the cradle of biblical, moral, liturgical, and systematic

---

3. William J. Abraham, "Inclusivism, Idolatry and the Survival of the (Fittest) Faithful," in Mark Husbands and Daniel J. Treier, eds., *The Community of the Word: Toward an Evangelical Ecclesiology* (Downers Grove, IL: InterVarsity Press, 2005), p. 145.

theologies. The recovery of patristic catechumenate offers much-needed resources for the curing of hearts, souls, and bodies of present-day Christians.

Robert W. Wall turns to the classroom to explore yet another effect of catechetical neglect in the contemporary church: biblical illiteracy. He notes that, in their attempt to foster healthy interpretive practices, Bible faculty often find that students are spiritually debilitated by the academic study of Christian Scripture. In response, Wall engages three theological terms — Scripture, canon, and sacrament — that provide a framework for understanding the essential place of the Bible in spiritual and intellectual formation.

Drawing on the vast resources of the church's worship practices, Geoffrey Wainwright shows that the Christian liturgy is reflective of God's work in healing a broken world. In particular, he suggests that God's gracious activity calls forth our cooperative participation through works of piety and works of mercy. Engaging Wesleyan and ecumenical sources, Wainwright develops the theme of healing as it is displayed in the liturgical practices of the Christian tradition.

Ellen T. Charry explores the formative and therapeutic roles of both civic and Christian symbolic rites. Her account of ritual ceremonies captures their pedagogical, social, and moral import for a given community and its members. By reflecting on the similarities and differences between civic and Christian ceremonies, Charry brings out the particular complexity of Christian life in a broader society that makes claims of national identity on its members.

In light of the theological and practical problem of disunity in the church, Douglas M. Koskela reflects on ecclesial reconciliation as a healing practice. With attention to both ecumenical and intra-ecclesial relationships, he examines the impetus toward and patterns of reconciliatory practice. Koskela outlines six categories of ecclesial reconciliation: dialogue, recognition of areas of agreement and disagreement, confession, forgiveness, commitment, and communion. He suggests that, by approaching reconciliation in a posture of humility and attentiveness to its own canonical riches, the church has genuine hope of restoration and revitalization.

Turning to the healing of our cognitive practice, Frederick D. Aquino examines the epistemological potential of patristic sources in identifying and developing crucial virtues of the mind. Building on the work in contemporary virtue epistemology, he engages the conception of deification proffered by Maximus the Confessor to show the link between proper belief-forming practices and well-formed character. Furthermore, Aquino argues that regulative practices for acquiring knowledge of God cannot be reduced merely to the accumulation of justified true beliefs about God, but involve the transformation and healing of cognitive capacities, such as discernment and judgment, in deification.

R. R. Reno reflects on the tension between the confessional demands of Christian faith and the deep wariness about such submission in modernity. He offers a critique of this modern suspicion from a surprising source: Friedrich Nietzsche's *On the Genealogy of Morals*. Reno suggests that Nietzsche recognized a posture of self-denial as inevitable even in the modern alternatives to Christian faith. In this light, the canonical practice of confession is illustrative of a fundamental feature of the human condition.

Immersion into the life of God has profound implications for our moral reflection, as Thomas D. Sullivan and Sandra Menssen suggest in their discussion of fundamental human rights. They develop what they call "the suicide argument" to show that a wholly secular case is unable to ground absolute human rights. Sullivan and Menssen contend that the inadequacy of ethical visions that do not appeal to the divine points out the essential place of divine revelation in moral reasoning.

Finally, Jerry L. Walls turns to the need for healing in a world where horrendous evil is prevalent. He notes the sense of moral outrage that emerges from our recognition that the world is not as it should be, even on the part of those who reject classical Christian theism. After considering a variety of options regarding the nature of reality, Walls suggests that only belief in a good and all-powerful God is able to acknowledge the reality of evil while still offering hope for the healing of the cosmos.

To Know and to Love God Truly:
The Healing Power of Conversion

Jason E. Vickers

In recent systematic theology, conversion is a topic that has fallen on hard times. Generally speaking, systematic theologians have left the topic to the sociology of religion and to popular Christian literature.[1] Critical and creative theological reflection on conversion is, to say the least, difficult to find.[2] The lack of interest among Christian systematic theologians in conversion is a regrettable development. Failing to pay attention to conversion abandons both the concept of conversion and the ecclesial practices associated with it to ambiguity, distortion, and — in the worst cases — to abuse.

After years of neglect, the time is ripe to reconsider this important concept and its attendant ecclesial practices. To that end, I will begin by identifying two causes for the neglect of conversion in much contemporary

---

1. The most important exception to this is Karl Barth, *Church Dogmatics,* trans. G. F. Bromiley (Edinburgh: T&T Clark, 1958), IV.2, pp. 553-84. For sociological perspectives on conversion, see Lewis R. Rambo, *Understanding Religious Conversion* (New Haven: Yale University Press, 1993). See also Robert W. Hefner, ed., *Conversion to Christianity: Historical and Anthropological Perspectives on a Great Transformation* (Berkeley: University of California Press, 1993).

2. There is a substantial body of recent work on conversion in the early church. What is missing is contemporary and constructive theological reflection on conversion. For conversion in the early church, see esp. the work of Thomas M. Finn, including *From Death to Rebirth: Ritual and Conversion in Antiquity* (Mahwah, NJ: Paulist Press, 1997) and *Early Christian Baptism and the Catechumenate: West and East Syria* (Collegeville, MN: Liturgical Press, 1992).

theology: the lingering effects of Christendom on the one hand, and the widespread association of conversion with a particular subculture within evangelical Protestantism on the other. I will then explain why the conception of conversion prominent within that subculture is theologically problematic.[3] Next, I will attempt to rehabilitate the concept of conversion for theological reflection by reworking the theological framework in which a Christian understanding of conversion is situated and by reconnecting conversion to the sacramental life of the church.

Conversion: Causes of Neglect

A good place to begin an inquiry into conversion is with the chief causes of neglect. Why do theologians avoid the topic of conversion, except perhaps to make disparaging remarks about worn-out caricatures of parking-lot or television evangelists? In my judgment, there are two primary causes for the neglect of conversion. Since it has received far greater attention in recent theology, I will deal with the first cause expeditiously. And while I will spend more time presenting and reflecting on the second cause, it should be noted that the two causes mutually reinforce one another.

The first cause for the neglect of conversion has to do with the effects of Christendom. For many centuries, Christendom has meant that being Christian and being a part of society were one and the same. On this model, Christianity was seamlessly woven into the fabric of Western civilization. Virtually everyone was presumed to be Christian by virtue of his or her membership in the Christian society at large.[4] Therefore, conversion was not thought about in some quarters in any substantial way.

The second cause for the neglect of conversion is a tendency to associate conversion with a way of practicing evangelism prominent in a subcul-

---

3. The subculture that I have in mind is not limited to any one Protestant denomination. It can be found within Baptist, Lutheran, Pentecostal, Reformed, and Wesleyan traditions. This subculture is also widespread in many nondenominational churches.

4. Among the many recent critics of Christendom, Stanley Hauerwas is surely the best known. For a presentation of the issues at stake, see his *After Christendom?* (Nashville: Abingdon, 1991). Of course, Hauerwas is not the first to see the problems with Christendom or with what some call "cultured Christianity." Indeed, similar critiques were made in very powerful ways by Karl Barth and Søren Kierkegaard with regard to the church in 20th-century Germany and 19th-century Denmark, respectively.

ture within evangelical Protestantism. Invoking caricatures of parking-lot and television evangelists is simply a way of indicting both a particular practice of evangelism and the network of supporting theological commitments that supports the practice within that subculture. And while the standard criticisms of both the understanding of conversion and the approach to evangelism in this subculture of evangelical Protestantism will be familiar to most (e.g., they are highly individualistic, other-worldly, and the like), a brief review is nonetheless in order.

In *The Logic of Evangelism,* William Abraham provides a splendid summary of the concept of conversion and the practice of evangelism within this evangelical Protestant subculture. In a passage worth quoting at length, he says:

> Pietists, Methodists, and Revivalists over the years have given the distinct impression that *the heart of evangelism has nothing to do with the rites and ceremonies of the classical liturgies of the church.* For them, evangelism is centered on the new birth and conversion; the individual stands alone before God in need of personal regeneration, which no church can supply; only God through the action of the Holy Spirit can meet this need. The church, rather than helping in this arena, has been at best indifferent and at worst thoroughly hostile. This is the impression one receives from reviewing the history of modern evangelism within the Protestant tradition.[5]

Abraham continues: "[Conversion] is now the badge of a party within Christianity; it is under a cloud of suspicion; and it is divorced from the sacramental life of the church." Moreover, the language of conversion "has become buried in a theological underworld that has strained it to its limits."[6] The outcome of these developments is predictable.

> Fruitless debates about the mechanics and logistics of divine grace in the soul have elbowed out the native sense that the language of new birth once transmitted. In addition, attempts to articulate the morphology of conversion have turned much of the theology of evangelism, which this

---

5. William J. Abraham, *The Logic of Evangelism* (Grand Rapids: Eerdmans, 1989), p. 118 (italics added).

6. Abraham, *Logic of Evangelism,* p. 122.

language fosters, into an introspective anthropocentrism that neglects the richer tapestry of Christian theology and encourages the development of a narrow and inadequate piety.[7]

Many will no doubt resonate with Abraham's summary. For example, David H. C. Read offers a very similar account of the understanding of conversion and the practice of evangelism prominent in many evangelical Protestant circles. Thus, like Abraham, Read is especially keen to say that "the message is directed to the individual *as if conversion has nothing to do with the holy, catholic church, nor the communion of saints.*"[8]

In the end, Abraham's analysis makes the same general point as the caricatures of parking-lot and television evangelists, albeit in more sophisticated terms. Indeed, Abraham himself cannot help resorting to the familiar caricatures:

> Evangelists offer friendship and love for sale through radio and television, and educational credentials are used as passwords into the lives of the gullible. The whole operation depends on a personality rather than on serious preaching. . . . In all, modern evangelism has become a kind of entrepreneurial industry organized, funded, and run like a modern corporation.[9]

Given this analysis, it is not difficult to see why contemporary theologians tend to neglect the concept of conversion. The concept of conversion is so widely associated with "a party within Christianity" that it is virtually irretrievable. The buildup of connotations, images, and stereotypes surrounding the concept of conversion prohibits its rehabilitation for persons who do not belong to the relevant party. Those who might wish to relocate the concept within a wider and richer theological tradition will first have to disabuse people of these deeply embedded stereotypes and images — stereo-

---

7. Abraham, *Logic of Evangelism,* p. 122.

8. David H. C. Read, "The Evangelical Protestant Understanding of Conversion," in H. Newton Malony and Samuel Southard, eds., *Handbook of Religious Conversion* (Birmingham: Religious Education Press, 1992), p. 142 (italics added).

9. Abraham, *Logic of Evangelism,* p. 200. Elsewhere he says: "In fact, much of modern mass evangelism has reached such a nadir of public scandal and disorder that one wonders whether the operation represents an evangelistic underworld of spiritual and theological corruption" (p. 10).

types and images confirmed in popular literature and film, mainstream news media, and a range of televangelism programs. Therfore, it should come as no surprise that some theologians regard the concept of conversion as more trouble than it is worth.

However strong the temptations to abandon the concept of conversion, I believe that it is worth a second look. The key here is not so to focus on familiar examples of the abuse of the practice of evangelism and the call to conversion that one misses the most crucial insight embedded in Abraham's analysis, an insight that can be developed in aid of a recovery of the concept of conversion for the church today. The insight I have in mind is that the concept of conversion has been "divorced from the sacramental life of the church," resulting in "the development of a narrow and inadequate piety."

What exactly is the problem with the separation of conversion from the sacramental life of the church? More specifically, how does this separation result in a narrow and inadequate piety? Before proposing an alternative conception of conversion, I want to explore these questions in greater detail.

Conversion and Theological Reductionism

What is really at stake in the separation of conversion from the sacramental life of the church is a theological reductionism that is spiritually disastrous. The reductionism I have in mind cuts right across the classical theological curriculum, including the doctrine of God as well as the doctrines of human nature, sin, and salvation. When conversion is not intimately related to the sacramental life of the church, one can expect to find a severe truncating of no fewer than five of the loci of systematic theology. To be sure, the theological implications are often unstated, but they are no less real and no less dangerous for it.[10]

10. Here I need to emphasize that I am speaking only of conceptions of and approaches to conversion that are not *intimately related to the fullness of the church's sacramental life.* Thus the following account of theological reductionism does not apply to all evangelical Protestant churches or to the Roman Catholic Church. On the contrary, many evangelical Protestant traditions conceive of and approach conversion in ways that are directly related to the sacramental life of the church. A good example of this can be seen in the conception of and approach to conversion in the Wesleyan tradition. See Kenneth J. Collins and John H. Tyson, eds., *Conversion in the Wesleyan Tradition* (Nashville: Abingdon, 2001).

First and foremost, there is a truncating of the Christian doctrine of sin. This is deeply ironic, because approaches to conversion divorced from the sacramental life of the church typically begin with the doctrine of original sin and total depravity, registering the need for forgiveness, for relief of one's debt to God, for pardon from punishment, and the like. The reductionism occurs not because sin is left out, but because the true nature and consequences of sin are not carefully considered. More specifically, the nature and consequences of sin are often conceived of in legal or juridical terms. Sin has to do with the transgressing of divine laws and not with the disordering of human desire and human love. What is missing here is what Ellen Charry, following Augustine, refers to as the "struggle to know, love, and enjoy God." This struggle is "basic to human life." It is "the one from which all other struggles arise and into which they dissolve."[11]

The really deep issue here concerns "the ambiguity of love and the instability of desire." The human struggle with sin is, at its root, a struggle with the disordering of the self that is the direct result of disordered desire and disordered love. Indeed, disordered desire and disordered love are the sources of "our misery and suffering in this life."[12] The problem here is straightforward. We desire and we love all kinds of things as though they were God. In the process, we fail to desire and to love the one thing that will truly bring happiness; the knowledge, love, and enjoyment of God.

Unfortunately, that is not the end of the matter. An even deeper problem is our inability to do anything about the situation in which we find ourselves. We continually desire and love things as though they were God, regardless of how many times the things that we love and desire turn out to be disappointments. We continually seek enjoyment and true happiness in all the wrong places. In essence, we cannot help ourselves.[13]

When conversion is separated from the life of the church, these dimensions of the "human situation" are often nowhere in sight. The point of conversion in this case is to secure forgiveness and pardon for our sins, but sin here is clearly a matter of doing the wrong thing. Unfortunately, *loving and*

11. Ellen T. Charry, "Augustine of Hippo: Father of Christian Psychology," *Anglican Theological Review* 88, no. 4 (2006): 577-78.

12. Charry, "Augustine of Hippo," p. 578.

13. What is most helpful about Charry's essay is the contrast that she draws between Augustine's Christian psychology and modern secular psychology. The latter tells us "you can do it!" The former comes clean, admitting that, without divine assistance, we cannot improve our situation.

desiring the wrong thing is an even more intractable and debilitating problem than *doing* the wrong thing.[14]

At this stage, we are already in the territory of the second theological reductionism accompanying understandings of conversion not intimately related to the sacramental life of the church. Reductionist views of sin mask reductionist views of human nature. The psychology at work is unbearably thin, foregrounding human intellect and will quite apart from desire, not to mention the deep springs from which human desires flow. The basic scheme works like this: humans somehow know God's law (the intellectual component), but they consistently choose to disobey God's law (the volitional component). What is missing here is any sustained reflection on why human beings willfully disobey the laws of God.

More specifically, what is missing from this account of human psychology is an appreciation of the extent to which humans are creatures of desire. Before we will, we desire. Unfortunately, many of our desires are misplaced. Either we desire the wrong thing or we desire things in inappropriate ways or to an inappropriate degree. This includes our desires for food, sex, political power, and celebrity status. Even more important are the deep springs from which misplaced human desires or disordered human loves flow. If we break God's laws, we do not do so because of a failure of will, as though being human were primarily a matter of grit and determination. The problem is deeper than that.

Unfortunately, we are getting ahead of ourselves. We need to continue our analysis of what has gone wrong theologically. We will return to the deep springs of misplaced desire later on.

A third kind of theological reductionism follows naturally from reductionist views of human nature and sin, namely, reductionist views of the atonement and of salvation. What humans need is pardon for transgression and the appeasement of the demands of God's righteousness. The good news on this analysis is that Jesus Christ has taken our place in meeting the demands of righteousness. He stands in for us as a substitute, suffering the punishment that is our due.[15] In doing so, he secures pardon for our sins;

---

14. For a more robust account of sin, see Cornelius Plantinga, Jr., *Not the Way It's Supposed to Be: A Breviary of Sin* (Grand Rapids: Eerdmans, 1995).

15. For complementary views of the atonement, see James Beilby and Paul R. Eddy, eds., *The Nature of the Atonement* (Downers Grove, IL: InterVarsity, 2006). For an extended critique of substitutionary views of the atonement, see J. Denny Weaver, *The Nonviolent Atonement* (Grand Rapids: Eerdmans, 2001); see also Paul Fiddes, *Past Event and Present Salvation* (Louisville: Westminster Press, 1989).

salvation is thus construed as pardon, as relief from debt, and so on.[16] Overcoming the real problem that truly haunts humanity — the problem of disordered love and disordered desire — is nowhere in sight.

A fourth area of theological reductionism has to do with humans' role in salvation. When conversion is separated from the sacramental life of the church, humans must do two things to lay claim to salvation (as pardon for sin). Put simply, they must confess their guilt, and they must confess Jesus Christ as Lord; upon making these two confessions, they are converted. Again, coming to grips with the problem of disordered love and disordered desire is not part of the equation, except insofar as loving and desiring the wrong things resulted in actions worthy of divine punishment. Apart from the sacramental life of the church, the human role in conversion is reduced from a deep struggling with the problem of disordered desire and love to a simple confession of guilt and a request for pardon. Indeed, being converted is often depicted as something simple or even "easy" to do.

The fifth and final area of reductionism has to do with the absence of the person and work of the Holy Spirit. Generally speaking, the Holy Spirit's role in conversion is reduced to an epistemic one. The Spirit confirms that the doctrines of original sin, total depravity, substitutionary atonement, and salvation as pardon are true. Apart from the sacramental life of the church, the means of grace through which the Holy Spirit assists people in coming truly to know, love, and to enjoy God is obscured from sight.[17] Without the presence and work of the Spirit to this end, conversion amounts to obtaining a pardon from a God one does not truly know and cannot possibly love or enjoy.

Having sketched the causes of neglect, I will now attempt to rehabilitate the concept of conversion for Christian theology today. To this end, my chief objective will be to develop an understanding of conversion on which a more adequate piety might be based. Doing so will require two things. First, we need to rework the theological framework for a Christian account of conversion, paying close attention to human nature and sin as well as to the work of Christ and salvation. Second, we need to think carefully about the vital relationship between conversion and the sacramental life of the church.

---

16. For an alternative view of salvation, see Vigen Guroian, "Salvation: Divine Therapy," *Theology Today* 61 (2004): 309-21.

17. For the means of grace in the life of the church, see especially William J. Abraham, Jason E. Vickers, and Natalie B. Van Kirk, eds., *Canonical Theism: A Proposal for Theology and the Church* (Grand Rapids: Eerdmans, 2008).

Unfortunately, in the space of this chapter I will only be able to make a start on both of these fronts. The descriptions of a theological framework for conversion and of the role of the sacramental life of the church in conversion that follow are rudimentary at best. Nevertheless, they are an indication of the direction in which I want to go.

Reworking the Theological Framework of Conversion

The first thing needed for an adequate account of conversion is a more substantive and compelling theological framework. Above all, we need a more substantial account of human nature and sin. We can cut to the chase here by focusing on the way in which sin is a manifestation of misplaced human desire.

On the basis of one of the most common definitions, sin is simply a willful transgression of a known law of God. Whatever the merits of this definition, its chief weakness is that it does not get at the deep cause of sin. To say that humans intentionally or volitionally sin does not tell us why they do so. At one level, sin is a manifestation of misplaced human desire. We choose to do certain things because we desire either the things themselves or some outcome that we believe will result from doing those things. To sin is to love or to desire the wrong thing; alternatively, it is to love or to desire things in inappropriate ways or to an inappropriate degree. Thus we might spend our lives pursuing fame and fortune without regard for other persons, not to mention God.

At a deeper level, however, we need to ask ourselves how this happens. How is it that we come to love and to desire the wrong things? How is it that we come to desire or to love things in inappropriate ways or to an inappropriate degree? What are the origins of misplaced human desire?

Among the deepest springs of misplaced human desire are fear and distrust.[18] Indeed, human psychology is beset by a vast range of fears. We fear for our lives. We fear that we will not have enough to eat or to drink, or we fear that someone will break into our homes and murder our families. We fear being victimized by those with power over us. We fear that no one

---

18. I am not arguing that fear and distrust are the only springs of misplaced desire; I would readily concede that pride is also among the deepest springs of misplaced desire. I am simply suggesting that fear and distrust play crucial roles.

will remember us when we are gone. We fear that terrorists will detonate a dirty bomb in our city. We fear that we will not measure up in the eyes of God.

Human fear is inextricably related to distrust. Indeed, the relationship between fear and distrust is so intimate that it is often very difficult to tell which comes first. At times our fears give rise to distrust. Because we fear for our lives, we do not trust our neighbors. At other times, distrust gives rise to fear: because we do not trust our neighbors, we fear for our lives.

Fear and distrust are the deep springs of misplaced human desires and therefore of sin. For example, if we fear that no one will remember us when we are gone, then we might seek out celebrity status, or we might spend our lives writing books that will remain on the shelves long after our demise. If we fundamentally distrust others in the workplace, then we might expend all of our energies scaling the corporate ladder so as to limit the number of people who have power over us. In essence, we spend our lives trying to gain control, to limit risks, to rise above or even to eliminate the competition. Deep down we know that human life really is the survival of the fittest.

With this more substantial analysis of human nature and sin in place, we can begin to develop a more substantial view of the life and work of Christ. Alongside substitutionary and satisfaction views of the atonement, we need to think carefully about how the Incarnation addresses the really deep problem of human fear and distrust. It does so in at least two ways.

One way that the Incarnation addresses the problem of fear and distrust is by giving us a glimpse of what a human life looks like when it is not ruled by fear and distrust. Put positively, the life and work of Christ show us what it means to trust God entirely. Indeed, whatever else we might want to say about the life and work of Christ, one thing is undeniable. Jesus trusts his heavenly Father. This is profoundly illustrated in Luke 4:1-13: after his baptism, Jesus sojourns for forty days and nights in the wilderness. During this episode, the devil tempts Jesus three times. Each temptation is fundamentally an appeal to fear and distrust. In the first temptation, the devil appeals to the human fear for life itself, urging Jesus to satisfy his hunger by acquiring food for himself. In the second temptation, the devil appeals to the human desire for political power and control, which is nothing if it is not an appeal to fear. In the third and final temptation, the devil appeals to the human desire for supernatural power and control.

In each of the three temptations in the wilderness, Jesus refuses to give in to fear and distrust. He is not given over to misplaced desires precisely because he trusts his Father in heaven. Because he trusts his Father in heaven, he does not live out fear; because he is not overcome by fear, he is not ruled by the need to take control of his circumstances. Nor is this the last time Jesus exhibits such fundamental trust. On the contrary, his trust in his heavenly Father manifests itself time and again throughout his life, most notably when he gives over his life to death on the cross.

Were we to stop here, the message would be clear enough. Conversion is not simply a legal matter of securing pardon for our sins. Nor is it simply an intellectual matter having to do with assent to basic Christian doctrines. To be sure, conversion involves both of these things. Yet, if we take the etymology of the word seriously, conversion also involves a fundamental change in the way that we live our lives. Etymologically, the word conversion means "to turn." More specifically, the Hebrew term from which the concept derives *(shub)* is often closely associated with another term, which means "to walk" *(halakah)*. Taken together, to be converted is to stop walking one way and to begin walking in another way. Nor is this simply a matter of direction. It has to do with the way one walks, which is to say, the way one lives. From a Christian point of view, conversion entails living life the way Jesus did. To be converted is to turn from a way of walking or living that is ruled by fear and distrust to a way of walking and living that is ruled by trust in God.

Unfortunately, this leaves one very important question unanswered. How is this possible? At this stage, the natural temptation is to object that Jesus was capable of overcoming fear and distrust because he was God. Suffice it to say, we are not God. Therefore, it is unreasonable to expect the same level of trust from us that we find exhibited in the life of Jesus. This is simply too much to ask.

The problem with this objection is that it runs the risk of denying the fullness of Jesus' humanity. It implies that, precisely when Jesus faced the deepest of human temptations, his divine nature somehow took over. Suppose for a moment that it did not. Suppose that Jesus wrestled with fear and distrust all the way down. How, then, was he able to resist the temptations of misplaced desire? How did he avoid giving himself over to the desire for control or for political power? Most importantly, how did he keep his desire rightly ordered and rightly directed toward his heavenly Father?

In raising these questions, we are really asking after the source of fear and mistrust. Why is it that fear and mistrust take hold in the first place? The answer is simple and straightforward. We are given over to fear and to mistrust because we are not sure that God loves us. We do not know or we do not believe that we are the object of God's affection and desire. We may even suspect that God is either a vengeful deity bent on our destruction or an indifferent deity who is not paying close attention to our needs.

Even a cursory reading of the life of Jesus reveals that the Son is aware that he is the object of the Father's affection and desire. It is precisely this awareness that enables Jesus fundamentally to trust his heavenly Father and therefore not to succumb to misplaced desire, most notably the desire to secure his own life. Thus it is no accident that, just prior to the wilderness temptations, the Father exclaims, "You are My beloved Son, in You I am well-pleased" (Luke 3:22, NASB).

This brings us to the other way in which the Incarnation addresses the deep problem of human fear and distrust. The Incarnation is about more than appeasing the divine wrath of God the Father. It is equally, if not more, the ultimate expression of the divine love that God the Father has for us. Thus in his prayer to the Father near the end of his time on earth, Jesus himself can say that he came "so that the world may know that You sent Me, and loved them, even as You have loved Me" (John 17:23, NASB).

It is even possible to think of Christ's death as exemplifying divine love rather than divine wrath. Indeed, Clement of Alexandria depicts the eternal begetting of the Son, the Incarnation and the death of Christ in terms of divine love:

> It was in his love that the Father became the nature which derives from woman, and the great proof of this is the Son whom he begot from himself, and the love that was the fruit produced from his love. For this he came down, for this he assumed human nature, for this he willingly endured the sufferings of humanity, that by being reduced to the measure of our weakness, he might raise us to the measure of his power. And just before he poured out his offering, when he gave himself as a ransom, he left us a new testament: "I give you my love" (John 13:34).[19]

To apprehend that "God so loved the world, that He gave His only begotten Son" (John 3:16a, NASB) is no small thing. On the contrary, seeing and knowing that we are the object of God's affection and desire is prerequi-

---

19. Clement of Alexandria, *Quis Dives Salvetur* 37 in G. W. Butterworth, ed., *Clement of Alexandria: The Exhortation to the Greeks,* Loeb Classical Library (Cambridge, MA: Harvard University Press, 1960), p. 346.

site to any change worthy of the name conversion. If we are to walk as Jesus walked, then our desires must cease to be ruled by fear and distrust. If we are to desire God above all and to sublimate all other desires to our desire for God, then we must first see and understand God's love for us in Christ. This is exactly the point made by Peter Abelard:

> Now it seems to us that we have been justified by the blood of Christ and reconciled to God in this way: through this unique act of grace manifested to us — in that his Son has taken upon himself our nature and preserved therein in teaching us by word and example even unto death — he has more fully bound us to himself by love; with the result that our hearts should be enkindled by such a gift of divine grace and true charity should now not shrink from enduring anything for him. . . . So does [Christ] bear witness *that he came for the express purpose of spreading this true liberty of love amongst men.*[20]

The problem, of course, is that we are constantly tempted to believe otherwise. We are tempted to believe that God does not love us. Even if we believe that God loves us, we are constantly tempted to think that God's love may not be enough in a world in which everyone is out to get us. After all, our lives consist of daily reminders that we cannot trust — that we dare not trust — the persons around us. God may love us, but we know only one way to live. Our conversion is perpetually interrupted.

Can anything be done about this? This question brings us to the second thing necessary for a more adequate understanding of conversion. Having begun to rework the theological framework of conversion, we need now to explore the role of the sacramental life of the church in conversion.

Conversion and the Sacramental Life of the Church

The good news is that God has not left us to our own devices. Giving up our fears and our distrust is not simply a matter of gritting our teeth or redoubling our efforts. Nor is coming to know we are truly the object of God's de-

---

20. Peter Abailard, "Exposition of the Epistle to the Romans," in Eugene R. Fairweather, ed., *A Scholastic Miscellany: Anselm to Ockham* (Philadelphia: Westminster, 1956), pp. 282-83.

sire. On the contrary, God has taken the initiative in the Incarnation of Jesus Christ and in the sending of the Holy Spirit to dwell among us and to sanctify us. In the Incarnation, God reveals to us the true likeness of humanity. In the sending of the Holy Spirit, God sets about both *awakening* us to God's love for us in Christ and *renewing* us therein. The work of Christ in revelation and the work of the Holy Spirit in awakening and renewing are intimately related to one another. Therefore, Karl Barth is exactly right when he says, "Revealed to him as truth, the reality that God is for him and he for God sets him in this movement, in the *conversio* which is as such his *renovatio*" [sic].[21]

Nor does God's initiative end with the Incarnation or with Pentecost. Rather, the Holy Spirit makes available in the sacramental life of the church the means whereby we can come to know and to enjoy God's love for us in Christ and to be liberated therein from the tyranny of fear and distrust. Indeed, as things turn out, the Holy Spirit has made available more than we could need or ask for.[22]

A good way to think about the person and work of the Holy Spirit in the sacramental life of the church is to regard our fear and distrust and the misplaced desires that result from these as a kind of spiritual sickness. Over against this, we can think of the Holy Spirit as a physician or healer and the church as a hospital for those who are spiritually sick. Moreover, we can think of the means of grace that make up the sacramental life of the church as the medicine through which the Holy Spirit works to facilitate our healing, that is, our conversion.

This is exactly how the presence and work of the Holy Spirit are often thought of in the Christian tradition. For example, in his defense of sacred images, John of Damascus says:

> Suppose I have few books, or little leisure for reading, *but walk into the spiritual hospital — that is to say, a church* — with my soul choking from the prickles of thorny thoughts, and thus afflicted I see before me the

---

21. Karl Barth, *Church Dogmatics*, trans. G. F. Bromiley (Edinburgh: T&T Clark, 1958), IV.2, 561. It is worth noting that Barth locates his very helpful discussion of conversion within the framework of a doctrine of sanctification. Thus, for Barth, conversion is from beginning to end the work of the Holy Spirit in the lives of humans.

22. For the Holy Spirit's provision of gifts to the church for our salvation, see Jason E. Vickers, "The Canonical Heritage of the Church: Medicine of the Holy Spirit," in Abraham, Vickers, and Van Kirk, eds., *Canonical Theism*.

brilliance of the icon. I am refreshed as if in a verdant meadow, and thus my soul is led to glorify God. I marvel at the martyr's endurance, at the crown he won, and inflamed with burning zeal I fall down to worship God through His martyr, and so receive salvation.[23]

The provision of sacred images is only one of the means of grace through which the Spirit is present and at work in the church, healing us of our fears and misplaced desires and bringing about our desire for God. Thus Irenaeus observes: "God established in the Church the apostles, the prophets, the doctors and all the other effects of the working of the Spirit in which those who do not run to the church do not share."[24] Indeed, the Holy Spirit gives such a plentitude of means for our healing that Irenaeus has to admit, "It is impossible to say how many charisms the church receives throughout the world from God in the name of Jesus Christ who was crucified under Pontius Pilate."[25] William Abraham echoes Irenaeus's judgment:

> From the beginning, there were charismatic gifts in the church. These were varied, serving the diverse needs of the body and her ministries. The gifts were so abundant that no formal list was adequate to capture their nature or number.[26]

While it is surely correct to emphasize the sheer generosity of the Holy Spirit, it is also the case that, over time, the church has identified certain means of grace as proven instruments of the Spirit. Through these means of grace, the Spirit brings about our conversion, enabling us to walk as Jesus walked in the sure knowledge that we are the objects of God's desire and affection. The proper term for this process of identification is *canonization*. Across the centuries, therefore, the church has canonized an entire range of materials, persons, and practices through which the Holy Spirit has been present and continually at work.

Through these means of grace, the Holy Spirit helps us taste and see that God truly loves and desires us. As a result of this, the Holy Spirit further

---

23. John of Damascus, *On the Divine Images,* trans. David Anderson (Crestwood, NY: St. Vladimir's Seminary Press, 1980), p. 39 (italics added). John is commenting on a sermon attributed to St. Basil that is entitled "On the Martyr Gordius."

24. Irenaeus, *Adv. haer.* 3.24.1.

25. Irenaeus, *Adv. haer.* 2.32.4.

26. Abraham, *The Logic of Renewal* (Grand Rapids: Eerdmans, 2003), p. 159.

enables us to love and to enjoy God and one another. These gifts of the Spirit include creeds and other catechetical materials; Scripture and doctrine; baptism, Eucharist, and other sacraments; sacred images, canonical liturgies, and hymnody; as well as canons of martyrs and saints, fathers and great teachers of the faith, and various forms of ministry. Taken together, the gifts of the Holy Spirit constitute the canonical heritage of the church.[27]

Four things are especially worth noting about the presence and converting work of the Holy Spirit in the canonical heritage of the church. First, the various components of the canonical heritage of the church do not all have the same function. Thus Scripture does not do the work of the Eucharist, and the Eucharist cannot do the work of episcopacy.[28] Chrysostom captures this point in the following:

> In adopting the best possible way of life, you may be spurred on to emulation by someone else's example; but when it is false doctrine that the soul is suffering from, words are urgently needed, not only for the safety of the Church's members, but to meet the attacks of outsiders as well.[29]

Second, some components of the canonical heritage of the church are more vital during the early stages of conversion, while others are more vital after the period of initiation. For example, catechesis and baptism play a crucial role early on. In catechesis, people come to know who God is and what God is like and to respond accordingly. Indispensable for this instruction, of course, are the canons of Scripture, creeds, and doctrine. Similarly, the Eucharist typically takes on great significance after baptism, as God's love for us is made manifest in the real presence of Jesus Christ. Thus Thomas M. Finn can identify four basic stages of conversion during which various components of the canonical heritage are more or less prominent. Finn says:

---

27. The term "canonical heritage of the church" was coined by William J. Abraham in *Canon and Criterion in Christian Theology: From the Fathers to Feminism* (Oxford: Oxford University Press, 1998), see esp. chap. 2. For an extensive treatment of the various components of the canonical heritage of the church, see Abraham, Vickers, and Van Kirk, eds., *Canonical Theism: A Proposal for Theology and the Church.*

28. See William J. Abraham, *Canon and Criterion in Christian Theology,* pp. 27-56.

29. John Chrysostom, *Six Books on the Priesthood,* trans. Graham Neville (Crestwood, NY: St. Vladimir's Theological Seminary Press, 2002), p. 115.

For those ancients who sought the Christian "Way," the journey had clearly marked stages: (1) a period of preparation that emphasized instruction and testing and involved personal struggle; (2) penultimate preparations for baptism also characterized by instruction, testing, and ritual struggle; (3) baptismal immersion; and (4) post-baptismal "homecoming" celebrations, which included the Eucharist.[30]

Third, while the various components of the canonical heritage of the church each have distinctive functions, they also should be seen as working cooperatively in our conversion. Consider Athanasius's remark concerning the importance of the lives of the saints for the profitable reading of Scripture.

> But for the searching and right understanding of the Scriptures there is need of a good life and a pure soul, and for Christian virtue to guide the mind to grasp, so far as human nature can, the truth concerning God the Word. One cannot possibly understand the teaching of the saints unless one has a pure mind and is trying to imitate their life.[31]

Similarly, consider Nicholas Cabasilas's marvelous description of the way prayers, psalms, Scriptures, and the Eucharist work together in the context of the liturgy:

> The prayers turn us towards God and obtain for us pardon for our sins; the psalms make God look favourably upon us, and draw to us that outflowing of mercy which is the result of such propitiation. . . . As for the lessons from the Holy Scripture, which proclaim the goodness of God, and his love for men, but also the severity of his justice and judgment, they instill in our souls the fear of the Lord, enkindle in us love for him, and thereby arouse in us great eagerness and zeal for the observance of his commandments. All these things, which make the souls of both priest and people better and more divine, make them fit for reception and preservation of the holy mysteries, which is the proper aim of the liturgy.[32]

---

30. Finn, *Early Christian Baptism and the Catechumenate*, p. 3.

31. Athanasius, *De Incarnatione* 57.

32. Nicholas Cabasilas, *A Commentary on the Divine Liturgy*, trans. J. M. Hussey and P. A. McNulty (London: S.P.C.K., 1983), p. 26.

Fourth, while all of the components of the canonical heritage ideally work together, it is not the case that conversion requires every component. It is to be expected that the Holy Spirit will use some means more than others in bringing about the conversion of particular persons. The early church fathers pick up on this when they note that sacred images are of special benefit for the illiterate. Thus John of Damascus says:

> For just as the words edify the ear, so also the image stimulates the eye. What the book is to the literate, the image is to the illiterate. Just as words speak to the ear, so the image speaks to sight; it brings understanding.[33]

Given the extent to which we suffer from misplaced desires born of fear and distrust, such a range of medicine is precisely what is needed. The truth is that we encounter on a daily basis situations that threaten to catapult us back into a life of fear and distrust, undermining our knowledge that we are the object of God's love and affection. At every turn we are tempted to do whatever it takes to get control of our lives, to eliminate risks, even to eliminate other persons who threaten us.

If this is true of us individually, it is equally true of our life together in the body of Christ. The church may be a hospital, but it is not immune to disease. Therefore, concerning the work of the priesthood, Chrysostom observes:

> People who are keen for athletic fitness need doctors and trainers and a careful diet and continual exercise and any amount of other precautions. For the neglect of a small detail in these matters upsets and spoils the whole scheme. Then what about those whose vocation it is to look after this Body which has to contend, not against flesh and blood, but against unseen powers? How can they keep it spotless and sound, unless they possess superhuman wisdom and fully understand the treatment suitable for the soul? *Or do you not realize that that Body is liable to more diseases and attacks than this flesh of ours, and is infected more quickly and cured more slowly?*[34]

33. John of Damascus, *On the Divine Images,* trans. David Anderson (Crestwood, NY: St. Vladimir's Theological Seminary Press, 1980), p. 25.
34. Chrysostom, *Six Books on the Priesthood,* p. 114 (italics added).

The church is most vulnerable when, as William Abraham puts it, she forgets that she is "from beginning to end a charismatic community brought into existence, equipped, guided, and sustained by the Holy Spirit." Unfortunately, this is precisely what has happened in the mainline Protestant churches of Western Europe and North America. Turning their backs on vast stretches of the canonical heritage, these churches are now beset by fear and distrust from top to bottom. Thus Abraham is exactly right when he says, "The key to the renewal of the church is the varied workings of the Holy Spirit, the Lord and Giver of Life."[35]

Unfortunately, the medicine available in the canonical heritage of the church does not result in a "quick fix." As Chrysostom observed, spiritual diseases are "cured more slowly." Yet even here there is good news. In fact, coming to grips with this aspect of conversion is itself a key for the renewal of the church today.

One of the reasons that the church is so badly in need of renewal today is that she has chased one quick fix after another. In an effort to make Christianity more attractive to a culture obsessed with instant gratification and quick-fix solutions, many churches have condensed the hard work of Christian initiation into a few short weeks. Many mainline Protestant churches do not even do this much, reducing the criteria for baptism to a minimal profession of faith that "Jesus is Lord" and ignoring the vital practices of self-examination, spiritual struggle, and instruction that are so crucial to conversion. Indeed, many churches have long given up on the hard work of instruction in basic Christian teaching (doctrine) for initiates.[36] Topping things off, a growing number of churches have made the Eucharist available to the baptized and unbaptized alike, obscuring the fact that the Eucharist is an especially strong medicine that is to be given only after adequate preparation.

Behind these developments is a failure to take seriously the importance of waiting on the Holy Spirit. This hardly comes as a surprise. Waiting is not something that very many people like to do. Yet a failure to prescribe and to practice the spiritual discipline of waiting is nothing less than a failure to understand adequately the dynamic undertaking that conversion truly is, especially when conversion is understood in terms of the reordering

35. Abraham, *Logic of Renewal,* p. 158.

36. For a penetrating analysis of the consequences of this move within United Methodism, see William J. Abraham, *Waking from Doctrinal Amnesia: The Healing of Doctrine in the United Methodist Church* (Nashville: Abingdon, 1995).

of human desire and love. Refusal to wait is symptomatic of our obsession with taking control of our lives.

In the midst of our wilderness wanderings, we want bread now. We are constantly fearful that there will not be enough to go around. By contrast, the ability to wait on the Holy Spirit is a sign that we have come truly to see and know that we are the objects of God's love. We can wait patiently because we know that at Christ's table there is truly bread enough for all.

Finally, the failure to situate conversion squarely within the sacramental life of the church results, to use William Abraham's expression, in "a narrow and inadequate piety" precisely because it cuts us off from the very means whereby we can come to know the love of God for us in Christ. It is tantamount to offering a band-aid as a cure for cancer when far more effective treatments are readily available. By contrast, to conceive of conversion as a matter of the Holy Spirit's bringing us to an apprehension of God's love for us in Christ through the sacramental life of the church is to open the way to a life of piety the depths of which are truly unimaginable. To "run to the church" is to avail oneself not simply of the church's resources, but of "the abiding resource behind all her resources," namely, "the grace and energy of the Triune God."[37] Only then will we be able to know and love God truly.

37. William J. Abraham, "Canonical Theism and the Life of the Church," in Abraham, Vickers, and Van Kirk, eds., *Canonical Theism.*

The Healing Process of Initiation:
Toward the Retrieval of Patristic Catechumenate

Paul L. Gavrilyuk

The structure of Christian education may be likened to a temple in which baptismal initiation serves as the foundation, church school as the walls, seminary as the roof, and postgraduate education as the cupola crowning the edifice. If this structure is to be durable, its foundation has to be solid, reaching into the deep resources of the patristic catechumenate.

Theology professors who teach in private Christian colleges and seminaries are painfully aware of the critical significance of catechumenate. We find to our dismay that undergraduate students from respectable Christian families are often blissfully ignorant about the very basics of their faith. It is even more lamentable when the future Church leaders enter graduate schools of theology considerably under-catechized. For such students a course in systematic theology becomes a "university-level catechesis."[1]

The scholarly effort toward recovering the wisdom and rich resources of the patristic catechumenate has continued unabated since the beginning of the twentieth century. This effort has owed much to the *Ressourcement* movement in Catholic theology, as well as the simultaneous advances of liturgical studies. It is noteworthy that, unlike the revival of catechesis during the Reformation, the present scholarly interest in catechumenate is largely ecumenical in character. Roman Catholic schol-

---

1. William Abraham, "Lectures on Systematic Theology" (unpublished). One hopes that these lectures will eventually be published.

arship has in many ways led the field, with Anglican, mainline Protestant, and Eastern Orthodox liturgical scholars joining in the endeavor. The long list of the seminal historical studies of the patristic catechumenate includes the works of Jean Daniélou, Michel Dujarier, Victor Saxer, Hugh Riley, Aidan Kavanagh, Edward Yarnold, Giuseppe Cavallotto, William Harmless, Thomas Finn, and Alexander Schmemann.[2] Taking the patristic catechumenate as both instructive and foundational, the Roman Catholic Church has implemented the Rite of Christian Initiation for Adults (RCIA). Other Christian communions followed suit by putting into practice the functional equivalents of the same.

What is at stake in the recovery of patristic catechumenate today is as much a matter of historical research as it is a matter of practical engagement with the realities of the contemporary church. My own historical work in this area has been inspired by the personal example of my friend and mentor, William Abraham. After the manner of the Oxford divines of the nineteenth century, Professor Abraham combines the rigor of an analytic philosopher in his scholarship with the fervor of a Christian missionary in his church work. Abraham's example was so captivating that, as a doctoral student at Southern Methodist University, I abandoned my dissertation research on the issue of divine suffering for two years, to produce a book on patristic catechumenate instead. I wrote the book in my mother tongue, Russian, largely with a post-Soviet Russian-speaking readership in mind.[3] Practically speaking, it was imprudent to put my doctoral work on hold for

---

2. J. Daniélou, *La catéchèse aux premiers siècles* (Fayard: École de la Foi, 1968); M. Dujarier, *Le parrainage des adultes aux trois premiers siècles de l'église* (Paris: Cerf, 1962); W. Harmless, *Augustine and the Catechumenate* (Collegeville, MN: Liturgical Press, 1995); A. Kavanagh, *The Shape of Baptism: The Rite of Christian Initiation* (New York: Pueblo, 1989); H. M. Riley, *Christian Initiation: A Comparative Study of the Interpretation of the Baptismal Liturgy in the Mystagogical Writings of Cyril of Jerusalem, John Chrysostom, Theodore of Mopsuestia, and Ambrose of Milan* (Washington, D.C.: Catholic University of America Press, 1974); V. Saxer, *Les rites de l'initiation chrétienne du IIe au VIe siècle. Esquisse historique et signification d'après leurs principaux témoins* (Spoleto: Centro italiano di studi sull'alto medioevo, 1988); E. Yarnold, *The Awe-Inspiring Rites of Initiation* (Collegeville, MN: Liturgical Press, 1994); G. Cavallotto, *Catecumenato antico. Diventare cristiani secondo i padri* (Bologna: Edizioni Dehoniane, 1996); T. M. Finn, *Early Christian Baptism and the Catechumenate,* 2 vols. (Collegeville, MN: Liturgical Press, 1992); A. Schmemann, *Of Water and the Spirit* (Crestwood, NY: St. Vladimir's, 1974).

3. *Istoriia katekhizatsii v drevnei tserkvi* (Moscow, 2001); a substantially revised French edition was published as *Histoire du catéchuménat dans l'église ancienne* (Paris: Cerf, 2007).

such a long time, but the combination of émigré nostalgia and the inspiration of my Doktorvater proved irresistible.

*   *   *

Over the first four centuries CE, Christian initiation developed into a network of practices in which the converts were purified in exorcism, disciplined by ascesis, edified in catechesis, joined to Christ in baptism, and illumined by the ever-present power of the Holy Spirit. The predominant pattern of conversion in the New Testament is that of a relatively swift decision to join the group of Jesus' disciples. Such a decision is usually prompted by hearing the word of God, being physically cured, or witnessing a miracle. While most New Testament instances of conversion do not imply anything amounting to a lengthy period of prebaptismal instruction, on occasions the traveling missionaries did spend considerable time in one locale, as attested by the one-year instruction that Paul and Barnabas offered to the Christian community in Antioch (Acts 11:26; cf. 19:8-10). In the apostolic times the preliminary study of Torah prepared the synagogue-frequenting convert to embrace the gospel. As the church was becoming predominantly gentile, the process of initiation had to be expanded, since a greater preparation was required to turn the pagan souls from idolatry to the worship of the one true God.

For the overwhelming majority, conversion was a gradual process, a lifelong pilgrimage toward the kingdom of God.[4] For some, conversion was deep and permanent; for others it was superficial and transitory. Some accepted the gospel as a result of a serious inner struggle that involved a deliberate choice to follow Christ. Others embraced the new faith on the spur of the moment, or joined their relatives and friends on the basis of a variety of mixed motives. Some, like the martyrs, adhered to their new religion so strongly that they were prepared to die for the faith; others were prepared to compromise in the times of danger. When Christianity became a part of the political establishment, some were not reluctant to use the methods of the persecutors against the unconverted.

Overall, the arrival of Christendom has been a mixed blessing. The historical picture is so complex and fragmentary that any metanarrative of the proud Roman Empire's conversion to the message of the Crucified God

---

4. For a discussion of conversion, see Jason Vickers's contribution to this volume.

is bound to remain contested. Most contemporary historians duly avoid both the triumphalism of Eusebius of Caesarea and the cynicism of Edward Gibbon. In order to strike the right balance, one could say that the Christianization of the empire was as much a process of transforming the pagan culture as it was, conversely, an exercise in domesticating the rebellious gospel. A historian has to consider these developments both as an insider and as an outsider, as a sympathizer and as a critic: to listen to the reports of those in charge of conversion, and to give her ear to the often muted voices of those who were reluctant to convert, so that she can enter into the minds of both.[5]

Since our knowledge of the past is inescapably based on highly selective memories, it would be misleading to set unrealistic epistemic standards of historical knowledge. It would be impossible to do justice to the contingencies of history in a short essay. Fortunately, this is also quite unnecessary, because my primary focus is on how initiation has functioned and continues to function as a means of grace and healing. Along the way I will give the reader some sense of the historical texture of the developments that I analyze. The historical picture from which I will derive my prescriptions for present-day Christianity will be admittedly idealized. Such an idealization, while inescapable, should not be interpreted as an appeal to return to some imaginary golden age in the church's past. I take seriously Georges Florovsky's insight that "the age of the Fathers" is as much a part of the church's past as it is a promise held for her future.[6]

The leadership of the early church made no systematic efforts to standardize catechumenate. Catechetical practices varied over time and space considerably. While the church councils made canonical decisions regarding specific catechetical practices, the fathers in general refrained from recognizing one local catechetical practice as binding upon the church at large. Nevertheless, the cumulative evidence of the first five centuries allows us to speak of many common elements that were shared by

---

5. The literature on conversion in antiquity is vast. Some important studies include: Thomas M. Finn, *From Death to Rebirth: Ritual and Conversion in Antiquity* (New York: Paulist Press, 1997); Ramsay MacMullen, *Christianity and Paganism in the Fourth to Eighth Centuries* (New Haven, CT: Yale University Press, 1997); Robin Lane Fox, *Pagans and Christians* (New York: Knopf, 1987).

6. Georges Florovsky, "St. Gregory Palamas and the Tradition of the Fathers," in *Bible, Church, Tradition: An Eastern Orthodox View* (Belmont, MA: Nordland Publishing Company, 1972), p. 111.

the geographically distant churches. I should reemphasize, of course, that there was no uniformity. Hence the stages of initiation discussed below do not correspond to any single historical instance of catechumenate. My overview represents a synthetic and thus somewhat artificial picture of what the historical catechetical process looked like. I distinguish five major stages of initiation: preliminary, remote, proximate, baptismal, and mystagogical. The exact number is not important, and other divisions are justifiable, too.[7]

The catechetical practices of the early church presuppose that the majority of those preparing for baptism were of relatively mature age. The level of catechetical sermons implies a target audience consisting of adults. This is not to say that children were not present or were not baptized at all. From the late second century we have solid evidence in some locales for the baptism of infants and young children. It was common in Christian families to make children catechumens, while postponing their baptism indefinitely.[8] From the middle of the fifth century, the baptism of children became so common in many areas that the initiation rites were curtailed to accommodate this change. Everything that I have to say below about patristic catechumenate will have to be considerably adjusted for circumstances when the baptism of adults became the exception rather than the rule.

Preliminary Stage

The preliminary stage of catechumenate is the most difficult to map with any precision. Future converts commonly made their first contact with the church with the help of friends. The pagan philosopher Celsus reports in the late second century that Christian slaves, even at work, cannot keep their mouths shut about their faith. These despicable characters, Celsus observes with indignation, keep disseminating their godless superstition among their coworkers, especially when the taskmasters are not watching them.[9] The inquirers could have been attracted by the bonds of charity and mutual help

---

7. See Edward Yarnold, *The Awe-Inspiring Rites of Initiation*, pp. 1-54.

8. To mention one well-known example, while Augustine became a catechumen in early childhood, he made the decision to be baptized much later in his life. How common or how universal this practice was cannot be established conclusively, since most of our evidence is anecdotal.

9. Origen, *Contra Celsum*, III. 44; cf. Minucius Felix, *Octavius*, VIII. 4.

that Christians showed to one another. In a time of persecutions, some future converts may have been inspired by the courage of the martyrs and by the willingness of the confessors to die for their beliefs. Others may have witnessed a miracle, or perhaps they heard about an incident of healing or exorcism performed in the name of Jesus.

Under Constantine, when Christianity was granted a privileged status among the religions of the empire, the motives of those entering the church for the first time became mixed.[10] Some inquirers were attracted by the grandeur of the newly built basilicas and the power of the holy places. Others were drawn by the favors that the ruling elites showered on the church and by the prospect of social promotion. Cyril, the fourth-century bishop of Jerusalem, addressed this sad reality in his catechetical sermons with considerable pastoral sensitivity. He challenged the fortune-seeking catechumens to turn their earthly aspirations to something more worthwhile during the time of their preparation for baptism.

Typically, there was no regular instruction at the preliminary stage. According to Augustine's *De catechizandis rudibus,* the preliminary informal discussion with the inquirers regarding the basics of faith was conducted in some parishes of Latin-speaking North Africa by a minister, most commonly a deacon. Augustine advises that, rather than offering the same message to everybody and getting profoundly bored in the process of repeating oneself a countless number of times, the catechist should instead listen to those who came to him and find out about their background and any previous encounters with the faith.[11] This is, of course, common sense. Still, the importance of such personal conversations should not be overlooked, because they often played a crucial role in the convert's decision to embrace the Christian way of life.

Remote Stage

Those inquirers who decided to become catechumens were signed with the sign of the cross. This ritual act served as the provisional means of protection against demonic influences. Thus the process of healing began with the

---

10. Recent liturgical scholarship rightly cautions against drawing a sharp contrast between the pre-Constantinian and post-Constantinian eras.

11. Augustine, *De catechizandis rudibus,* 2.

first sacramental action of the church on behalf of the catechumens. In addition, hands were laid on the catechumens as an indication of their future vocation. In the West, the enrollment rite was also accompanied by a brief exorcistic prayer and the tasting of salt, which symbolized a foretaste of the words of the gospel. Candidates of all ages could participate in this rite.

It is difficult to ascertain the degree of commitment that was expected from the catechumens at this stage. Unlike the rite of baptism, no version of the rite of the making of a catechumen that has come down to us includes the following two markers of conversion: the rite of the renunciation of Satan and the rite of adhesion to Christ.[12] The evidence of the puzzle-ridden church order known as *The Apostolic Tradition* (the date, origins, and redaction history of which are much disputed) suggests that some churches did impose rigorous moral requirements on those who considered joining the church as catechumens. It was more realistic to expect the reform of character to begin with, rather than to be a prerequisite for, this stage. We also know that penance applied to the baptized Christians was more severe than that applied to the catechumens. For example, baptized believers who lapsed underwent a longer period of reintegration into the church than did catechumens for the same transgressions.

The remote stage often lasted for a long time. In some locales a one- to three-year period was considered optimal. In cases of mass conversions, attested both in the apostolic times and later centuries, the desideratum of at least a one-year catechumenate could not have been realistically enforced.[13] The church canons legislated against inordinate haste in the advancement from the status of the catechumen to that of a baptized Christian.[14] It was important that the catechumens undergo a trial period of considerable length before making the fateful decision to enter the church as full members and receive communion.

The more pressing problem that the fourth-century shepherds of the church faced was quite the opposite: many catechumens postponed their baptism indefinitely, some even until their deathbed. The sermons of Cyril

12. On the rites of renunciation and adhesion see "Baptismal Rite" below.

13. I should point out that at least in the fourth century, for which we have the most comprehensive evidence, mass conversion did not necessarily involve baptisms on the spot. St. Martin of Tours, for example, would convert pagan villages en masse by making country folk catechumens, not baptized Christians.

14. While we can be certain that these canons were violated by some, there is no way of telling how often such violations could have occurred.

of Jerusalem, John Chrysostom, Gregory of Nyssa, Augustine, and others are filled with exhortations to catechumens not to procrastinate.[15] Summoning all of his rhetorical skill, John Chrysostom presented "clinical" or deathbed baptism in the worst imaginable light.[16] Many, especially the highest-ranking government officials, remained undeterred and conveniently delayed the rite that washed away all sins to the indefinite future. To be a life-long catechumen in the fourth century was the equivalent of being a nominal, nonpracticing Christian in today's church. Some historians see this development as a sign of the post-Constantinian church's laxity, worldliness, and corruption. This is only partially true, since the reverse side of this coin is the obvious implication that the moral performance of the baptized Christian was taken with the utmost seriousness and the fear of ecclesiastical punishment was very real indeed.

At the remote stage the catechumens were expected to participate in the charitable work of the church: attending to the needs of the poor, taking care of the sick, visiting those in prison, protecting the widows, and so on. They took part in corporate worship, though they most commonly stood apart from the baptized Christians. The catechumens attended the Liturgy of the Catechumens, sang hymns, heard Scripture proclaimed and explained, and then were dismissed before the beginning of the Liturgy of the Faithful.[17] It is possible that the word "hearers" *(audientes, auditores)* came to be applied to the catechumens precisely because they had the status of the auditors whose primary task was to hear and be fed by the word of the gospel. In the Liturgy of St. John Chrysostom, used in the Eastern Orthodox Church to this day, one finds the following litany before the dismissal of the catechumens:

15. See H. Thurston, "When Baptism Was Delayed," *The Month* 152 (1928): 529-41; Everett Ferguson, "Exhortation to Baptism in the Cappadocians," *Studia Patristica* 32 (1997): 121-29.

16. John Chrysostom, *In Johannem*, 18 (PG 59, 115B); *In act. apost.* 1 (PG 60, 25A); *Baptismal Instructions* Montf. 1.4-11.

17. In my judgment, the term "the liturgy of the sacrament" often applied by Western liturgists to the liturgy of the faithful is a bit problematic, since it appears to presuppose that the Liturgy of the Word is nonsacramental, or at least less sacramental. Such a distinction would be alien to the patristic understanding of both parts of the liturgy as belonging to the church's sacramental life. On this point, see Robert Wall's contribution to this volume, the section entitled "The Bible as Sacrament."

Pray unto the Lord, ye catechumens.
>   [Each petition is accompanied by "Kyrie eleison"]
Ye faithful, pray ye for the catechumens, that the Lord
>   may have mercy upon them.
That He may teach them the word of truth.
That He may reveal to them the Gospel of righteousness.
That He may unite them unto His holy, catholic, and
>   apostolic Church.
Save them, have mercy upon them, preserve them, and protect them,
>   O God, by Thy grace.
Bow your heads unto the Lord, ye catechumens.

This prayer is an intercession of the faithful (i.e., baptized Christians) on behalf of those who have not yet fully joined the church. The prayer emphasizes the agency of God as the primary teacher and revealer of Scripture. The bowing of the heads is a ritual recommitment of the catechumens to new life with God. The exclamation that the priest subsequently utters on behalf of the catechumens expresses the longing of the baptized members of the community to be fully united with the catechumens when they receive baptism.

Some ancient sources also envision a regular catechetical instruction offered specifically for the catechumens as an identifiable group within the local community. Irenaeus's *Proof of the Apostolic Preaching* serves as a good illustration of what such an instruction could typically involve. The catechumens were introduced to the biblical history of salvation, which began with creation, continued as a drama of human transgression and divine redemption, culminated in the coming of Christ, and would go on in the church till the eschaton.[18] The catechumens were invited to become a part of this history, to relive it as their own.[19]

---

18. Cf. Augustine's advice on what constitutes a good catechesis: "The narration is full when each person is catechised in the first instance from what is written in the text, 'In the beginning God created the heaven and the earth,' on to the present times of the Church," Augustine, *De catechizandis rudibus*, 3.5, trans. S. D. F. Salmond, *On the Catechizing of the Uninstructed*, NPNF, vol. 3 (Grand Rapids: Eerdmans, 1993), p. 285. Augustine adds that such a narration ought to be selective, not to test the patience of the audience with long expositions.

19. Today we are painfully aware of the fact that the biblical narrative can be deconstructed if the logic of the canon formation is forgotten or jettisoned. It was especially in Christian preaching and the baptismal instruction that the story of the Bible was told as sal-

Moral catechesis, one instance of which is preserved in the *Didache,* was not separated from the Christocentric account of the history of salvation. The author of the *Didache* builds on the Deuteronomistic teaching about the Two Ways, developing it as a commentary on the Beatitudes. Those seeking initiation were presented with a clear choice: either to choose the way of death by persisting in the habits of their pagan past or to choose the way of life by striving after the perfection of the gospel. The motivation to embrace a new way of life came from their newly found faith in Christ. The new adepts were not left alone in their struggles but were encouraged "to seek daily the company of the saints."[20] The catechumens were introduced to people whose lives had been thoroughly transformed by the power of God. Communion with living saints provided the best medicine for the souls of catechumens at this stage.

Proximate Stage

Most of our historical evidence related to initiation in the early church focuses on this critical stage. Those wishing to be baptized in the near future had to appear before the local bishop: baptismal instruction was generally one of his primary responsibilities. It is telling that the surviving baptismal homilies were in so many cases written by the bishops: Irenaeus of Lyons, Cyril of Jerusalem, Ambrose of Milan, Augustine of Hippo, and Theodore of Mopsuestia, to name only some notable examples. While John Chrysostom probably preached his baptismal sermons while still a priest in Antioch, he continued his catechetical work after having been appointed the archbishop of Constantinople. Many centuries later, when Pope John Paul II began to offer weekly homilies, he showed a great example to the church at large: he was reminding the hierarchs that their primary responsibility was not the art of political intrigue but the initiation of new members into the life of the church.

During the interview with the candidates, the bishop spoke with each of the catechumens seeking baptism about that individual's motives for en-

---

vation history. Whether or not the unity of the Bible can be derived from the biblical text itself, it was the theological achievement of the ancient preachers and catechists to present the story of the Bible as a metanarrative of salvation history.

20. *Didache,* 4.2; *Epistle of Barnabas,* 19.6.

tering the church. He inquired about the individual's current occupation in order to determine whether it was compatible with the Christian life. He also asked some searching questions about the candidate's private life.[21] While the mores of pagan society dictated otherwise, the church essentially allowed only two options regarding marital status: either celibacy or monogamous marriage. In practice, the concubinage involving one permanent partner was allowed for slaves whose masters remained pagan. Penance for adultery and other forms of fornication was strict, though it is difficult to judge with what success the punishment could have been realistically enforced. In addition, sponsors had to testify before the bishop that their spiritual child was of good repute. The decision to be baptized bespoke a serious commitment to pursue a life of holiness.

The names of those who passed the interview with the bishop were inscribed in the church register. In the West they were called the "chosen ones" *(electi)* or those preparing [for baptism] *(competentes)*. In the East they were more commonly referred to as those preparing for illumination *(phōtizomenoi, illuminandi)*. It is significant that a key metaphor for baptism in the early church was illumination, or enlightenment *(phōtismos)*. Behind this metaphor one may discern the living experience of the transformation of one's cognitive capacities, desires, and affections by the power of the Holy Spirit. The following prayer before the reading of the gospel in the Liturgy of St. John Chrysostom captures well the importance of illumination:

> Enlighten *[ellampson]* our hearts, O Master who lovest mankind, with the pure light *[phōs]* of thy divine knowledge, and open the eyes of our mind *[tēs dianoias ophthalmous]* to the understanding of thy Gospel teachings; implant in us also the fear of thy blessed commandments, that trampling down all carnal desires we may enter upon a spiritual manner of living both thinking and doing such things as are well-pleasing unto thee: for thou art the illumination *[phōtismos]* of our souls and bodies, O Christ our God, and unto thee we ascribe glory, together with thy Father who is from everlasting, and thine all-holy, good, and life-giving Spirit: now and ever, and unto ages of ages. Amen.

---

21. *Loci classici* for this practice include: *Apostolic Tradition*, 16; Egeria, *Itinerarium*, 45.2-4. It should be noted that in contrast to most other church orders, the *Apostolic Tradition* puts the inquiry into lifestyles and professions at the preliminary, rather than at the proximate, stage.

The prayer calls for a thorough transformation of the cognitive capacities that enabled believers to perceive the things of God: the enlightenment of the heart, the opening of the eyes of the mind, the illumination of souls and bodies, and the education of desire. The proximate stage of initiation was an especially intense period of preparation for the reception of illumination.

This stage normally lasted from three weeks to forty days. It was common to baptize the catechumens as a group on Easter Eve or on other important church feasts, such as Pentecost, Christmas, and Epiphany (Baptism of Christ). As is well known, the liturgical cycle of Lent was shaped in many ways by the circumstances of the ancient initiatory practices. While baptisms were performed on demand in extreme circumstances, the dominant practice in the fourth century appears to have favored the baptisms of large groups on major feast days.

During this time the catechumens and the accompanying faithful were offered special instructions on a regular basis. The instruction was either preceded or concluded by corporate prayers and individual exorcisms. Certain ministers were specifically appointed as exorcists. Strict fasting and other lessons in self-discipline, including the guarding of one's tongue and thought, as well as refraining from attending theatrical shows and other questionable entertainments, were also an integral part of this stage.

While the content of prebaptismal catechesis varied considerably from place to place, three main patterns can be distinguished. The prebaptismal homilies of Cyril of Jerusalem and Theodore of Mopsuestia were mainly detailed expositions of the articles of the creed. As much as doctrine owed its development to heated controversies, it should not be overlooked that theology's proper home is baptismal instruction. Systematic theology was the very stuff that prebaptismal catechesis was made of. There was no disjunction in the early church between the speculative theology produced in the academy and the pastoral theology that provided nourishment for souls seeking Christ. The main loci of modern systematic theology, no matter how revisionist, are still based on the main articles of the creed (though this connection often becomes very tenuous). In this sense, systematic theology should function as a "university-level catechesis."²² The second pattern of

22. I should emphasize that this is not to extol indoctrination as a paradigm of theological training. Perish the thought! Nevertheless, the legitimate fear of indoctrination should not turn into an antitheological phobia of imparting any doctrine at all (alas, this

prebaptismal catechumenate included a brief commentary on the creed joined to moral instruction, which was also, as the reader might recall, a part of the remote stage. This particular catechetical pattern is attested by the baptismal instructions of John Chrysostom and Ambrose of Milan. The third and final pattern of the prebaptismal catechumenate focused on the history of salvation, again continuing the instruction begun during the previous stage.

Whatever the overall pattern of instruction, the exposition of the creed or creedlike formulae was a crucial part of the catechumenate at this stage. In some areas the bishop imparted the creed to the candidates in a solemn ceremony *(traditio symboli)* and directed them to memorize its words so that they could subsequently recite the creed back *(redditio symboli)* in the presence of the representatives of the local church. In most churches the Lord's Prayer was likewise expounded upon and imparted to the candidates for baptism. This tradition goes back at least to Tertullian — and perhaps much earlier. It is also attested by Origen and Cyprian, among others.[23] The candidates were likewise asked to memorize this prayer. In some locales there developed a custom of *traditio et redditio* of the Lord's Prayer, similar to the *traditio et redditio symboli.*[24]

Baptismal Rite

The details of the baptismal rite varied significantly, depending on local customs. For example, the so-called rite of the opening of ears and nostrils *(ephphatha)* is found only in Latin sources, and not in Eastern ones. The purpose of this rite, which refers to the story of Jesus' healing of the deaf-and-dumb person in Mark 7:32-33, was the activation of the mode of perception that would allow the adepts to breathe in "the aroma of Christ" (2 Cor. 2:15) and to attune their ears to the understanding of the truths imparted in the mystagogical catechesis. In order to experience the union with Christ in baptism, one's sense perception had to be transformed and enlightened.

---

phobia reigns supreme in some post-Protestant schools of theology today). My point is rather that contemporary systematic theology needs to come to terms with its original raison d'être as the medicine offered to those seeking incorporation into the church.

23. See Tertullian, *De oratione;* Cyprian, *De dominica oratione;* Origen, *De oratione.*

24. A parallel practice of *traditio* and *redditio* of the Psalms seems to have been in use solely in Naples.

The renunciation of Satan and his minions was sometimes separated from baptism proper by a day, but in most cases it was a part of the rite. While repeated exorcisms purified the soul from demonic influences with little cooperation from the believer, the renunciation of Satan was an expression of the believer's determination voluntarily to tear up her pact with the devil and to become a possession of Christ. The renunciation was a dramatic act, accompanied in some cases by the believer's turning toward the west and literally spitting in the direction of an invisibly present Satan. This act accentuated the decisive break with the pagan past and the readiness of the believer to embrace a new life in Christ. The rite of adhesion to Christ (or, according to one variant of this rite, adhesion to the triune God) became, in time, an element distinct from the three baptismal immersions. The teaching about the Two Ways that was a part of moral catechesis became lived experience through *ascesis* and was ritually reenacted in the rite of baptism.

Before entering the baptismal font, the candidates were stripped naked and anointed. The function of the prebaptismal anointings varied, but the most widely assumed one was exorcistic. The anointings purified and protected the baptizand from potential demonic influences. The triple immersion in the name of the Father, Son, and Holy Spirit followed.[25] Assisted by ministers, the baptizands emerged out of the baptismal font to be clothed with resplendent white robes. They were subsequently given the seal of the Holy Spirit in chrismation; they were then welcomed with the laying on of hands and were invited to join the faithful for their first communion. In the early medieval West, chrismation and the laying on of hands evolved into a separate rite called confirmation. While it is problematic, from the standpoint of patristic sacramental theology, to think of baptism as somehow incomplete and having to be confirmed at a later stage, we must recognize that the sacrament of confirmation is a valuable signpost in contemporary Western practice, and that it marks the importance of continuing instruction after baptism.

Drawing on the treasury of biblical imagery, the church fathers used a constellation of powerful metaphors to describe what happened in the rite of baptism. The baptizands emerged out of the darkness of idolatry into the light of true faith. They tore apart the contract with Satan and entered into a

---

25. It should be noted that the precise number (either one or three) and meaning of the baptismal immersions remained contested during the christological controversies of the fourth and earlier centuries.

new covenant with Christ. They were no longer the slaves of demons but were now liberated from prison by the power of the cross. They left Egypt, the house of slavery, in order to enter the Promised Land. Their sins perished in the water of baptism after the manner of the pharaoh's chariots and horses, which drowned in the Red Sea. They were born from above, from water and the Spirit, and they were created anew through the womb of the primeval water. They were adopted as God's children. Before immersion, they were anointed like wrestlers preparing for the decisive match. They became the soldiers of Christ, ready for the future spiritual battle. Like sheep, they were branded with the seal of Christ's ownership in chrismation. They entered into the sacred marriage with Christ, the celestial bridegroom. They were baptized into Christ's death in order to emerge from the baptismal water destined for immortality. They took off the old Adam and put on the new Adam, Christ. They embarked on the lifelong journey toward deification and were now ready to commune with Christ in the Eucharist.[26]

Mystagogy

In her pastoral wisdom, the ancient church realized that the spiritual nourishment of the newly baptized had to be continued after baptism. While there were some echoes of the postbaptismal catechesis in the earlier period, toward the beginning of the fourth century such a catechesis became a clearly identifiable part of the initiation process. One fourth-century pilgrim to Jerusalem reports that the local bishop dedicated the full week after Easter to the exposition of the sacraments specifically for the benefit of the neophytes.[27] Such sermons included the explanation of the theology and ritual details of baptism, chrismation, Eucharist, and — in some quarters — a comprehensive exposition of the Lord's Prayer.

Present-day Christians may wonder how the ancient candidates for baptism were supposed to participate in the sacraments, initially having no clear idea about what was being done to them. We have a difficult time understanding how one can meaningfully participate in something that one does not understand, but the ancients approached the matter very differ-

---

26. Compare the discussion of this issue in Geoffrey Wainwright's contribution to this book.

27. Egeria, *Itinerarium*, 47. 1-2.

35

ently. The experience of the Eucharist was offered prior to its explanation precisely because the eucharistic participation was something defying any exhaustive explanation. To be joined to Christ in baptism, to taste him in the Eucharist, was more foundational than to hear the explanations of what was involved in joining and tasting. The experience of a baptizand's entering into the church's sacramental life was certainly not prelinguistic. At the same time, initially at least, the transformative power of the Eucharist was not constrained by what the bishops taught about it.[28] It was more important to perceive God in the Eucharist by means of the spiritual senses than to understand the logic of the sacrament. One received the medicine of immortality without initially being taught how this medicine worked.

*   *   *

What are contemporary theologians and churchmen to do with this embarrassment of initiatory riches? Admittedly, this program may prove hard to swallow in our age, since many people have become so immune to the power of the ritual (despite the resurgence of interest in ritual in some religious quarters). It is tempting to become defensive and argue that these rites presuppose a rather dated worldview. For example, what are we to make of repeated references to daily exorcisms? Can anyone today seriously pay that much attention to the power of the demonic? Actually, the answer to this question is far from obvious. There are now, according to the latest count, about 500 million charismatics in the world.[29] The worldview of these Christian believers is thoroughly supernaturalist, including being populated with angels and demons. It would be rather cavalier, à la Richard Dawkins, to dismiss any and all supernaturalism as delusional.[30] Many factors, including the ever-present reality of horrendous evil, make the demonstration of the nonexistence of demons a tough call.

It is a telling coincidence that Renaissance, Reformation, Enlightenment, and New Age happen to be the forgotten names of Christian initiation. In baptism one is born again, one is reformed into a new creature, one is illumined by the power of the Holy Spirit, and, finally, one enters a new es-

---

28. I owe this insight to an exchange with Prof. Ellen Charry during her Summer Seminar at Calvin College in July 2006.

29. David Barrett et al., *World Christian Encyclopedia* (New York: Oxford University Press, 2001).

30. See R. Dawkins, *The God Delusion* (London: Bantam Press, 2006).

chatological aeon of the kingdom of God. Therefore, baptism is renaissance, reformation, enlightenment, and the dawning of the new age all in one. As G. K. Chesterton famously put it, "the world is full of old Christian virtues gone mad."[31] Similarly, the proud self-appellations of modernity turn out to be nothing but the forgotten baptismal metaphors run amok.

When the logic of initiation is misunderstood or forgotten, the possibilities for abusing the sacraments increase exponentially. Consider, for example, the present-day practice, endorsed by some Christian groups, of admitting unbaptized visitors to communion. While the road to justifying this practice is paved with good intentions, and those promoting it "can cite Scripture for their purpose," the consequences of this liturgical revolution are dire. The practice is detrimental to the spiritual life of both the uninitiated and the baptized. The uninitiated do not receive the gift of forgiveness, for they are hardly aware of their estrangement from God. The baptized are thrown into spiritual confusion, because what the practice implies is that baptism makes no difference in their communion with God. In the name of welcoming the stranger, faith and agape are reduced to sentimental fellow-feeling. Sobornost, or the fullness of unity in Christ, is turned into a vague and cheap togetherness. To violate the logic and order of initiation is to wreak chaos in the spiritual life of the church.

The opposite temptation is to apply the patristic catechetical model too literally and directly to the present circumstances. For example, I know of some Orthodox priests in Russia today who at one point experimented with mightily expelling the uninitiated from the Liturgy of the Faithful, zealously reproducing the venerable patristic practice. The result was an immense confusion and the protest of those expelled. To police the Eucharist in this way is almost as bad as to promote the communion of the unbaptized. The spirit of patristic catechumenate should not be reduced to the letter of individual rules, though discipline and the ordering of desire are indispensable in the spiritual life.

I am also told that a few Russian clerics (either out of residual liturgical fundamentalism, or, if we are to interpret their intentions more charitably and less realistically, out of unbounded trust in the power of God to guard his people from carnal temptations) have boldly resumed the practice of baptizing adults in the original state of Adam, that is, naked. According to one report, the sight of those baptized in this way was rather unedifying for

---

31. G. K. Chesterton, *Orthodoxy*, chap. 3.

all involved. Fortunately, common sense soon prevailed, and they quietly dropped this particular element of the ancient ritual.

To parrot the work of the ancient liturgists (a typically Eastern Ortho-dox temptation) would be as detrimental to the life of the Spirit in the church as to ignore this work altogether (a temptation of the Western com-munions). If we are to drink from the wells of patristic wisdom, we should keep our feet firmly on the ground of present ecclesiastical realities, so that we can avoid falling into those sacred wells. We need to enter into the posses-sion of patristic liturgical treasures as children, not as slaves. In order for us to inherit the patristic tradition in freedom, it is important that we learn how to think and pray with the fathers, to acquire a patristic, scriptural, and ecclesiastical mind.[32]

One of the striking features of a patristic mind is its ability to hold vari-ous aspects of theological education in profound unity. The proclamation and interpretation of the Bible was thus an indispensable part of the ancient catechumenate. Moral theology developed as a series of answers to the existen-tial concerns of those entering the church. The creedal pattern of systematic theology acquired its main contours in baptismal instruction. The newcomers learned how to pray while being initiated into the Christian community. The two main parts of the liturgy, the Liturgy of the Catechumens and the Liturgy of the Faithful, reflected a catechetical concern both to bring together in prayer and at the same time keep a clear distinction between the baptized and the un-initiated. While prebaptismal catechesis prepared the catechumens for the re-ception of the sacraments, postbaptismal catechesis was the cradle of liturgical theology. All these pieces — biblical, moral, dogmatic, pastoral, and liturgical theologies, so commonly at odds with each other in the curricula of modern theological schools — were once harmoniously interconnected parts of one existential reality: the healing process of initiation.

For many believers through the centuries, this process has meant a profound reorientation of life. It was in this process that souls wounded by sin received their first cure; repentant hearts were opened to accept the love of God and share it with others; humbled minds were enlightened by the Holy Spirit to comprehend the word of God; docile bodies were trained to become vessels of holiness; spiritual senses were attuned to discern the hand of God in all things; and the lifelong journey toward deification began.

32. See Georges Florovsky, "St. Gregory Palamas and the Tradition of the Fathers," pp. 107-12.

Appendix: Stages of Initiation

The table reflects more developed catechetical practices of the fourth and fifth centuries.

stage of initiation	length & time	groups of adepts	content	requirements & expectations
preliminary	indefinite	inquiring pagans	Inquirers were attracted by conversations with Christian friends, examples of saintly life and martyrdom; charity and imperial favors; healings, exorcisms, and other miracles; beautiful church buildings, holy places, and awe-inspiring worship	none
remote	commonly, one to three years	"hearers"	Catechumens attended the Liturgy of the Catechumens and were dismissed before the Liturgy of the Faithful; read Scriptures and were instructed in Christian morals	Catechumens were expected to abandon idolatry; reform morally; read Scripture; pray and participate in the charitable work of the local Christian community

Table continues on page 40.

stage of initiation	length & time	groups of adepts	content	requirements & expectations
proximate	normally from three to eight weeks of Lent ("forty days")	West: "the chosen ones" or "preparing for baptism"; East: "those preparing for illumination"	The candidates were instructed in the creed, Christian morals, and the Bible; exorcised regularly; fasted and performed other ascetic exercises	The fulfillment of the expectations of the remote stage was a prerequisite for the proximate stage. The bishop interviewed the candidates, testing their motives and reform of character. In addition, the candidates were required to memorize the creed (and in some cases the Lord's Prayer) and recite them in the presence of the bishop
baptismal rite	often during the Easter Vigil	baptizands	Baptizands renounced Satan and united themselves to Christ; were anointed; were immersed three times in the name of the Trinity; were chrismated	N/A
mystagogical	during the Easter (Bright) Week	newly illuminated (neophytes)	Neophytes were instructed daily about the sacraments and other liturgical practices	fully participated in the sacramental life of the church; were expected to receive communion regularly and were required to do penance for serious transgressions

A Theological Morphology of the Bible:
A Prescription for "Spiritually Disabled" Students

Robert W. Wall

My chapter in this book proposes to define the three essential terms used by biblical scholars to express the purpose of their theological appropriation of biblical texts. I offer my reflection on this special glossary as a tribute to the work of my friend William Abraham, who more than anyone else in my experience has alerted me to the importance of hammering out a more precise definition of the practical but unwieldy relationship between Scripture and theology. He has also been a fierce champion of the theological catechesis of rank-and-file believers as a crucial congregational practice: the view that every believer is initiated into a more animated life with God through richer theological understanding. In this regard, Abraham has been critical of the guilds of biblical scholars and academic theologians, as have I, not so much because of their modernist intellectual commitments, but because their exaggerated commitments to the protocols and precepts of academic guilds have typically shortchanged the needs of ordinary believers. Serious believers seek an experience of God's love and grace, and they turn to the Bible to mediate such an experience.

Abraham's timely criticism corresponds to a recent survey of Seattle Pacific University students, who were asked to evaluate the required three-course theological curriculum, entitled "University Foundations," at our university. While they generally express gratitude for what they have learned, a significant number of those student respondents report a loss of interest in Bible study as an unexpected result of their theological education. Rather than learning material that left them feeling empowered, they report finishing their courses feeling, in the words of one student, "spiritually disabled." This feeling is partly the effect of being overwhelmed by the sheer amount of new information they are being taught. But it is also because they believe that they are being required to learn more than they possibly can learn in order to read the Bible with "skill and grace" — the stated goal of our Bible courses. Therefore, while they are duly impressed with the scholarly competence and tempers of their Bible faculty, they leave the classroom confused and convinced that serious Bible study is something that faculty members do with their scholarly peers, but it is not anything students can — or even should — do to cultivate their life with God.

Moreover, their faith in God is sometimes left destabilized because the different emphases of the classroom conflict with those taught them by their churches and parents. The spiritual effect on students is often substantial and debilitating: quite a few report that the Bible has lost its magic, its mystery, its capacity to comfort, to correct, and to guide. While this finding haunts and discourages us, it does not surprise anyone on our faculty. We have long known that this is often the effect produced when students encounter academic approaches that train them to become observers of demystified literary texts. They become more knowledgeable about the social worlds that shaped them and the audiences who first heard them, but they are more detached from their own spiritual benefaction. And in their teaching of the texts, our Bible classes tend to create distance between those very texts we love and study and the students we love and teach. The problem in our case is not what Mark Schwehn reports in his stirring book *Exiles from Eden:* that today's faculty members pursue their scholarly interests to the exclusion of a concern for the well-being of students or a deep desire to cultivate friendships with them. Nonetheless, many students leave our classrooms feeling disabled and with a sense that the Bible is no longer accessible to them.[1]

John Wesley's use of the therapeutic idiom *(therapeia psychēs)* to characterize a gracious God "healing our sin-diseased souls, restoring the vitality of life that God intended for us,"[2] cues a constructive response to this peda-

---

1. Mark R. Schwehn, *Exiles from Eden: Religion and the Academic Vocation in America* (Oxford: Oxford University Press, 1993).

2. Randy Maddox, *Responsible Grace: John Wesley's Practical Theology* (Nashville: Kingswood Books, 1994), p. 145.

gogical problem. Although hardly caused by sin, the cognitive dissonance they report upon being initiated into an academic reading of the Bible presents itself as a kind of academic disability that requires a therapeutic response. The working model I have in mind is when a patient requires postsurgery "rehabilitative therapy" to learn to use new muscles that enable different movements that the surgery has made necessary.[3] While successful surgery has corrected some malformation or excised something harmful, it has also left the patient momentarily disabled. She must fashion new muscles through repeated exercise and over an extended period of time — with a therapist's help and often with considerable pain. After a course of rehabilitative therapy, these muscles make necessary movements possible that allow the patient to negotiate her world.

Similarly, we can agree that students become momentarily "disabled" by necessary surgery: a critical reading of biblical texts that a student learns in the classroom exposes and corrects an array of misreadings and faulty perceptions. One might be inclined to argue, then, that the most suitable surgical procedure is one that best excises the problem at hand: in this case, the functional illiteracy and array of misunderstandings, sometimes compounded by the Protestant "Scripture principle," which misuses or neglects the full range of biblical teaching. The relevant pedagogical question, then, is this: How do faculty members teach the Bible with intellectual honesty while helping move students into a deeper, more satisfying life with God? How do we build bridges that allow them back into the mystery and delights of the symbolic world forged by Scripture with a sense of Ricouer's "second naiveté"?

Text-centered approaches to Bible study practiced by most scholars leave little wiggle room for their students, who must deal with what the text actually says, a kind of "radical surgery" on prior beliefs and expectations that requires rehabilitative therapy to exercise different muscles for new movements to and from biblical texts. In the modern period this procedure has come to be charted by the historian's prognosis: "For modern commentators, theology is the result of historically determined exegesis."[4] A text's normative meaning is retrieved from its point of origin, in light of its "origi-

3. My thanks to Prof. Richard B. Steele, who patiently helped me work out this model, though I am certain he would want to qualify it more carefully at every turn.

4. Stephen Fowl, *Philippians*, Two Horizons New Testament Commentary (Grand Rapids: Eerdmans, 2005), p. 2. Fowl notes the premodern notion of "literal sense" is different because it was based on what the text actually says rather than on what the text meant for its author and first audience.

nal" author's communicative intentions and the "original" audience's reception of his intended meaning, both of which are shaped within a particular sociopolitical location. Whatever theological interest is vested in the text, then, is derivative of the "original" beliefs of its author and his or her first audience. And what a text may teach us about God is restricted to the meaning it had for the communities that produced it. While historical criticism is certainly a muscular approach to the text, it tends to create rather than bridge the distance between it and today's reader.

Those who rehearse the current state of affairs in the scholarly guilds typically cite J. P. Gabler's articulation of the modernist project, whose unrealistic goal was to construct the Bible's historical referent with theological neutrality, as hermeneutical of the present impasse between biblical studies and the theological disciplines. Indeed, if scholars are intent on retrieving the literal sense of biblical texts from their point of origin, which favors the communicative intentions of authors for their first audiences, then it is difficult if not impossible to bridge the distance between the text and current audiences. Ironically, at the very moment when the Protestant Scripture principle was formulated during the Magisterial Reformation, the modernist seeds were planted, which, when harvested centuries later, would make the application of that principle to contemporary theology more untenable. In the West the situation is even more desperate, if William Abraham's analysis of the "epistemology of theology" is correct, and biblical teaching about God, a resource of singular importance for theologians, is regarded as largely irrelevant for a modern culture. If the Bible functions as *the* rule of faith, its interpretation is no longer regulated by the Rule of Faith, and thus teachers are free to turn to ideology or idiosyncratic prompts to craft their theology for culture and church.

This chapter proposes an initial round of therapy, sometimes called "patterning," framed by the simple recognition that Bible faculty would help their students by teaching them — consistently and persistently — a morphology of the theological terms that would more adequately articulate Scripture's importance for Christian formation. If the philosophical muses that shaped Bultmann's hermeneutic have taught us anything, it is that how we speak and think of the Bible hard-wires our approach to and from the Bible when we seek to make meaning for life and faith. A lack of clarity and self-criticism about our presuppositions leads to confusion and cognitive dissonance. If students leave a Bible class "feeling spiritually disabled" rather than empowered by what they have learned, perhaps the therapy should include a steady diet of clearly stated and developed definitions, served up in every class, that would help forge a perspective that would facilitate the Bible's role in enriching a believer's life with God.

This leads me to another reason for this study. Especially among confessing Bible scholars who are compelled by the Protestant Scripture principle — though buffeted by the strong historical and metaphysical currents of modernity — the heavy lifting required to move sacred texts toward theological ends in service of the church continues. Yet the recent publication of *The Dictionary of the Theological Interpretation of Scripture*[5] envisions a confusing array of proposals that are shaped by competing epistemic and theological interests.[6] Clearly, even this sustained conversation among those scholars most keen to move beyond modern criticism's failures and approach biblical studies as a theological discipline exhibits a muddled complex of presumptions and protocols. I would like to make the reasons for this initiative more clear.

The Bible as Scripture

The affirmation that the Bible is a sacred book for Christians is unpretentious if removed from the culture wars between the academic guilds and the church. "Scripture" has become an important catchword in the current renewal of interest among scholars who are interested in the theological appropriation of the Bible in service of the church. Those same scholars often lament the loss of the Bible's importance within the church, where blame is posited on those who fail to regard the Bible as God's word. The more edgy, polemical subtexts of this use of Scripture regard modern biblical criticism as a failure, not only on epistemic grounds (more widely admitted) but also for religious reasons. That is, modern critics have come to read biblical texts as though their referent is not the living God but rather ancient history; or they retrieve meanings from biblical texts as though they are not revelatory

5. Kevin J. Vanhoozer, Craig G. Bartholomew, Daniel J. Treier, N. Thomas Wright, eds. (Grand Rapids: Baker, 2004).

6. I find it striking that an encyclopedia dedicated to "the theological interpretation of the Bible" includes no article that defines "the Bible" but a series of articles that seek to define the "authority," "clarity," "sufficiency," and "unity" of Scripture. At the same time I would also note that no other article examines how "Scripture" is variously used by the contributors to this volume.

of God's word for today but rather are merely descriptive of an ancient author's beliefs and intentions; or these critics substitute critical methods for ecclesial practices, supposing that the scholar's work rather than God's Spirit is the principal constraint in protecting the Bible's perspicuity.[7]

Some even note, with biting irony, that many who now seek to tame biblical texts with religious blinders on were initiated into their discipline as an act of spiritual devotion, motivated in their study by the very beliefs they now set aside. Indeed, one inference of this irony is a judgment about modernity's humanism that has forsaken a deeply religious way of thinking about the Bible and its study. For this reason it seems logical for us to assume that the rehabilitation of the Bible's influence within the church is tied to the recovery of a religious grammar about the Bible's essential character, namely, that the Bible is sacred Scripture. This may in turn reshape the exegete's prior judgments about the Bible and even about the practices of biblical criticism as holy work.

But what else stands behind this locution? What is meant by the distinction — often made today but rarely defined — between the Bible and Scripture? What must be said initially is that this distinction is hardly conciliatory of the present divorce between the church and academy that I have noted above: "the Bible" is what the scholarly guild seeks to tame, whereas "Scripture" is what the church seeks to hear as a timely word from God brought near by the Holy Spirit. In making this comparison, the church presses the ecclesial location as the Bible's legal address: there its texts are read and heard differently than in the academy; they are read as sacred lections that frame and form a vital faith in God. There and only there, where believers congregate together to worship God, is the Bible faithfully engaged as a sacred text. For true believers, then, the Bible is no ordinary text; it is the Scripture whose very property is to mediate the word of the Lord God Almighty to those people who belong to God.

As a metaphor of the sacred, "Scripture" implies a very different sense from that of a precious artifact placed in a museum for its members to look at with respect for its age and reverence for its cultural importance. The sa-

---

7. John C. Poirier, who appeals to James Barr's scathing criticism of Brevard S. Childs's "canonical approach" for moral support, calls this use of Scripture "definition-rigging," and he argues that locating the Bible's meaning in the church is a variety of reader-response criticism that, in the end, is "an abuse of categories set by the NT writers themselves." Poirier, "The Canonical Approach and the Idea of 'Scripture,'" *Expository Times* 116, no. 11 (2005): 366.

cred nature of Scripture is more a sense or spiritual temper apprehended through its inspired and profitable use within the life of a congregation — for "teaching, reproof, correction, training in righteous living" (2 Tim. 3:16b). Moreover, while "Scripture" has become an essential idiom in current objections to Gabler's modernist project noted above, it has also become the edgy catchword of the church's take on the academy's work with the Bible, which is deemed "arbitrary, uncontrollable, and finally moot."[8]

Now I readily admit, if only parenthetically, that the above appraisal is meant for an academic setting and reflects the mindset of professional scholars whose work seeks to underwrite a faithful engagement of the Bible as the Scripture of God's church. Within most congregations, earnest believers look to the Bible as a sacred book without a passing worry about what scholars think. They "incense it, swear by it, parade it around in processions, anoint it, bow before it, sing from it, pound on it, lay it on wounds of head and heart. Sometimes they even read it."[9] But the subtext of my chapter here is that the church's rank-and-file *should* worry about what the academy has done with its Scripture, since many of their leaders have been shaped by modernity's "hermeneutics of suspicion," and that has had deleterious results in the teaching and preaching ministry of the church.

Consider, for example, the Bible's most evident properties: the Bible is a literary collection of ancient and theologically diverse writings. Given the material character of biblical texts, scholars are trained to approach the Bible as a time-conditioned ancient text, each of whose author's communicative intentions was shaped by the currents of his own day and in response to the circumstances of his particular audience. Again, the historical distance created by the passage of time is a challenge for us all. But the challenge to those who pick up the Bible as Scripture — as a medium of God's eternal word brought near — is different from that of the historian. For the critic, the challenge is to navigate what Barth called "the strange world of the Bible," often with a scarcity of landmarks to guide her, in order to understand and retrieve a text's "original" meaning as somehow normative. Sharply put, then, the critic's challenge is to *create* distance between today's readers and the text's ancient audience, and thus to detach the text from its ecclesial set-

---

8. Robert W. Jenson, "Scripture's Authority in the Church," in Ellen F. Davies and Richard B. Hays, eds., *The Art of Reading Scripture* (Grand Rapids: Eerdmans, 2003), p. 27.

9. Luke T. Johnson, "Fragments of an Untidy Conversation: Theology and the Literary Diversity of the New Testament," in S. J. Kraftchick, C. D. Myers, and B. C. Ollenburger, eds., *Problems and Perspectives: Biblical Theology* (Nashville: Abingdon, 1995), p. 277.

ting, where an "original meaning" might be contaminated by a faithful people's appropriation of it.

An epistemology of the Bible that is linked to this myth of originality is doomed from the beginning. Besides an array of practical problems associated with criticism's preoccupation with indeterminate historical prolegomena, it remains unclear to me why the compositional moment should be favored over the canonical moment, say, when a text is first regarded as Scripture by the faith community. Given the scarcity of information about the authorial moment, no one can honestly claim that a text's meaning is at its clearest or most relevant at its point of origin. In the hands of suspicious critics, if the perspicuity of biblical texts at their point of origin is debatable, the texts themselves become irrelevant and dispensable.

To safeguard the epistemology of Scripture against this sort of nihilism, conservative interpreters add a variety of metaphysical claims about the production of its divinely inspired texts. If a biblical text is written by divine inspiration, then its "original meaning" — that is, the meaning intended by its divinely inspired author — is revealing and normative. While such a belief is taken on faith and in the abstract, it still asks questions of the modern historical project that largely go unanswered.[10]

My purpose is neither to disparage nor to celebrate the critic's work; rather, it is to point out that her challenge is different from those who approach the biblical text as Scripture. When an ordinary believer appeals to a Pauline text using the formula "Paul says," he is not really interested in the historian's Paul or in his intended meaning for first-century auditors/readers; he is interested in recovering the text's plain sense for its living readers. The stark contrast between retrieving a time-conditioned meaning frozen in some distant, strange, and ancient past and recovering the timeless teaching of a biblical text to make it ever-present for its ever-changing audiences envisions very different approaches to, even judgments about that text — and about the historical, metaphysical, and spiritual distances its meanings must travel to its present readers.[11] Simply put, then, speaking of the Bible as

10. Perhaps it would be more helpful for conservatives to argue for the theological (and hermeneutical) importance of written texts: Scripture is *graphē* (e.g., 2 Tim. 3:16; 2 Pet. 3:16). While the act of writing a text stabilizes fluid traditions for the benefit of posterity, the locus of authority is the text per se and not the act of writing or reading texts. For this reason, NT writers frequently introduce Scripture (often rewritten for a new audience!) with the formula "it is written."

11. The apt distinction between "retrieving" the past meaning of a classic text to study

Scripture entails an optimism of faith that the church catholic offers a setting of worship and magisterial guidance for navigating the distance of time between a biblical text and its current audience: "The word is near you, on your lips and in your heart" (Rom. 10:8).

While modern biblical criticism has successfully clarified the Bible's literary and theological diversity, the overall effect has been to detach and isolate texts from each other. Rather than a Bible whose teaching presents a coherent and unified understanding of God, critics have reduced it to a fragmented anthology of unrelated bits. The modern challenge to the Bible's sacred nature and inherent capacity to bear witness to God, which is predicated by this keen awareness of its massive diversity, is not at all evident to the critic whose principal interest is to speak honestly about it. But it is a challenge for faithful readers whose theological engagement of the Bible as Scripture presumes to hear the word of *one* God within the bounds of the *one,* holy, catholic, and apostolic church. That is, the singularity of the church's theological grammar does not anticipate well the Bible's own diversity.

Perhaps the best response to this challenge is a straightforward one: while admitting that the Bible consists of many different parts that do not easily fit together in a coherent way, one might propose new strategies by which the interpreter can reconnect the Bible's diverse parts into an integrated, coherent whole: Old Testament *and* New Testament; Pauline *and* Catholic Epistles; Synoptic *and* Johannine Gospels — and so forth. My own work in constructing "intracanonical conversations" between theologically and literarily diverse biblical witnesses has sponsored but one response to the material problem of the Bible's disunity.[12] And I admit that my motive in doing so looks toward a theological or metaphysical assumption about the unity of Scripture — of the "sacred" — whose referent is the same God who has lived with and who stands over a profound diversity of congregations across space and time.[13] It is this theological affirmation more than any

---

it in the past — the work of modern critical scholarship — and "recovering" some present meaning for the benefit of its living readers is made by Michael Walzer, "Philosophy, History, and the Recovery of Tradition," *Chronicle of Higher Education* (June 16, 2000): A56.

12. See, for example, my "Toward a Unifying Theology of the Catholic Epistles: A Canonical Approach," in J. Schlosser, ed., *Catholic Epistles and the Tradition,* BETL 176 (Leuven: Peeters, 2004), pp. 43-71.

13. See L. T. Johnson, "Fragments of an Untidy Conversation," for a brilliant statement about the theological problem of Scripture's literary diversity.

other idea that critiques the distance created by biblical criticism between the sacred text and those very congregations.

But another reflection of this problem is still more challenging than devising new interpretive strategies to reckon with the Bible's diversity: if the Bible is not at all unified but presents very different and even contrary articulations of God's gospel, the tendency is to treat it as a "grab-bag" (George Lindbeck's term), choosing bits and pieces according to self-interest or sectarian doctrine. For this reason I have also suggested the application of an external apparatus — namely, the Rule of Faith — to tame and unify disparate biblical witnesses. The Bible's own unity does not exist at its literal level but is finally envisaged in its different utterances about the church's core theological agreements.[14] In this sense, the unity of Scripture is both regulated and discerned by something outside the text itself: by what the one church confesses to be true about the one God. In this way, it is the Rule that prevents the grab-bag mindset, and it is the Rule that enables faithful readers to put "Humpty-Dumpty back together again."

The Bible as Canon

Considerable attention has recently gathered around the very idea of a biblical canon, not only as a carrier of theological freight but also as a hermeneutical medium.[15] This attention has more specifically concentrated in two areas: on the Bible's final literary, or "canonical," form (e.g., Childs, Seitz, Trobisch), which instantiates a particular articulation of God's word, and on the canonical process itself (e.g., Sanders, Gamble, McDonald), which is guided from start to finish by the community's "canon consciousness" — a sense of additional performances of certain sacred texts in forming and framing Christian life (e.g., Abraham, Vanhoozer). In both places one is likely to find scholars interested in a theological appropriation of the Bible, whether for today's faithful readers or within the framework of a history of receiving and interpreting biblical texts as authoritative for Christian theology.

14. See, for example, my essay on this point, "The Rule of Faith in Theological Hermeneutics" in J. B. Green and M. Turner, eds., *Between Two Horizons: Spanning New Testament Studies and Systematic Theology* (Grand Rapids: Eerdmans, 1999), pp. 88-107.

15. See my fuller discussion of this point, "The Significance of a Canonical Perspective of the Church's Scripture," in L. McDonald and J. A. Sanders, eds., *The Canon Debate* (Peabody, MA: Hendrickson, 2002), pp. 528-40.

Moreover, the biblical canon, whether in final form or during its formation, was not regarded as a loose collection of writings from which any one may be read in a way that is isolated from the other writings with which it is collected and to which it is joined within the biblical canon. That is, collections of individual writings were formed over time and fitted into an authoritative biblical canon to serve future generations of believers as a guide to their understanding of God. And using such a guide productively requires the readers to be ever alert to the unity (or "canonical shape") of each text, typically cued by the precanonical history of that text and the reasons for its reception as canonical, but, more importantly, to the grouping of texts into collections and the relationships between these collections as parts of an integral whole (e.g., Wall).

These cursory observations about the idea of a biblical canon and the canonical process that produced it raise considerable questions. Not the least of these questions is a clear working definition of a biblical canon, for as McDonald points out, "much of the controversy surrounding canon formation has to do with the lack of agreement on the meaning of canon."[16] In fact, the ancient church's choice of the metaphor "canon" to assign — or to "sign" — authority to a particular collection of sacred texts merits our attention, since the reasons for doing so, to the extent that they may be discerned from its initial usage, may help us understand its present value as a theological metaphor for the Bible's religious authority.

Furthermore, the selection of "canon" when speaking of the Bible's special authority is logically linked to the reasons for selecting certain writings from among other sacred writings to form a canon of Scripture. It would seem crucial to our project to observe that, while all canonized texts were first deemed Scripture, whether because of their usefulness or their apostolic origins, not all Scripture finally became canonical (see below). I take it, then, that the idea of a biblical canon must confer some "value added" to Scripture that may help us understand how to use the term "canon" more precisely. Again, my interest is not to reconstruct the history of the Bible's formation, which other scholars have done (notably, von Campenhausen, Bruce, Metzger, Gamble, McDonald, Trobisch). Rather, my interest is to retrieve clues from it to inform our present use of "canon" as metaphorical of the Bible's religious authority. And Gamble correctly notes that the meaning of a biblical canon "can be estimated only against this background."[17]

---

16. L. McDonald, *The Biblical Canon* (Peabody, MA: Hendrickson, 2006), p. 40.
17. H. Gamble, *The New Testament Canon* (Philadelphia: Fortress, 1985), p. 15.

According to Bruce Metzger, the word "canon" came to be used in reference to material things — a canon of confessed beliefs, of sacred texts, of conciliar decisions, of spiritual leaders — only "little by little" over time, borrowing freely from its widespread secular usage especially among the philosophers and rhetors of antiquity.[18] While these layers of meaning were not added to an evolving idea of a religious canon in arbitrary ways but were intentional and reflected changes in the church's perception of its canonical heritage, at its root the referent of "canon" was to a stout reed or firm rod that was used to measure cloth or timbers consistently and accurately. Within its ecclesial setting, "canon" typically indicated the use of a certain standard of accepted truth, of right conduct, of useful practices, and of those who exemplified or personified these things to others.[19]

The earliest Christian uses of *kanōn* are found in a Pauline benediction (Gal 6:16) in reference to a prior theological saying (cf. 6:15), and then more formally in the second century by Clement of Alexandria of a rule of theological beliefs.[20] We should note that these uses are well prior to the church's invention and formation of a Christian biblical canon. In these initial uses, the concept of "canon" carries a more dynamic, functional meaning detached from a biblical canon in which a "canon of faith" inculcated a way of believing, of behaving, of thinking within a particular community that was saturated with stories about Jesus, his apostles, and other sainted exemplars of the faith, and where sacred texts were read aloud.

Irenaeus's use of the "rule of faith" (*Adv. Haer.* 1.9.4) in supplying all believers with a *permanent* theological grammar uses "canon" for a medium of Christian unity and continuity. For him, the notion of apostolic succession had less to do with apostolic hagiography and more to do with the perpetual relevance of the theological Rule of Faith that the original apostles received directly from Jesus to pass on to others. Indeed, their salvation depended on people coming to a knowledge of that version of the truth and repenting based on it. Such a "canon" is also used to clarify contrasting items

---

18. B. Metzger, *The Canon of the New Testament* (Oxford: Clarendon Press, 1987), pp. 289-93. For different ways in which the word "canon" was used in Second Temple Judaism and by Greco-Roman literati, from whom the early church learned and borrowed for its uses, see H. Beyer's illuminating article on *kanōn* in *TDNT* 3:596-602; cf. Gamble, *NT Canon*, pp. 15-18.

19. Contra William J. Abraham, *Canon and Criterion in Christian Theology* (Oxford: Clarendon Press, 1998), pp. 19-21,

20. Clement of Alexandria, *Strom.* IV. xv. 98.

of differing quality. According to this nuance, whatever was stipulated as "canonical" becomes a plumb line between good and bad, right and wrong, truth and false, superior and inferior things. In antiquity, the measurement of a straight line, whether materially or its salutary effect, was sometimes clarified by a crooked line.

My point is that the essential inference of "canon," whether of a canonical heritage inclusive of theological ideas, sainted exemplars, moral practices, sacred objects or more particularly of a canon of sacred writings, is that of some standard by which the content of what a community believes or how its members behave is measured. This canonical standard is apropos with catholic scope (i.e., for any and all current believers) and prospectively so (i.e., for any and all future generations of believers).[21]

But as McDonald points out, the church's choice of *kanōn*, as a principal metaphor of religious authority should be distinguished from other terms available from the Greco-Roman world that went unused, especially a *pinax* (lit., "tablet") of specific things.[22] That is, the primary metaphor of the religious authority was not envisioned as a catalogue of certain things, fixed for all time — a creed of core beliefs or a collection of texts — to mark out clear boundaries around the faith community for all to see.[23] The church's measuring stick was not first of all a *pinax* that circumscribed faith and practice by means of lists of things; rather, religious authority was something affective and internal, unwritten and thus apprehended in faith and by persistent use during public worship. Again by inference, then, the orienting concern of a biblical canon is not framed by an authoritative listing of books, which remains contested between faith communities in any case; rather, the concern is for a more dynamic and practical performance of the Bible during worship with the effect of cultivating right patterns of faith and life in its interested readers/auditors.

Only later, when the idea of a "catalogue" *(pinax)* was added to these principal inferences of "canon" did our current, more formal idea of a self-contained — some would even say "closed" — catalogue of canonical books emerge. The first to articulate this expanded idea, at least according to extant literature, was Athanasius during the fourth century (ca. 367), when he famously presented lists of the church's canonical books in response to Nicaea's

21. Cf. Abraham, *Canon and Criterion,* pp. 26-56.
22. McDonald, *Biblical Canon,* pp. 54-55.
23. McDonald, pp. 43-44.

detractors. I take it that his reason for doing so was purposeful, consistent with the circumstances that convened the Council of Nicaea in the first place and not incidental to the history of this idea. While not wishing to subvert the primary inferences of a biblical canon noted above, I believe that the idea of a fixed canon and the hermeneutics tied to such are worth pondering. But I leave this project to others and offer only a couple brief observations.

First, what we gain in understanding the idea of a biblical canon qua *pinax* is a more precise recognition of which sacred texts actually work best for those "who wish for instruction in the word of godliness."[24] Athanasius's point fully recognizes the *functional* authority of those books he lists — those texts that have proved to work best for holy instruction — and in this sense adapts the church's earlier use of "canon" in a concrete and rational way. Second, however, the problem with making lists is to misplace this more functional recognition of the Bible's religious authority, dependent on the Spirit and worship for application, for something more static. As Gamble notes, the very idea of "canonical" became linked first of all to the Bible and then, second, to being included "in the list." The list itself was reified into a sacred thing, and the "status" of a canonical book became a more important matter of its authority than its use.

Furthermore, the concrete typically overwhelms the ineffable in human operations, and so it is that the community historically has concentrated the Bible's authority "in the list," absolutizing it and finally making it the one and only articulation of the church's theological "rule" (despite the loud protestations for doing so!). Rarely does the community consider the lack of evidence that the canonical process was ever closed down and the list of sacred writings fixed; the list per se has become the norm. Ultimately, not only did the Bible come to do most if not all of the heavy lifting for the church's theologians, but the list of writings itself took on the character of the divine.[25] The reason for my insistence that the earlier definition of canon be adapted as the primary inference drawn from a biblical canon is to safe-

24. Athanasius of Alexandria, *Ep.* 39. 7.

25. Gamble, p. 18. I take it that the Bible's canonical authority is limited in at least two senses: (1) The Bible is one among other articulations of the church's rule of faith. (2) The Bible is not self-interpreting but must always be subjected to faithful interpretation. The multivalence of biblical texts is reflected by their multiple interpreters of differing spiritual maturity and intellectual talent; and while always aimed at the one God, biblical interpretation also responds to the issues found in ever-changing settings where faithful readers are interested in hearing God's word afresh.

guard the Bible and the church's understanding of its religious authority from this kind of hagiography in which being counted "in the list" becomes a more important matter than actually using the books therein.

Athanasius's commentary on the biblical canon is also useful to observe that the biblical canon is the literary byproduct of a process of selection. What interests me is not the familiar emphasis of most historical constructions of the canonical process that it identified and selected those sacred texts whose content and effect agreed with the church's Rule of Faith over others that were judged heretical: the sacred from the profane to mark out insiders from outsiders. This is how the church's Apologists read the results. But the church's historians, such as Eusebius, and its theologians, such as Athanasius, are more subtle. They often speak of a process that distinguishes Scripture from other scriptures, canonical texts from those judged merely sacred. While Athanasius also distinguishes those writings he lists "in the canon and handed down as sacred" (par. 3) from those "apocryphal writings that are the invention of heretics" (par. 7), he also distinguishes between canonical and those "other books not included in the canon but appointed by the Fathers to be read by those who newly join us" (par. 7), such as the *Shepherd of Hermas*. Athanasius uses the idiom of catechesis when characterizing the *Shepherd's* sacred nature: new believers would find in it instruction for godly living. What is clear to him, however, is that "scripture" and "canon" are not synonymous metaphors for the Bible, but each infers different properties of the one book.[26]

Sharply put, then, what is true of a canonical text that need not be true of its sacred nature? The answer to this question can hardly be reduced to a critical matter of authorship or date, or to a lack of intrinsic value or theological perspicuity. Ironically, my answer is found "in the list" and perhaps also in the canonical process that produced the list (or lists). That is, what finally must distinguish our use of "scripture" and "canon" as theological metaphors concerns the manner by which "the list" articulates the Bible's authorized role as a theological rule. Of course, because this list is comprised of texts already recognized as Scripture, some of what is discussed earlier under the rubric "The Bible as Scripture" may also be useful in a discussion of the Bible's authority as canon. For example, the Bible's characteristic literary or theological diversity, if we include every part of the list as canonical,

26. Cf. Charles Wood, *The Formation of Christian Understanding* (Philadelphia: Westminster, 1981), pp. 82-105.

makes it impossible to reduce or absolutize the importance of any one part of the whole canon.

But what distinguishes the biblical canon from those very scriptures it includes is the list itself: the biblical canon articulates the church's theological rule in the literary form of a catalogue of books or collections of books. While I am aware of most of what must finally qualify this definition, let me plunge ahead to make two related and relevant observations about it. First, the list of Old Testament and New Testament books forms a self-contained and singular whole. The ancient rubrics "old" and "new," while problematic, nonetheless imply this wholeness: there is nothing beyond a list that includes what is "old" and what is "new." There is no third category. Every part of the whole must be taken together with every other part of the whole, Old and New, Gospel and Letter, Pauline and Catholic, Genesis and Revelation, and so on. Further, the different parts form a sequential and unfolding whole, so that the Old is read prior to and is continued by the New, the Gospel is read prior to and is continued by Acts, and Acts by the Letters, the Old and the New are read prior to and are assumed by the Revelation. That is, the ordering of collections is precise, not arbitrary in the manner of a careful and practiced performance of the sacred word — a performance that anticipates a good result.

Second, the list was produced and made complete over time as people observed the spiritual benefaction when using sacred books. A canon becomes a canon only by use, and canonical lists took shape by accounting what texts worked well *together* and even to some extent in what particular arrangement of texts. The entire list, then, unfolded not as an arbitrary assemblage of odd bits but of tested bits collected and related together in a particular fashion to do their authorized work more effectively. I have argued elsewhere that books were added to an emergent New Testament for reasons consistent with its canonical role: Acts is added because its narrative freighted the spiritual authority of the "canonical" authors of the letters that follow it; the collection of Catholic Epistles was formed and then added to the list in part to correct widespread misreadings of the Pauline witness (by insiders and outsiders) as well as to add a fresh interpretation of God's gospel.[27] That is, books were added to the list in order to make its performance of God's

27. *Called to Be Church: The Book of Acts for a New Day,* with Anthony B. Robinson (Grand Rapids: Eerdmans, 2006), pp. 266-73; "Toward a Unifying Theology of the Catholic Epistles; "The Function of the Pastoral Letters within the Pauline Canon of the New Testament: A Canonical Approach," in S. E. Porter, ed., *The Pauline Canon* (Leiden: Brill, 2004), pp. 27-44.

word more robust, more persuasive, more useful, more articulate. A final orienting concern when approaching the Bible as canon, then, is of a carefully crafted book constructed from various scriptures to form a complete and integral whole for its use among believers as a theological medium.

The Bible as Sacrament

The primary purpose in this portion of my essay is not to make the case that the Bible should be added to the list of approved sacraments, but rather to suggest that "sacrament" provides a viable metaphor for the effects of the Bible's performance within the worshiping community, which are sacrament-like. In making this point, I'm alert to the problems inherent in discussing "the Bible as sacrament" in a classroom where Protestant students have deep suspicions that sacramentalism is not a biblical notion and may even be subversive of the Magisterial Reformation's "Scripture principle." And in any number of Protestant congregations in North America, which participate in a renewal of interest in liturgical reform where an interest in artful symbolism sometimes displaces biblical exposition, this worry may be well-founded. In any case, definitions of "sacrament" are complicated things: How does one define a sacred mystery or make sense of divine grace? And they are difficult for any teacher to exploit in clarifying the Bible's purchase for confused students. What follows, then, is a modest proposal.

Sandra Schneiders claims that "Scripture, like the Eucharist, is best understood as sacrament."[28] Following Augustine's more narrow definition of a sacrament, she explains that the Bible is a material "symbol" that signifies God's encounter with human life preeminently in Christ. Any biblical text or story, when read aloud (i.e., preached, studied, discussed) as a congregational practice, becomes a medium of the real presence and power of the resurrected Lord in its midst. In fact, it is the living Jesus who through the Spirit enters into conversation with believers through the medium of a biblical text. It is the biblical text, whether read or heard, studied or contemplated, that carries the mystery of God's truth to those who receive it. By analogy, then, the biblical text per se is like the bread and wine of the Eucharist, a faithful proclamation of the text's witness to the gospel is like the priestly act of consecrating the table, and hearing that proclamation in faith is like re-

---

28. S. Schneiders, *The Revelatory Text* (San Francisco: Harper, 1991), p. 40.

ceiving and ingesting the wafer and wine in that auditors "ingest" the eternal truth of the incarnate Word. Schneiders puts it sharply: "Scripture is the sacrament of the word of God."[29]

Typically, however, this orientation toward the Bible is lacking in Protestant worship, where the familiar rubric "word and sacrament" sees dissimilar referents of differing effects: "word" refers to the proclamation of Scripture, while "sacrament" refers primarily to the Eucharist and baptism. And in line with the Protestant "Scripture principle," word almost always trumps sacrament. In fact, different Protestant communions contest whether what is signified by a sacrament is also caused and realized in those who receive it. Sacrament is an add-on, some symbol of another spiritual reality; and thus it can only supplement the gospel's truth but is not equated with it. Word is not sacrament. But my point is that when Scripture is rendered and received as a sacrament of the word, not merely added to it but representative of it, then we can reimagine a communicative moment in which the very presence of the living Jesus is mediated and experienced by its faithful auditors.

The focus of sacramental theology, besides linking the physical sign with the spiritual signified, has always been on the efficacy of a sacrament for those who receive it. And that is where my focus lingers as well.[30] At least for my purposes here, canon as "sacrament" works best as a metaphor for the Bible's role when defining the spiritual benefits to the communities that use it. In his review of sacramental theology, Alister E. McGrath considers the "essential" role of sacraments in Christian formation in terms of four benefits they effect.[31] When relating each benefit to the community's reception of the Bible, especially in worship, we can see the sacrament-like nature of its role become more evident.

Sacraments Carry God's Grace. Most agree that a sacrament's most essential role is as a means of God's grace for those who receive it. Of course, this assumes that a sacrament's gracious effect is real and not merely the public symbol of an inward operation of God's grace: that is, the effect of mediated grace is a discrete experience of God's salvation-creating power. If this human experience, however mysterious its cause, occurs in a way similar

29. Schneiders, p. 41.

30. The fuller definition of sacrament proffered by post-Augustinian theologians such as Hugh of St. Victor or Peter Lombard emphasizes the real benefits sacraments confer on those who partake of them.

31. A. E. McGrath, *Christian Theology: An Introduction,* 2nd ed. (Oxford: Blackwell, 1997), pp. 502-09.

to the sacrament itself, then one should expect that our receiving of the biblical text results in coming to a knowledge of the truth of God's gospel and issues in God's salvation (cf. 1 Tim. 2:3-7). A more functional definition of "inspiration" (*theopneustos,* "God-breathing") in 2 Timothy 3:16 may help to illustrate this point. The word considered in its canonical context is read as an intertext that recalls and reinterprets antecedent stories of God breathing new life into Human (Gen. 2:7) and Israel (Ezek. 37:1-10). As a *typos* of divine agency and the present force of the implied action of the 2 Timothy passage, "inspiration" envisions a God who is continually enlivening the congregation that uses its Scripture in "teaching, correction, reproof, training," as the medium through which the Spirit of the resurrected Christ conveys God's life-giving power to those who humbly receive it.[32] The use of Scripture is not merely a "sign" of divine agency, but its use effects the believer's Christian formation, since the text goes on to claim that "the man of God (= Timothy) may be made complete (presumably by God's grace), equipped for every good work" (2 Tim. 3:17).

Sacraments Cultivate Faith. Among the most important literary features of the New Testament's so-called Pastoral Epistles is the repeated exhortation to remember what Paul taught, which is then summarized in creedal formulae and stipulated as the church's "sound doctrine" (cf. 1 Tim. 1:11; 2:3-7), which establishes the pattern of Christian faith and life (cf. 2 Tim. 1:9-14). The biblical witness of prophets and apostles is not merely a visible sign that supplements God's word but is itself an articulation of that word that guides the life of faith.

The way the sacrament is received is important, since grace has a variable effect on those who receive it. Adapting the Pauline warning that believers should not receive the Eucharist "in an unworthy manner" (1 Cor. 11:27), the spiritual effect of receiving the biblical word depends on the extent the communicant "gets rid of every moral vice and every trace of spiritual impurity, and receives the word with meekness" (James 1:21a). Like the book of James, which considers doubt subversive of faith, when the Reformers insisted that believers turn with complete confidence to Scripture to find God's prognosis of our spiritual ills, they did not imagine that the church's sacred text would be

---

32. "2 Timothy 3:16 as an Anti-Gnostic Polemic," unpublished paper presented to the Society of Biblical Literature at its annual meeting in New York, 1984. I intend to develop this reading of 2 Tim 3:16 in my forthcoming commentary on the Pastoral Epistles in the Two Horizons New Testament Commentary series (Grand Rapids: Eerdmans).

read by a hermeneutics of suspicion or subjected to modernity's ideological criticisms! Whether read to afflict the comfortable or to comfort the afflicted, the sacramental regard of the Bible's performance among those who receive its word with meekness enables God "to save your souls" (James 1:21b).

Sacraments Constitute Christian Unity. Stanley Hauerwas laments the divisiveness generated by unregulated, individualistic interpretations of the Bible in the American Protestant church, and calls for the return of a magisterial office to restore church order.[33] Douglas Koskela echoes Hauerwas and proposes that what is needed is a "formal teaching office of the church" that is similar to the function of the magisterium in the Roman church.[34]

I take their point: the exercise of mature priestly leadership when interpreting the Bible for a community, especially when consecrated and offered as a sacrament of God's word, is a critical feature of its constructive effect. My principal concern in underwriting this element of the Bible-as-sacrament metaphor is not what ecclesiastical apparatus or seminary education best guarantees the spiritual maturity and intellectual preparation of those who teach the Bible for the church, though those may be critical bits of the larger solution. Rather, it is to emphasize with Koskela a congregation's oversight in selecting teachers whose character is "mature, patient, wise and who are deeply immersed in the life of faith."[35] One is reminded of 1 Timothy's instructions of the Christian woman whose religious virtue is evinced in part by the choices she makes in her instructors (1 Tim. 2:11-12).

Sacraments Confirm God's Promises. The final effect McGrath discusses in his theological summary of sacrament regards the distinctively Protestant emphasis on sacrament as correlative of God's biblical promises. That is, there is always this sense of time in the celebration of the sacrament that integrates the past (Jesus) and the present (church) eras of salvation's history with its future. So, for example, the Pauline liturgy of the Eucharist, which testifies to the past death of Jesus as presently efficacious of the believer's reconciliation with God, concludes with the exhortation to ingest the bread and wine as public testimony of the gospel now in effect "until he comes" (1 Cor. 11:26b).

---

33. S. Hauerwas, *Unleashing the Scripture: Freeing the Bible from Captivity to America* (Nashville: Abingdon, 1993).

34. D. Koskela, "The Authority of Scripture in Its Ecclesial Context," in William J. Abraham, Jason E. Vickers, and Natalie B. Van Kirk, eds., *Canonical Theism: A Proposal for Theology and the Church* (Grand Rapids: Eerdmans, 2008), pp. 210-223.

35. Koskela, "The Authority of Scripture," pp. 217-20.

To perceive the Bible's role as sacrament-like is to understand that its proclamation as a worship practice must be organized by the deep logic of the story itself, which is plotted from Genesis to Revelation by God's faithfulness to promises made. But this is not an easy perspicuity, for the Bible is not an easy book to render clearly: its teaching is often confusing and contradictory and requires the most mature and competent of guides. And here is where the church fathers, especially Origen, are the best guides of all because, while they are alert to the Bible's offense, their practice of digging down to the text's spiritual meaning recovers in the clearest way its essential meaning: in Christ God has acted faithfully to the promise to deliver all of creation from the ravages of human folly and sin. When every sermon, every teaching, every lection, every lecture makes this point, over and over again, the Bible will have its most profound sacramental effect.

Conclusion

This essay is prompted by a pedagogical problem: How do teachers introduce the study of Scripture to support the intellectual and theological formation of students? I contend that the use of Scripture in the service of religious ends requires a clear-headed — and I would argue, a prior — articulation of what Scripture is. Confusion in the troubled souls (and minds) of students is often the result of a teacher's failure to set out from the start what core commitments will regulate the class's approach to Scripture. (In fact, incoherent interpretation among biblical scholars sometimes results from this same failure.) Instruction that seeks to aim students at God will make sense to students only when a theology of Scripture requires it.

The reader of this chapter may imagine still other metaphors or typologies to use with respect to the Bible, to which biblical studies may neatly cohere. The ones I have used in this study — Scripture, canon, sacrament — are traditional ones, routinely used by Christians to confirm or anticipate performances that serve sacred ends.[36] The limited task of this chapter has been to offer robust definitions of each metaphor with the aim of preparing introductory students at a church-related university for healthy Bible study.

---

36. I develop a biblical theology of Scripture from the book of Acts that relates these three terms together in Robinson and Wall, *Called to Be Church*, pp. 260-69.

Axiomatic in the modern academy is an ethics of reading shaped by the intentions of the author or community that produced the studied text. I have here favored the church over the modern academy when introducing the Bible for serious instruction, not only because it is apropos for my particular academic location to do so but because it is the right thing to do. That is, the Bible belongs to the church, and its intentions ought to inform — at the very least — the orienting concerns of the wider academy. Without denying the legitimacy of any approach to Scripture or the critical interests of any interpretive strategy, I would simply ask that all teachers introduce the Bible to their classes with a careful articulation of those ecclesial beliefs and practices of the religious community that produced it. Such civility would then allow for an equally careful and honest introduction of an instructor's commitments to the Bible and how those commitments cohere to a particular course of study. Perhaps such an introduction to a teacher's instruction of Scripture will present itself to students as a *therapeia psychēs*.

The Healing Work of the Liturgy

Geoffrey Wainwright

"In a broken world. . ." begins the text on ministry in *Baptism, Eucharist and Ministry*, the landmark document passed by the Faith and Order Commission of the World Council of Churches in Lima, Peru, in 1982: "In a broken world, God calls the whole of humanity to become God's people." A fallen humankind is implicated in so many ways — individually and collectively, physically and spiritually — in the sickness of a world fragmented through the rupture of its relationship with the Creator, whose saving purpose yet remains firm. In my Yorkshire youth, the local idiom had it that a person recovering from illness was "on the mend." God's work for the mending or healing of this broken and ailing world is recounted in Trinitarian terms by the Lima text in paragraphs that received practically unanimous endorsement in the official responses of the churches:

1. In a broken world God calls the whole of humanity to become God's people. For this purpose God chose Israel and then spoke in a unique and decisive way in Jesus Christ, God's Son. Jesus made his own the nature, condition and cause of the whole human race, giving himself as a sacrifice for all. Jesus' life of service, his death and resurrection, are the foundation of a new community which is built up continually by the good news of the Gospel and the gifts of the sacraments. The Holy Spirit unites in a single body those who follow Jesus Christ and sends them as witnesses into the world. Belonging to the Church means living in communion with God through Jesus Christ in the Holy Spirit.

2. The life of the Church is based on Christ's victory over the powers of evil and death, accomplished once for all. Christ offers forgiveness, invites to repentance and delivers from destruction. Through Christ, people are enabled to turn in praise to God and in service to their neighbours. In Christ they find the source of new life in freedom, mutual forgiveness and love. Through Christ their hearts are directed to the consummation of the Kingdom where Christ's victory will become manifest and all things made new. God's purpose is that, in Jesus Christ, all people should share in this fellowship.

3. The Church lives through the liberating and renewing power of the Holy Spirit. . . . The Spirit calls people to faith, sanctifies them through many gifts, gives them strength to witness to the Gospel, and empowers them to serve in hope and love. The Spirit keeps the Church in the truth and guides it despite the frailty of its members.

4. The Church is called to proclaim and prefigure the Kingdom of God. It accomplishes this by announcing the Gospel to the world and by its very existence as the body of Christ. . . . Christ established a new access to the Father. Living in this communion with God, all members of the Church are called to confess their faith and to give account of their hope. They are to identify with the joys and sufferings of all people as they seek to witness in caring love. . . . In so doing they bring to the world a foretaste of the joy and glory of God's Kingdom.

5. The Holy Spirit bestows on the community diverse and complementary gifts. These are for the common good of the whole people and are manifested in acts of service within the community and to the world. They may be gifts of communicating the Gospel in word and deed, gifts of healing, gifts of praying, gifts of teaching and learning, gifts of serving, gifts of guiding and following, gifts of inspiration and vision. All members are called to discover, with the help of the community, the gifts they have received and to use them for the building up of the Church and for the service of the world to which the Church is sent.[1]

These opening paragraphs from the "Ministry" section of *BEM* (the acronym for "Baptism, Eucharist and Ministry" by which the Lima text became universally known) incorporate in a remarkable way the entire range

---

1. *Baptism, Eucharist and Ministry,* Faith and Order Paper No. 111 (Geneva: World Council of Churches, 1982).

of themes that make up the present book on the "healing resources of the Christian faith." Moreover, the quoted paragraphs are loaded with hints, echoes, and indeed direct mentions of the worshiping life and practice of the church. My purpose in this chapter is to display the Christian liturgy as the paradigm of God's healing work toward a fallen human race — and our co-operation with it.

First, a few linguistic remarks. Etymologically, one component of the word "liturgy" is the Greek word *ergon,* or "work"; the other half of the word derives from *laos,* or "people." This combination was used by many in the twentieth-century liturgical movement to expound the worship assembly as "the work of the people," in which all members of the church, in their respective roles, took a "full, conscious, and active part" in the offering of praise and prayer to the triune God.[2] The Greek *leitourgia* also had an earlier, secular meaning: it was closer to our own "public works" or "public service," that is, duties performed on behalf of the wider society. Along that line, one might think of the church's liturgy as celebrated for the sake of the world — on its behalf and for its benefit. In any case, the Greek stem *erg* will repay attention as we consider the "work" of healing.

Shifting languages, we note that the usual German word for "worship" is *Gottesdienst,* or "divine service." This can be, and often is, expounded bidirectionally: Protestant theologians especially like to show that the "upward" movement of our service before God is preceded, and indeed enabled, by the "downward" movement of God's service to us. In *The Knowledge of God and the Service of God according to the Teaching of the Reformation* (1938), Karl Barth puts the "Church Service as Divine Action" before the "Church Service as Human Action"; and in the great work by the Lutheran theologian Peter Brunner, *Der Gottesdienst der im Namen Jesu versammelten Gemeinde* (1952), the chapter on "worship as the service of God to the congregation" precedes the chapter on "worship as the congregation's service before God." In a work that he edited, *L'Église en prière* (1961), the French Catholic Aimé-Georges Martimort still followed a traditional medieval pattern in giving to the chapter on "the twofold movement of the liturgy" the sequence "worship of God and sanctification of man" *(le double mouvement de la liturgie: culte de Dieu et sanctification des hommes),* but he had already recognized the divine initiative in the chapter on "the dialogue between God

---

2. The adjectives are those used in the Constitution on the Sacred Liturgy of the Second Vatican Council, *Sacrosanctum Concilium,* 14; cf. 26-30, 41.

and his people" *(le dialogue entre Dieu et son peuple: la Parole de Dieu dans l'assemblée; la réponse à la Parole de Dieu).*

Enough of foreign linguistics. Let us turn to Wesleyan theology, homiletically expressed and therefore appropriate to our liturgical interest. The crucial text is John Wesley's Sermon 85, "On Working Out Our Own Salvation," which is based on Philippians 2:12-13: "Work out your own salvation with fear and trembling; for it is God that worketh in you, both to will and to do of his good pleasure."[3] The gist of Wesley's sermon is that "God works, therefore you *can* work; God works, therefore you *must* work." It is by virtue of God's work for us and in us that we are enabled and obliged to "co-operate" with God (cf. 2 Cor. 6:1). Our works take shape as works of piety and works of mercy.

It is not my intention to offer here a detailed account of Wesley's theology in these matters; my principal concerns are not historical but systematic and practical. As is appropriate in a tribute to William Abraham, John Wesley will figure as stimulus rather than as subject. Whereas Wesley here thinks chiefly of the individual believer, I shall characteristically think in corporate, ecclesial terms. In my own style, I will bring out the liturgical dimension. And I will, as my opening appeal to *BEM* suggests, enlarge the scope to the ecumenical.

Abraham himself, in his *Canon and Criterion in Christian Theology,* recognizes that the treasures of the liturgy — its materials, practices, persons — rank high in "the canonical heritage of the Church."[4] Not only did "use in worship" play a part in the determination of the canon of Scripture,[5] but "sacraments, doctrinal summaries, particular forms of internal structure, liturgical materials, the designation of certain individuals as Fathers, saints, and teachers, ecclesiastical regulations about fasting — all these constitute

---

3. KJV; Wesley notes that the original sense becomes clearer with the transposition of a phrase: "It is God that of his good pleasure worketh . . ."). Sermon 85, "On Working Out Our Own Salvation" (1785), in *The Works of John Wesley,* Bicentennial Edition, vol. 3, ed. Albert C. Outler (Nashville: Abingdon Press, 1986), pp. 199-209. Outler remarks that "in any dozen of his sermons most crucial for an accurate assay of Wesley's theology, this one would certainly deserve inclusion": "it stands as the late Wesley's most complete and careful exposition of the mystery of divine-human interaction, his subtlest probing of the paradox of prevenient grace and human agency" (p. 199).

4. William J. Abraham, *Canon and Criterion in Christian Theology: From the Fathers to Feminism* (Oxford: Clarendon, 1998).

5. Abraham, *Canon and Criterion,* pp. 140-41, 156.

canonical material and practice, in that they are acknowledged as binding within the life of the Church across the board."[6] The "ultimate goal of this whole process" — which may be likened to "the production of a grand symphony" — "is to participate in the very life of God, so that the mind and character of Christ may be formed in those who have turned to God for salvation and healing. Hence the canonical materials and practices of the Church are intimately related to the whole sweep of God's action in salvation and sanctification. Properly received and used, they are means whereby we are enabled to love God and neighbour, whereby we are renewed in the image and likeness of God, whereby we become by grace what Christ was by nature, and whereby we are made perfect in holiness."[7]

The Work of God

The two "grand heads of doctrine" concerning the work of the Triune God for human salvation "relate," says Wesley in Sermon 85, "to the eternal Son of God, and the Spirit of God — to the Son, giving himself to be 'a propitiation for the sins of the world' [1 John 2:2], and to the Spirit of God, renewing men in the image of God wherein they were created [cf. Col. 3:10]."[8] These are brought home to individuals in an unfolding sequence of grace and its reception: first, by "preventing grace," which brings "the first wish to please God, the first dawn of light concerning his will, and the first slight, transient conviction of having sinned against him"; next comes "convincing grace," which prompts "repentance" or "a larger measure of self-knowledge, and a further deliverance from the heart of stone"; and at last "we experience the proper Christian salvation, whereby 'through grace' we 'are saved by faith' [Eph. 2:8], consisting of those two grand branches, justification and sanctification. By justification we are saved from the guilt of sin, and restored to the favour of God; by sanctification we are saved from the power and root of sin, and restored to the image of God."[9]

6. Abraham, *Canon and Criterion*, p. 40.
7. Abraham, *Canon and Criterion*, pp. 54-55.
8. Sermon 85, intro. 2 (*Works* 3: 200).
9. Sermon 85, II. 1 (*Works* 3: 203-204). According to Sermon 5, "Justification by Faith" (1746), II.1, justification "implies what God *does for us* through his Son," while sanctification implies "what he *works in us* by his Spirit" (*Works* 1: 187). According to Sermon 43, "The Scripture Way of Salvation" (1765), I.3-4, "[j]ustification is another word for pardon. It is the

Liturgically, the question is that of the relationship between the above and the sacrament of baptism or, more broadly, the ritual process that twentieth-century liturgical scholars called "Christian initiation." Wesley does not so much as mention baptism in Sermon 85. Elsewhere he endorses the definition of a sacrament, given in the Church of England catechism and echoed in the Articles of Religion, as "an outward and visible sign of an inward and spiritual grace, and *a means whereby we receive* the same." In his *Explanatory Notes upon the New Testament,* at Acts 22:16, he comments that "baptism, administered to real penitents, is both a means and a seal of pardon. Nor did God ordinarily in the primitive Church bestow this on any, unless through this means." In his sermon entitled "The New Birth," Wesley refers explicitly to the baptism of adults and puts as the condition of its efficacy that they "repent and believe the Gospel," while affirming that "those who are baptized in their infancy" — he is assuming a covenantal context of believing parents — "are at the same time born again."[10]

A way to understand baptism as both a work of divine grace and its experiential human appropriation in justification and sanctification is indicated in the "Baptism" section of *BEM:*

8. Baptism is both God's gift and our human response to that gift. It looks towards a growth into the measure of the stature of the fullness of Christ (Eph. 4:13). The necessity of faith for the reception of the salvation embodied and set forth in baptism is acknowledged by all churches. Personal commitment is necessary for responsible membership in the body of Christ.

---

forgiveness of all our sins, and (what is necessarily implied therein) our acceptance with God. The price whereby this hath been procured for us . . . is all that Christ hath done and suffered for us. . . . [A]t the same time that we are justified, yea, in that very moment, sanctification begins. In that instant we are 'born again', 'born from above', 'born of the Spirit'. There is a *real* as well as a *relative* change" (*Works* 2:157-58). In Sermon 23, "The New Birth" (1760), intro. 1, Wesley says that "the doctrine of justification" relates to "that great work which God does *for us,* in forgiving our sins," and that the doctrine "of the new birth" relates to "the great work which God does *in us,* in renewing our fallen nature" (*Works* 2:187).

10. Sermon 45, "The New Birth" (1760), in *The Works of John Wesley,* Bicentennial Edition, vol. 2, ed. Albert C. Outler (Nashville: Abingdon, 1984), pp. 186-201. The grounding of infant baptism by analogy with circumcision under the Old Covenant is found in a writing that John Wesley in 1756 borrowed from his father's pen, "A Treatise on Baptism," included in Thomas Jackson, ed., *The Works of John Wesley,* vol. 10, 3rd ed. (London: Wesleyan Methodist Book Room, 1872), pp. 188-201.

9. Baptism is related not only to momentary experience, but to life-long growth into Christ. Those baptized are called upon to reflect the glory of the Lord as they are transformed, by the power of the Holy Spirit, into his likeness, with ever increasing splendour (2 Cor. 3:18). The life of the Christian is necessarily one of continuing struggle yet also of continuing experience of grace. In this new relationship, the baptized live for the sake of Christ, of his Church and of the world which he loves, while they wait in hope for the manifestation of God's new creation and for the time when God will be all in all (Rom. 8:18-24; 1 Cor. 15:22-28, 49-57).

The official responses of the churches to *BEM,* made over the following decade,

> reveal remarkable agreement on the conviction that God gives the Holy Spirit to those who die and rise with Christ in baptism. They show lack of agreement about how the anointing and the sealing of the Spirit is to be expressed in the baptismal rite, and how it relates to confirmation and participation in the Eucharist. The churches, in fact, demonstrate changing attitudes and actions concerning confirmation in accordance with an increasing awareness that originally there was one complex rite of Christian initiation. Confirmation is still seen to be serving two different purposes. Some churches see confirmation as the special sign of the gift of the Spirit in the total process of initiation, others take confirmation above all as the occasion for a personal profession of faith by those baptized at an earlier age. All are agreed that the first sign in the process of initiation into the body of Christ is the rite of water baptism; all are agreed that the goal of initiation is nourishment in the eucharist. Whichever emphasis is made in the understanding of confirmation, each is related to baptism and holy communion. This might be taken as a hopeful sign that the churches are coming to an understanding of initiation as a unitary and comprehensive process, even if its different elements are spread over a period of time. The total process vividly embodies the coherence of God's gracious initiative in eliciting our faith.[11]

11. *Baptism, Eucharist and Ministry 1982-1990: Report on the Process and Responses,* Faith and Order Paper No. 149 (Geneva: World Council of Churches, 1990), p. 112.

Perhaps the most impressive ritual expression and enactment of God's redemptive work and its existential appropriation is the normative *Ordo Christianae Initiationis Adultorum* of 1972, the fruit of liturgical reform in the Roman Catholic Church after the Second Vatican Council.[12] Initial evangelization is followed by a catechumenate, which, "while presenting Catholic teaching in its entirety, also enlightens faith, directs the heart toward God, fosters participation in the liturgy, inspires apostolic activity, and nurtures a life completely in accord with the spirit of Christ" (#78). As the time approaches for their baptism, the "elect" — supported by sponsors — undergo "scrutinies" that "are meant to uncover all that is weak, defective or sinful in the hearts of the elect; to bring out, then strengthen all that is upright, strong, and good" (#141). Immediately prior to their baptism, the candidates decisively renounce sin and profess faith in Christ and the Trinity. They undergo the baptismal washing and receive the strength and seal of the Holy Spirit in confirmation. They enter into the eucharistic community and for the first time receive the body and blood of the Lord. The postbaptismal period is to be one in which "the community and the neophytes together . . . grow in deepening their grasp of the paschal mystery and in making it a part of their lives through meditation on the Gospel, sharing in the Eucharist, and doing the works of charity" (#244).

The matter of entry into God's saving work is put for the individual by the apostle Paul in Romans 10:8-10: "The word is near you, on your lips and in your heart (that is, the word of faith which we preach); because, if you confess with your lips that Jesus is Lord and believe in your heart that God raised him from the dead, you will be saved. For man believes with his heart and so is justified, and he confesses with his lips and so is saved." The ecclesial context — with sacramental and liturgical resonances — is supplied by the First Letter to the Corinthians. Confessing, by the Holy Spirit, that "Jesus is Lord" (12:3), believers are "baptized into one body" (12:13), "the body of Christ" (12:27), and "made to drink of one Spirit" (12:13). In that "one body" (12:12-13) there are "varieties of gifts, but the same Spirit; and there are varieties of service, but the same Lord; and there are varieties of operations *[diaireseis energēmatōn]*, but it is the same God who works all in all *[ho energōn ta panta en pasin]*" (12:4-6) — and that "for the common good" (12:7). The determinative gift is that of love (1 Cor. 13). It is to be exer-

12. See *Rite of Christian Initiation of Adults* (Washington, DC: United States Catholic Conference, 1988).

cised in the worship assembly for the edification of the church: "Since you are eager for manifestations of the Spirit, strive to excel in building up the church" (14:12). This edification may be done by way of "a hymn, a lesson, a revelation, a tongue, or an interpretation" (14:26-33; cf. 14:6). It may involve prayer, thanksgiving, song (14:13-19). The fractious Corinthians, when they "assemble[d] as a church," were debasing "the Supper of the Lord," the instituted purpose of which was to "proclaim the Lord's death until he come" (11:17-34), the "one loaf" being for "the many" who make up the "one body" the means of participation in "the body of Christ" (10:16-17).

Faithful Cooperation

Coming now to the precise Pauline text on which Wesley's Sermon 85 is based, we find it both stating the work of God and exhorting believers to cooperation with the divine initiative and action: "Work out *[katergazesthe]* your own salvation with fear and trembling, for it is God that of his good pleasure worketh *[ho energōn]* in you both to will and to do *[to energein]*" (Phil. 2:12-13).

Wesley emphasizes the indispensable prior action of God: "Seeing all men are by nature not only sick, but 'dead in trespasses, and sins' [Eph. 2:1], it is not possible for them to do anything well till God raises them from the dead. It was impossible for Lazarus to 'come forth' [John 11:43] till the Lord had given him life. And it is equally impossible for us to 'come' out of our sins, yea, or to make the least motion toward it, till he who hath all power in heaven and earth calls our dead souls into life."

Next, however: "[I]f God 'worketh in you', then 'work out your own salvation.' The original word rendered, 'work out', implies doing a thing thoroughly. 'Your own' — for you yourselves must do this, or it will be left undone for ever." Wesley expounds "to will" and "to do" in this way: "*To thelein,* which we render 'to will', plainly includ[es] every good desire, whether relating to our tempers, words, or actions, to inward or outward holiness. And *to energein,* which we render 'to do', manifestly implies all that power from on high; all that energy which works in us every right disposition, and then furnishes us for every good word and work [cf. 2 Thess. 2:17]." The "proverbial" expression "with fear and trembling" implies two things: "first, that everything be done with the utmost earnestness of spirit, and with all care and caution, perhaps more directly referring to the former word, *meta phobou*, 'with fear'; secondly, that it be done with the utmost diligence, speed, punctuality, and exactness — not improbably referring to the latter word, *meta tromou*, 'with trembling.'" Because God works in you, Wesley tells his hearers and readers, not only *can* you work, but you *must* work — and continue to do so: "You must be 'workers together with him' (they are the very words of the Apostle [cf. 2 Cor. 6:1]); otherwise he will cease working." And for good measure, the preacher adds an imperfectly remembered dictum of St. Augustine: "*Qui fecit nos sine nobis, non salvabit nos sine nobis:* he that made us without ourselves, will not save us without ourselves" (cf. Augustine, Sermon 169; PL 38: 922-33).

The peroration of Wesley's Sermon 85 is a catena of scriptural texts that exhort believers to "cooperate" with the God who works first: "'Labour *(ergazesthe)*', then, brethren, 'not for the meat that perisheth, but for that which endureth to everlasting life' [John 6:27]. Say with our blessed Lord, though in a somewhat different sense, 'My Father worketh *(ergazetai)* hitherto, and I work *(ergazomai)*' [John 5:17]. In consideration that he still worketh in you, be never 'weary of well-doing' [cf. Gal 6:9; 2 Thess. 3:13]. Go on, in virtue of the grace of God preventing, accompanying, and following you, in 'the work of faith *(tou ergou tēs pisteōs)*, in the patience of hope, and in the labour of love *(tou kopou tēs agapēs)*' [cf. 1 Thess. 1:3]. 'Be ye steadfast and immovable; always abounding in the work of the Lord *(en tō ergō tou kuriou)*' [cf. 1 Cor. 15:58]. And 'the God of peace, who brought again from the dead the great Shepherd of the sheep', — Jesus — 'make you perfect in every good work to do his will, working in you what is well-pleasing in his sight, through Jesus Christ, to whom be glory for ever and ever!' [cf. Heb. 13:20-21]." Missing only, perhaps, is one of Wesley's favorite texts, by which he often encapsulates the believer's cooperation with God: "faith working through love: *pistis di' agapēs energoumenē*" (Gal. 5:6).

Faithful cooperation, according to Wesley's Sermon 85, takes shape as "works of piety" and "works of mercy." To these we now turn, and first to "works of piety," since these help more directly to constitute our liturgical paradigm for healing; but we shall also come to see that "works of mercy" are not without a liturgical connection.

The Works of Piety

In Sermon 85, Wesley lists the works of piety thus: "Use family prayer, and cry to God in secret. Fast in secret, and 'your Father which seeth in secret, he will reward you openly' [cf. Matt. 6:4, 6, 18]. 'Search the Scriptures' [cf. John 5:39]; hear them in public, read them in private, and meditate therein. At every opportunity be a partaker of the Lord's Supper. 'Do this in remembrance of him' [cf. Luke 22:19; 1 Cor. 11:24], and he will meet you at his own table. Let your conversation be with the children of God, and see that it 'be in grace, seasoned with salt' [cf. Col. 4:6]."

Three of these "works of piety" are mentioned in Wesley's Sermon 16, "The Means of Grace," and precisely as "means of grace," with an emphasis on the work of God in them and through them:

> The chief of these means are prayer, whether in secret or with the great congregation; searching the Scriptures (which implies reading, hearing, and meditating thereon) and receiving the Lord's Supper, eating bread and drinking wine in remembrance of him; and these we believe to be ordained of God as the ordinary channels of conveying his grace to the souls of men. . . . It is he alone who, by his own almighty power, worketh in us what is pleasing in his sight. And all outward things, unless he work in them and by them, are mere weak and beggarly elements. . . . We know that there is no inherent power in the words that are spoken in prayer, in the letter of Scripture read, the sound thereof heard, or the bread and wine received in the Lord's Supper; but that it is God alone who is the giver of every good gift, the author of all grace; that the whole power is of him, whereby through any of these there is any blessing conveyed to our soul.[13]

Exactly because they are "ordained of God," these "means" *must* be used. Thus those who have joined the Methodist societies in order to "work out their own salvation" are held by Wesley to be under obligation to follow "the General Rules of our societies; all which we are taught of God to observe, even in his written Word, the only rule, and the sufficient rule, both of our faith and practice." At this point we note, in particular, "attending upon all the ordinances of God. Such are: the public worship of God; the ministry

---

13. Sermon 16, "The Means of Grace" (1746), in *The Works of John Wesley*, Bicentennial Edition, vol. 1, ed. Albert C. Outler, pp. 376-97; here II.1-3, pp. 381-82. The same three — together with "using such a measure of fasting or abstinence as our bodily health allows" — are mentioned as "works of piety," "good works . . . necessary to sanctification," in Sermon 43, "The Scripture Way of Salvation," III.9 (*Works* 2:166).

of the Word, either read or expounded; the Supper of the Lord; family and private prayer; searching the Scriptures; and fasting or abstinence."[14]

From these three Wesleyan passages we may selectively construct our liturgical paradigm for faithful cooperation with the healing work of God in all its salvific aspects: (a) the reading, hearing, exposition, and absorption of Scripture; (b) the prayer of the congregation; (c) the exercises of mutual discipline, help and encouragement; (d) the celebration of the Eucharist, or Lord's Supper.

Scripture

One of the loveliest collects in the Church of England's *Book of Common Prayer* runs thus: "Blessed Lord, who hast caused all holy Scriptures to be written for our learning: Grant that we may in such wise hear them, read, mark, learn, and inwardly digest them, that by patience, and comfort of thy holy Word, we may embrace, and ever hold fast the blessed hope of everlasting life, which thou hast given us in our Saviour Jesus Christ." Traditionally, this prayer belonged to the Second Sunday in Advent, on which the Epistle reading was Romans 15:4-13 ("Whatsoever things were written aforetime, were written for our learning, that we through patience, and comfort of the Scriptures, might have hope"). Appropriately, the Sunday became known as Bible Sunday.

The various traditions of the church have not always provided for wide reading from Scripture. In the Middle Ages, neither the East nor the West included much reading from the Old Testament in their eucharistic liturgies. Among modern Protestant Evangelicals, the preaching service often limits the Bible to the brief passage that the preacher will expound. The twentieth-century liturgical movement greatly encouraged the use of enhanced lectionaries. In its Constitution on the Sacred Liturgy, the Second Vatican Council declared that "the treasures of the Bible are to be opened up more lavishly so that a richer fare may be provided for the faithful at the table of God's word."[15] Sustained courses of readings from the history of salvation,

---

14. "The Nature, Design, and General Rules of the United Societies," 1, 6-7, in *The Works of John Wesley,* Bicentennial Edition, vol. 9, ed. Rupert E. Davies (Nashville: Abingdon, 1989), pp. 68-75, esp. pp. 69, 72-73.

15. *Sacrosanctum Concilium,* 51.

using a comprehensive lectionary, provide a healthy, variegated diet for the congregation.

The Prayers of the Faithful

The early Fathers called prayer "hard work," a "heavy task" *(kopos):* "There is no labor greater than that of prayer to God."[16] In the Benedictine tradition, the "daily office" or "liturgy of the hours" is understood as *opus Dei,* the "work of God" — performed in community (*Rule of St. Benedict,* 8-19). The order's motto *(ora et labora)* can be practiced as alternating between the two activities: prayer and manual or studious or domestic work. But did not the apostle Paul both give the instruction to "pray without ceasing" (1 Thess. 5:17) and himself claim to "work night and day" (2 Thess. 3:8)? More subtly, then, work and prayer can be allowed to "compenetrate," as in the *Rule of St. Basil,* whom Benedict called his "holy father": "While our hands are occupied in work, we can praise God with psalms and hymns and spiritual songs, with the tongue if it is possible, but if not, then in the heart. In this way we thank Him who has given both strength of hand to work and wisdom of brain to know how to work, and also bestowed means by which to work both in the tools we use and the arts we practice, whatever the work may be. We pray moreover that the works of our hands may be directed towards the mark of pleasing God" (37). This is, indeed, a holistic picture of health.

The general prayers of intercession, whatever the precise form they take, are an integral part of communal worship, in accordance with 1 Timothy 2:1-4: "I urge that supplications, prayers, intercessions, and thanksgivings be made for all men, for kings and all who are in high positions, that we may lead a quiet and peaceable life, godly and respectful in every way. This is good, and it is acceptable in the sight of God our Saviour, who desires all men to be saved and to come to the knowledge of the truth." Clearly, such prayers aim — from several directions — at the healing of a broken world.

---

16. Agathon, 9, in *The Sayings of the Desert Fathers: The Alphabetical Collection,* trans. Benedicta Ward (Kalamazoo, MI: Cistercian Publications, 1975), pp. 18-19.

Geoffrey Wainwright

Communal Paraclesis

In early Methodism the gathering in classes and bands, instances of the *ecclesiolae in Ecclesia,* was a locus for the "conversation with the children of God" that Wesley numbered among the works of piety. A "society" was no other than "a company of men 'having the form, and seeking the power of godliness', united in order to pray together, to receive the word of exhortation, and to watch over one another in love, that they may help each other to work out their salvation."[17] The agenda of the "bands" was set out thus:

> The design of our meeting is to obey that command of God, "Confess your faults one to another, and pray one for another that ye may be healed" [James 5:16]. To this end we intend:
>
> 1. To meet once a week, at the least.
>
> 2. To come punctually at the hour appointed, without some extraordinary reason.
>
> 3. To begin (those of us who are present) exactly at the hour, with singing or prayer.
>
> 4. To speak, each of us in order, freely and plainly the true state of our souls, with the faults we have committed in thought, word, or deed, and the temptations we have felt since our last meeting.
>
> 5. To end every meeting with prayer, suited to the state of each person present.
>
> 6. To desire some person among us to speak his or her own state first, and then to ask the rest in order as many and as searching questions as may be concerning their state, sins, and temptations.[18]

The cited passage from the Letter of James makes complex links among sin and sickness, confession and prayer, forgiveness and healing, the work of the Lord and faithful cooperation with it: "Is any one among you suffering? Let him pray. Is any cheerful? Let him sing praise. Is any among you sick? Let him call for the elders of the church, and let them pray over him, anointing him with oil in the name of the Lord; and the prayer of faith will save the sick man, and the Lord will raise him up; and if he has committed sins, he will be forgiven. Therefore confess your sins to one another, and

---

17. "General Rules," 2, in *Works,* 9:69.
18. "Rules of the Band Societies," in *Works,* 9:77.

76

pray for one another, that you may be healed. The prayer of a righteous man has great power in its effects" (James 5:13-16). This text underlies a long and varied history of ecclesial practice — both sacramental (penance and anointing) and nonsacramental — in the face of sickness among the church's members.[19]

Another of Wesley's works of piety, "fasting or abstinence," also has ecclesial and liturgical resonances. The individual's exercise appropriately fits into a weekly discipline of Wednesdays and Fridays (chosen as early as the *Didache* in reference to Christ's betrayal and crucifixion) and the annual season of Lent. While Wesley's qualification, "as our bodily health allows," must be respected, such ascesis may — in the other direction — serve both physical and spiritual well-being, and it is dominically ordained (Matt. 6:16-17).

The Lord's Supper

While, according to the apostle Paul in 1 Corinthians 11:17-34, a faithless celebration of the Lord's Supper could have lethal consequences, for St. Ignatius of Antioch the Eucharist was properly "the medicine of immortality, the antidote against dying, so that one may live in Christ Jesus for ever" (*Letter to the Ephesians*, 20.2). For St. Cyprian of Carthage, the Eucharist was "the food of health, or salvation" *(cibus salutis)*, and he appeals to John 6:51-58 for the view that only those who communicate will live eternally (*On the Lord's Prayer*, 18). Traditional prayers for a fruitful communion mention healing of body and soul. The teaching of the "Eucharist" section of *BEM* runs in sequence:

2. The Eucharist is essentially the sacrament of the gift which God makes to us in Christ through the power of the Holy Spirit. Every Christian receives this gift of salvation through communion in the body and blood of Christ. In the eucharistic meal, in the eating and drinking of the bread and wine, Christ grants communion with himself. God him-

---

19. See Karen Westerfield Tucker, "Christian Rituals Surrounding Sickness," in Paul F. Bradshaw and Lawrence A. Hoffman, eds., *Life Cycles in Jewish and Christian Worship* (Notre Dame, IN: University of Notre Dame Press, 1996), pp. 154-72; Patrick Prétot, "Sacraments and Healing: A Typology of the Relationship between Two Dimensions of Healing," in *Studia Liturgica* 36 (2006): 34-59.

self acts, giving life to the body of Christ and renewing each member. In accordance with Christ's promise, each baptized member of the body of Christ receives in the Eucharist the assurance of the forgiveness of sins (Matt. 26:28) and the pledge of eternal life (John 6:51-58). . . .

8. . . .The Church, gratefully recalling God's mighty acts of redemption, beseeches God to give the benefits of these acts to every human being. . . .

23. The world, to which renewal is promised, is present in the whole eucharistic celebration. The world is present in the thanksgiving to the Father, where the Church speaks on behalf of the whole creation; in the memorial of Christ, where the Church, united with its great High Priest and Intercessor, prays for the world; in the prayer for the gift of the Holy Spirit, where the Church asks for sanctification and new creation.

26. . . . The eucharistic community is nourished and strengthened for confessing by word and action the Lord Jesus Christ who gave his life for the salvation of the world.

The Eucharist is not only a gift from God but also an offering to God. "We make him an offering," says St. Irenaeus of Lyons, "not as if he were in need of it, but in order to give him thanks with the aid of his gifts and to sanctify the creation" (*Adversus Haereses*, IV.18.6). The literary structure of the Wesleyan *Hymns on the Lord's Supper*[20] makes clear that the Eucharist not only "implies a sacrifice" (that of Christ) but entails "the sacrifice of our persons":

> While faith th'atoning blood applies,
> Ourselves a living sacrifice
> We freely offer up to God. (Hymn 128, v. 3)

20. John and Charles Wesley, *Hymns on the Lord's Supper* (Bristol, UK: Felix Farley, 1745). A facsimile reprint has been issued by the Charles Wesley Society (Madison, NJ, 1995). The texts can also be found in G. Osborn, ed., *The Poetical Works of John and Charles Wesley*, 13 vols. (London: Wesleyan-Methodist Conference Office, 1868-1872), 3:181-342; and in J. E. Rattenbury, *The Eucharistic Hymns of John and Charles Wesley* (London: Epworth Press, 1948). The last-mentioned did most to promote renewed *textual* interest in the *Hymns on the Lord's Supper*, which now extends ecumenically; but their *sung* use in worship practice lags sadly far behind.

Whate'er we cast on Him alone
Is with His great oblation one;
His sacrifice doth ours sustain,
And favour and acceptance gain. (Hymn 137, v. 3)

Father, on us the Spirit bestow,
Through which Thine everlasting Son
Offer'd Himself for man below,
That *we,* even *we,* before Thy throne
Our souls and bodies may present,
And pay Thee all Thy grace hath lent. (Hymn 150, v. 1)

Although the Wesleyan eucharistic hymns themselves are shamefully neglected in current Methodist practice, these realities come to expression in the normative Great Thanksgiving of "Word and Table" in *The United Methodist Book of Worship,* a prayer that also brings out well the role of the ecclesial community as sign and act in faithful cooperation with God for the benefit of the world:

And so,
in remembrance of these your mighty acts in Jesus Christ,
we offer ourselves in praise and thanksgiving
as a holy and living sacrifice,
in union with Christ's offering for us,
as we proclaim the mystery of faith.
Christ has died; Christ is risen; Christ will come again.
Pour out your Holy Spirit on us gathered here,
and on these gifts of bread and wine.
Make them be for us the body and blood of Christ,
that we may be for the world the body of Christ,
redeemed by his blood.
By your Spirit make us one with Christ,
one with each other,
and one in ministry to all the world,
until Christ comes in final victory,
and we feast at his heavenly banquet.[21]

21. *The United Methodist Book of Worship* (Nashville: United Methodist Publishing House, 1992), p. 38.

As early as the account in St. Justin Martyr of the Sunday assembly of the church in Rome in the middle of the second century, we find that the elements of communion "are sent through the deacons to those who are not present. And the wealthy who so desire give what they wish, as each chooses; and what is collected is deposited with the president. He helps orphans and widows, and those who through sickness or any other cause are in need, and those in prison, and strangers sojourning among us; in a word, he takes care of those who are in need" (*First Apology*, 67). British Methodism long had a lay office of "poor steward," whose responsibilities included not only preparation of the bread and wine for the Lord's Supper but the collection of alms at the service for the "poor fund."[22]

With that we are moving into what twentieth-century Orthodox theologians liked to call "the liturgy after the Liturgy," which might also be conceived of as "the liturgy before the Liturgy," inasmuch as existing diaconal and evangelistic concerns are already brought into the worship assembly.[23] In any case, we come in our Wesleyan scheme to "the works of mercy."

The Works of Mercy

In Sermon 85, "On Working Out Our Own Salvation," Wesley says quite generally concerning the required "works of mercy" only this: "Do good unto all men, to their souls and to their bodies."[24] In Sermon 43, "The Scripture Way of Salvation," he is much more specific, listing not only the traditional corporal works of mercy based dominically on Matthew 25:31-46 but also, in characteristically Wesleyan language, those that "relate to the souls of men."[25] In describing "The Character of a Methodist," Wesley formulated things this way:

[H]e "does good unto all men" [Gal. 6:10] — unto neighbours, and strangers, friends, and enemies. And that in every possible kind; not

22. Beginning with Wesley's own practice and the references in *The Sunday Service*, Karen Westerfield Tucker has provided ample continuing documentation in her article "Liturgical Expressions of Care for the Poor in the Wesleyan Tradition: A Case Study for the Ecumenical Church," *Worship* 69 (1995): 51-64.

23. See Ion Bria, ed., *The Liturgy after the Liturgy: Mission and Witness from an Orthodox Perspective* (Geneva: WCC Publications, 1996).

24. Sermon 85, II.4, *Works*, 3:206.

25. Sermon 43, III.10, *Works*, 2:166.

only to their bodies, by "feeding the hungry, clothing the naked, visiting those that are sick or in prison" [cf. Matt. 25:35-36], but much more does he labour to do good to their souls, as of the ability which God giveth [cf. 1 Pet. 4:11]: to awaken those that sleep in death; to bring those who are awakened to the atoning blood, that "being justified by faith" they may have peace with God [cf. Rom. 5:1]; and to provoke those who have peace with God to abound more in love and in good works [cf. 1 Thess. 3:12; 2 Cor. 9:8]. And he is willing to "spend and be spent herein" [cf. 2 Cor. 12:15], even to be offered upon the sacrifice and service of their faith" [cf. Phil. 2:17], so that they may "all come unto the measure of the stature of the fullness of Christ" [cf. Eph. 4:13].[26]

Quoting the passage from Matthew 25, St. Irenaeus (again) says: "This God, who needs nothing, accepts our good actions, in order to repay us with his own good gifts. . . . He asks for these things, not because he needs them, but for our sake, in order that we may not be unfruitful" (*Adversus Haereses,* IV.18.6).

Between the liturgy, on the one hand, and the "works of mercy" of the individual Christian and the works of the ecclesial community in mission and service, on the other, there is a relationship of correspondence or reciprocity: either can figure as the inspiration, the pattern, or the result of the other. The apostle Paul speaks of his own "work of an evangelist" (see 2 Tim. 4:5 for the *ergon euangelistou*) in liturgical terms: By the grace of God given to him, he is a minister *(leitourgos)* of Christ Jesus to the Gentiles, serving as a priest *(hierourgountos)* for the gospel of God, so that the offering *(prosphora)* of the Gentiles may be acceptable *(euprosdektos)*, sanctified *(hagiasmenē)* by the Holy Spirit (Rom. 15:15-16), whereby the nations would come to praise and glorify God along with his people of the old covenant (vv. 8-12). As to diaconal service, its ritual embodiment is the washing of feet (see John 13:14-15). Prayer and anointing can inspire or accompany medical ministry. The kiss of peace can motivate or seal reconciliation. Or again, from the "Eucharist" section of *BEM:*

Signs of [the final] renewal [of creation] are present in the world wherever the grace of God is manifest and human beings work for justice, love and peace. The Eucharist is the feast at which the Church gives

---

26. "The Character of a Methodist" (1742), 16, in *Works* 9:30-46 (here p. 41).

thanks to God for these signs and joyfully celebrates and anticipates the coming of the Kingdom of Christ (1 Cor. 11:26; Matt. 26:29)." (#22)

The Eucharist embraces all aspects of life. It is a representative act of thanksgiving and offering on behalf of the whole world. The eucharistic celebration demands reconciliation and sharing among all those regarded as brothers and sisters in the one family of God and is a constant challenge in the search for appropriate relationships in social, economic and political life (Matt. 5:23-24; 1 Cor. 10:16-17; 1 Cor. 11:20-22; Gal. 3:28). All kinds of injustice, racism, separation, and lack of freedom are radically challenged when we share in the body and blood of Christ. Through the Eucharist the all-renewing grace of God penetrates and restores human personality and dignity. The Eucharist involves the believer in the central event of the world's history. Therefore, as participants in the Eucharist, we prove inconsistent if we are not actively participating in this ongoing restoration of the world's situation and the human condition. The Eucharist shows us that our behaviour is inconsistent in face of the reconciling presence of God in human history: we are placed under continual judgment by the persistence of unjust relationships of all kinds in our society, the manifold divisions on account of human pride, material interest and power politics and, above all, the obstinacy of unjustifiable confessional oppositions within the body of Christ. (#20)

As God in Christ has entered into the human situation, so eucharistic liturgy is near to the concrete and particular situations of men and women. . . . The place of [diaconal] ministry between the table and the needy properly testifies to the redeeming presence of Christ in the world. (#21)

In some German churches in the late decades of the twentieth century, the traditional "hunger cloth" *(Hungertuch),* a Lenten drape, became, through its pictorial design, a sign of commitment to the Protestant work of "Bread for the World" or the Catholic relief agency "Misereor."

Conclusion: Liturgy and Life

In the Methodist tradition, there is no finer statement of the relationship between worship and work — itself in the mode of an address to God — than a hymn of Charles Wesley:

> Forth in thy name, O Lord, I go,
> My daily labour to pursue;
> Thee, only Thee, resolved to know
> In all I think, or speak, or do.
>
> The task Thy wisdom hath assigned
> O let me cheerfully fulfil,
> In all my works Thy presence find,
> And prove Thy acceptable will.
>
> Thee may I set at my right hand,
> Whose eyes my inmost substance see,
> And labour on at Thy command,
> And offer all my works to Thee.[27]

That offering of the individual believer is set in a more formally liturgical and fully ecclesial context by the Orthodox theologian Alexander Schmemann in a little book, *For the Life of the World,* that constituted an ecumenical opening for many in the mid-twentieth century. With baptism, says Schmemann, "the life which now begins is a life of offering and sacrifice, the life constantly transformed into the *liturgy* — the *work* of Christ": "The whole man is now made the temple of God, and his whole life is from now on a *liturgy.* . . . The only true temple of God is man and through him the world. Each ounce of matter belongs to God and is to find in God its fulfillment. Each instant of time is God's time and is to fulfill itself as God's eternity." Corporately, "the Church itself is a *leitourgia,* a calling to act in this world after the fashion of Christ, to bear testimony to Him and His Kingdom." The Eucharist is "the journey of the Church into the dimension of the Kingdom," and "the mission of the

---

27. No. 315 in *A Collection of Hymns for the Use of the People Called Methodists;* see *Works* 7:545-46.

Church begins in [this] liturgy of ascension, for it alone makes possible the liturgy of mission."[28]

If that may sum up "the healing *work* of the liturgy," let me conclude with a word on "the *healing* work of the liturgy." "Salvation" has figured in these pages, but with little linguistic notice. In the Gospels, the verb *sōzō* is used both for the healings performed by Jesus upon people who were ailing in body, mind, or spirit (often in response to faithful appeals) — *and* for salvation in a more ultimate sense.[29] The same range is found in the Christian usage of the Latin stem *salvus*. In hymnic mode and enactment, Charles Wesley ascribes salvation, in the comprehensive sense that it bears in the book of Revelation, to God as its source and pleads for its completion in ourselves as its object and beneficiaries (Rev. 7; cf. 12:10-12; 19:1f.). First:

> Ye servants of God,
> Your Master proclaim,
> And publish abroad
> His wonderful name;
> The name all-victorious
> Of Jesus extol;
> His kingdom is glorious,
> And rules over all.
>
> God ruleth on high,
> Almighty to save;
> And still He is nigh,
> His presence we have;

28. Alexander Schmemann, *For the Life of the World* (New York: National Student Christian Federation, 1963); fragments here quoted from pp. 14, 30, 54-55, 56. Schmemann developed his arguments more fully — with a view toward renewal also in Orthodoxy — in *Of Water and the Spirit: A Liturgical Study of Baptism* (Crestwood, NY: St. Vladimir's, 1974), and in *The Eucharist: Sacrament of the Kingdom* (Crestwood, NY: St. Vladimir's, 1987). The latter book receives sympathetic treatment in W. J. Abraham, *The Logic of Renewal* (Grand Rapids: Eerdmans, 2003), chap. 6.

29. In his little book *Sin and Salvation* (1956), first written for village teachers in South India, Lesslie Newbigin connects *sōzō* with the Sanskrit root *sarva*, taken to imply wholeness and found in many words commonly used in Tamil with the nuances of healing what is wounded, mending what is broken, setting free what is bound. Newbigin sees salvation as the overcoming of four contradictions in the fallen condition of humankind: contradiction with the natural world, with one's fellows, within oneself, and against God.

The great congregation
His triumph shall sing,
Ascribing salvation
To Jesus our King.

Salvation to God,
Who sits on the throne!
Let all cry aloud,
And honour the Son.
The praises of Jesus,
The angels proclaim,
Fall down on their faces,
And worship the Lamb.

Then let us adore,
And give Him his right,
All glory and power,
All wisdom and might,
All honour and blessing,
With angels above,
And thanks never-ceasing,
And infinite love.[30]

And then, from "Love Divine, All Loves Excelling," the prayer for completion:

Finish then Thy new creation,
Pure and spotless let us be;
Let us see Thy great salvation,
Perfectly restored in Thee;
Changed from glory into glory,
Till in heaven we take our place,
Till we cast our crowns before Thee,
Lost in wonder, love, and praise.[31]

---

30. No. 21 in *Hymns on the Great Festivals* (1746); it has become one of the most widely adopted of all Charles Wesley's hymns.

31. No. 374 in *A Collection of Hymns for the Use of the People Called Methodists;* see *Works* 7:545-46.

Ceremonies That Consecrate and Heal

Ellen T. Charry

Symbolic ritual practices are not simply conventions. They work both for the public good and for the flourishing of individuals. Here we will examine both civic and Christian ritual practices to ask what they effect.[1] We begin by broadly defining symbolic rituals as formal ceremonies that form people in the virtues needed for healthy functioning and, where persons are the object of the action, lay moral claims on their lives. They edify and formally bind people to a society and, in the case of some Christian rites, to God. Minimally, they educate women and men for public and personal well-being; maximally, they unite people with the power and goodness of God.

Although they differ in performance, both civic and Christian ritual practices preserve and nourish the community performing them, the persons for or on whom they are performed, and the persons witnessing them. To this end, rituals teach and reinforce virtues, values, and standards needed by individuals for the well-being of the society. Some civic ceremonies enact a new status or relationship. Others encourage or press individuals to confess to shared values and virtues that sustain the common good. Christian sacraments, perhaps the most dramatic of all, do this and set persons in

---

1. It is impossible not to stand in a specific place when talking about liturgical rituals. I write as an Anglican standing in the center of the spectrum of Christian communions, liturgically speaking: to my right are the Roman Catholic Church and the Eastern Orthodox churches; to my left are the Lutheran, Reformed, and Radical Reformation churches.

God's saving work in Israel and in Jesus Christ. Both civic and Christian rituals intend to so mark the person's character with a national or theological identity that s/he internalizes the values of and virtues for the identity being enacted.

That is, formal ceremonies edify, instruct, consecrate, and nourish people to become ensigns of the community's best portrayal of itself. Some rituals will embody all of these aspects, others some of them. What they all do is embed humans in moral narratives that are social matrices for the mutual flourishing of self and community so that people become its hands and feet. In this way, lives are uplifted, nobly directed, and rewarded. We begin with civic examples, and then we will turn to Christian ones.

Civic Ceremonies

While all public ceremonies edify, they do so in different ways that may be distinguished as follows. Some, like civic holidays, inform in hopes of inculcating loyalty to national values and history. Others, like saluting the flag, press the participants to profess loyalty to the nation through some action. Others, like dedicating buildings, inform and consecrate. Finally, some public rituals, like swearing-in ceremonies, inform, require a profession of loyalty, and consecrate. The strength of the moral claim advances along this continuum. Let us consider one category at a time.

Pedagogical Civic Ceremonies

Although all civic ceremonies inform in hopes of promoting national values and ideas, and most lay moral claim to people's lives, some — civic commemorations for example — do only that. In the United States, Memorial Day, the Fourth of July, Labor Day, Thanksgiving, Martin Luther King Day, and President's Day inform the public by promoting and recalling national history, dignity, and honor. Parades, broadcasts, and public gatherings all instruct the public in the nation's moral identity by extolling its values and heroes. Even if some of this instruction is now buried under partying and shopping, by setting aside annual days of remembrance to honor events and persons, and recalling them with speeches, reading of honored texts, music, and perhaps pictures or film, these celebrations help each new generation receive and carry forward the tradition of these noble causes and persons who serve as models for them. The dedication of these days highlights the ideals of the nation, honors those who died to protect and improve it, and encourages those who continue to labor in its vineyards to sustain the national heritage honorably, though no specific action is required whereby the audience attending these functions makes a definitive response affirming the values being promoted.

Confessional Civic Ceremonies

Pedagogical rituals edify passively. Another type of public ritual edifies actively by having the people involved profess virtuous intentions through formulaic summations of their loyalty to the common good through vows or gestures — or both. These include oath-taking, the making of vows, saluting and pledging allegiance to the flag, singing the national anthem, shaking hands, and bachelor parties. Here persons profess loyalty to the nation or to individuals and declare their intention to undertake or uphold certain standards.

In oath-taking in a court of law, the person professing is pledging to be honest, faithful, and diligent in upholding standards and principles of professional and personal conduct. When one pledges allegiance to the flag, one is publicly confessing one's loyalty to the nation that the flag symbolizes, and that calls for more than bare compliance with the law. Allegiance to the nation will also involve voting, or voluntarily coming forward, for example, with information that protects the community. Singing the national anthem at a sporting event that is about to commence is similar to a confession that identifies the event as an activity undertaken by both players and fans in good faith and honor that well bespeaks the national dignity.[2] A handshake can either signify the opening of a new social relationship or commit one to an agreed-upon joint course of action to be honorably undertaken by the parties involved, as do written contracts. Even when buried under silly — or even dangerous — behavior, the bachelor party marks the end of a period in a man's life, for the groom is about to "forsake all others" and pledge sexual, emotional, and financial loyalty to his bride.

All but the last are accompanied by formulaic language and specific

---

2. Interestingly, the national anthem is sung at baseball games but not at boxing or wrestling matches, since these do not express the national ethos.

gestures, such as saluting, placing one's hand over the heart, facing the flag, placing the right hand on a Bible and raising the left with open palm, which symbolize the virtuous intention. In all these promises, professions, pledges, and confessions, the person publicly commits to uphold the common good in one form or another.

Consecratory Civic Ceremonies

A third type of public ritual actively confers a new status or identity on persons or dedicates places for specific purposes. Here, gathered before witnesses, authorized representatives of the community raise certain people to a new status or inaugurate the use of buildings or public spaces for public use. Usually there are formal words that affirm the status. Thus, in graduation ceremonies that mark the completion of a course of study or special preparation, students officially close a chapter of their lives and receive a diploma or certificate from the educational institution's leaders. This publicly certifies them as now eligible for advanced employment, study, or promotion. They do not make vows or profess loyalty because no new relationship or specific set of responsibilities is being granted. Graduation parties not only celebrate the demonstrated accomplishments of the individuals but also the services and productive use the person will make of his/her new skills and knowledge for the common good in an anticipatory way.

Park and building dedications use gestures and sometimes formulae and symbols to consecrate places for certain uses. Cutting ribbons and breaking ground inaugurate new uses of space, while laying cornerstones and unveiling plaques and monuments create a permanent visible reminder of the purpose for which the place is set apart and honor those who made it possible. Public consecrations, with the appropriate speeches that accompany them, empower, dignify, and ennoble people and places, and they draw the attention of witnesses to the values, learning, and fine goals intended for the persons or places.

Covenantal Civic Ceremonies

A fourth type of public ritual, the most complex, is covenantal. It does everything that the other three do, plus it establishes formal relationships between individuals or between individuals and the state. It is the most interactive of rituals, and all participants — officiant, recipients, and witnesses — have roles to play for such an enactment to be correctly accomplished. The officiant consecrates, the consecrated ones profess, and the witnesses confirm the covenant that is being enacted simply by their presence. The effect of all this is to establish new relationships and identities.

Weddings, installations, and the swearing-in of public servants are all covenantal. In these ceremonies persons are consecrated for special responsibilities and duties by being given not only a new status but also new powers or duties. They verbally profess their loyalty and pledge to uphold their responsibilities and use their power appropriately. A uniform, ring, or badge given to the person to wear daily is the instrument that symbolizes this covenantal relationship: it visibly announces the individual's consecrated status and trustworthiness to strangers, and it is a permanent reminder to him/her of the vows taken. For the enactment to have its desired consecratory effect, specific words, gestures — such as placing a ring on a finger, pinning on a badge, or delivering a certificate — and tokens must function together.[3]

Weddings, of course, sanctify and inaugurate a new intimate relationship not only between two individuals but between two families, in some cases, even two nations, and they express the community's support for the couple and their future family. Swearing-in, installation, and investiture ceremonies publicly impart power to those who have successfully completed a course of study or have been elected to public office. Through the officiant, the granting institution declares the person fit and prepared for a new use of power with specific authority and responsibilities.[4]

At least that is what these civic ceremonies intend. The moral, pedagogical, and social dimensions of civic rituals are inseparable. They form persons in virtue. The social dimension of the ritual acknowledges and authorizes, while the pedagogical dimension internalizes the authority and responsibility extended by the public trust. If one breaches that trust, s/he may be legally prosecuted, as in cases of perjury, insubordination, desertion, or contempt of court. Civic rituals impart limited and specific forms of power

3. Of course, a lot of invisible work has gone on behind the scenes to be sure that the procedure is completely authoritative and appropriate.

4. To be married, for example, one must have demonstrated that one is not already married to someone else and that the couple is not prohibited from marrying by laws of consanguinity.

that establish relationships that guide both community and individuals through life. They enact virtues that propel one along life's way, as much by ending previous stages of life as opening new ones.

The degree to which participants in and witnesses to these ceremonies grasp what is happening in the event varies and is, to a great extent, influenced by how well prepared they all are and how well the ritual is performed. Failure to internalize the virtues being enacted by the rites signals that the means of public transmission of the values and goals of the culture and the responsibilities of its members has broken down. Therefore, physicians, judges, jury members, firemen, police officers and rescue workers, members of the armed forces, and so on, who do not understand the import of their vows and do not internalize the virtues to which their responsibilities call them, should not be serving in these capacities.

Christian Ceremonies

Christian ceremonies are similar in many respects to civic ones, and in North America they overlap in marriage.[5] Like civic ceremonies, Christian ceremonies nourish, encourage professions of loyalty, and enact covenantal relationships. They also provide persons with a larger identity that imparts a moral mandate. However, Christian liturgical rituals differ from civic rituals in three important ways. First, the community performing the practice is not the state or an arm of the state (such as a public educational institution) but a religious society with distinctive beliefs, values, and loyalties. Second, and more importantly, the community's sacraments graft people into the life of God, uniting them with the saving work of Christ and making them living members of it. Finally, in addition to formally inaugurating one's relationship to the saving work of God in Christ, some Christian liturgical rites can restore that relationship when it becomes damaged. They also seek to comfort and strengthen individuals in and for the commitments they have made. That is, as rites of healing they are reparative. Thus Christian rites have a heightened cosmic dimension lacking in the civic sphere that has but a national dimension. The cosmic dimension is a buffer against the fragile identity of personal narrative alone.

---

5. In the United States the civic and religious aspects of marriage are indissolubly joined, since clergy are authorized to act as agents of the state.

In nonsacramental ecclesial rites, the community is enacting, authorizing, and certifying in its own name. Some of these, such as the imposition of ashes and the washing of feet, look like sacraments in some ways, but are not, because they do not enact union with God but simply recall aspects of the Christian vocation initiated by that union enacted in baptism. The imposition of ashes calls one into an important episode in Jesus' life and inaugurates a penitential season. The washing of feet carries one into another fateful moment in Jesus' life and highlights the Christian life as one of service. Still others, such as the Stations of the Cross and Holy Week services, are special liturgical practices that reenact historic episodes in the church's life that enrich one's understanding but do not enact anything themselves or point to specific aspects of the Christian vocation, as do the imposition of ashes and the washing of feet.

It has been difficult for Christian theologians to find categorizing rubrics through which to interpret the church's ceremonies, because some rites developed apart from theological formulation, customs have differed significantly, and different ceremonies intend different effects. Liturgics and sacramentology may be the most contended area of Christian theology. Although liturgical and sacramental practices and rationales may change, the continuing attempt to find frameworks of interpretation for them should not be viewed as simply seeking to justify practices, but to understand them better. The endurance of Christian rites and rituals over millennia roots those participating in them in a long and dignified tradition of memory that itself shapes identity.

My purpose here is not to rehearse or assess the contentious history of liturgy and sacraments but to ask what liturgical rites accomplish socially and spiritually. I have argued that civic ceremonies accomplish several purposes for the common and individual good, and I will show that liturgical ceremonies do the same. But as I have already noted, Christian ceremonies, because they march to a different drummer, do things that civic ones cannot. They make people living members of the life and work of God and they restore persons and relationships that suffer damage to that identity and the high calling that abiding in communion with God establishes. Unlike their civil counterparts, many Christian rituals heal. Indeed, the whole point of the Christian enterprise is to heal a perishing creation. Christianity's very reason for being is medicinal.

While the schema we used to sort through civic ceremonies will help us here, medical imagery may also be clarifying because it highlights the reparative aspect of Christian ceremonies lacking in the civic ones. The medical arts distinguish prophylactic from therapeutic methods. The first tries to avoid or prevent damage to the mind and body, the second tries to restore health when damage occurs. The civic body does not think as clearly in these terms, but they are present. Mandatory public education and inoculations do recognize the importance of an educated and healthy public for the welfare of the whole. Civic pedagogical ceremonies, examined above, attest to the importance of creating a common public narrative through the nation's history and heroes to weave a strong social fabric. But the confessional, consecratory, and covenantal ones also protect the social health of the whole. They all function prophylactically, just as good nutrition, exercise, and good personal hygiene do for the individual.

So it is with liturgical practices. Some are prophylactic, while others are restorative. More elaborate Christian ceremonies serve more than one purpose, so no tight typology could work. Here, however, since our interest is in healing, I will use the categories employed for civic ceremonies to try to understand Christian ones, and then ask after the therapeutic power that several of them have, sometimes explicitly, at other times unintentionally or occasionally.

Pedagogical Christian Ceremonies

For the most part, the feast days and seasons of the church year instruct her members in the history and meaning of the faith and socialize them into its virtues and values. Advent, Christmas, Epiphany, Lent, Holy Week, Easter, and Pentecost, which begins ordinary time, annually recall the Christian narrative, just as civic commemorations do for the nation. Additional feast days, such as All Saints' Day and the recollection of Christian heroes and luminaries, enrich this nourishing fare intellectually and historically. These celebrations socialize the community and the content of its beliefs by enabling today's members to stand behind those who have come before. It is a nutritive measure that prevents Christians from thinking about their life in the divine drama of salvation asocially, a situation in which the emphasis is on a private relationship between self and God, and the past and the world disappear.

Special services on Ash Wednesday, during Holy Week, and various vigils and processions (with fire or palms, for example) dramatically reenact events in the life and death of Jesus. These invite people to stand with him in his temptation in the desert, in his agony in the garden, during and following his capture by the police, in his humiliation, death, and burial, and in his glorious resurrection. The spiritual often sung on Good Friday asks, "Were you there when they crucified my Lord?" Dramatic liturgical reenactment of the story enables people to say "yes" with better understanding than their own imagination might furnish.

These dramatic forms of worship are prophylactic because they educate people to know the God they worship. Should winds of doctrine blow in unseemly directions, the people will be fortified and prepared to resist them. Further, and more important, they give people an identity that is noble and glorious, yet scarred and tragic. It is not the private personal narrative that the modern notion of the self so highly prizes, or even the communal narrative of a single nation. Rather, it is the cosmic narrative of the redemption of the world by God. Successfully placing one's personal narrative into the broader scope of God's story checks self-preoccupation and idolatrous forms of nationalism.

Confessional Christian Ceremonies

Confessional rites edify, but people who speak their loyalty to God demonstrate that they have committed themselves. Christian ceremonies often involve personal vows and pledges of loyalty to God, but many of them also consecrate. We will consider such practices under the category of covenantal ceremonies.

Exclusively confessional Christian practices are basically of two kinds, both of which are done as part of public worship services: the singing of hymns and the recitation of creeds. Here people are instructed in and profess the faith of the church in the same breath. The singing of hymns is often the most active role worshipers have in the service. Singing three or four theologically sophisticated hymns, with four to six stanzas each, is perhaps the most pervasive form of Christian education there is. Adult education hours cannot compete with it. Contemporary worship, having songs with few words and oft-repeated choruses, will deeply embed in singers the few themes articulated (mostly praise); but it risks creating theologically shallow worshipers.

The other confessional ritual in Christian worship is the recitation of one of the creeds of the church. The Apostles' Creed is normally used at baptisms, and the later, more developed Nicene Creed is spoken at celebrations of the Lord's Supper. A common notion is that the people confess their faith by reciting the creed; but the recitation of the Creed is not a statement of personally crafted belief but of the faith of the church.[6] Confessing the faith of the church, whether in historic or contemporary form, may be seen by some as disingenuous, if individuals cannot yet personally affirm every clause. But it is a more humble approach, for it recognizes the failure of individuals to grasp the mystery of God and holds out the hope of growing into the faith of the church with ever-deepening insight.

Consecratory Christian Ceremonies

Consecratory rites edify and designate or dedicate persons and things for special use, purpose, or relationship. Consecrating is the same as sanctifying in the Hebrew sense of *qādāš*. Israel is set apart from the nations, dedicated by God to worship him only. Israel is sanctified or made "holy" by the status and expectations laid upon her. She is special to the Lord, but that expresses no moral approval, only the designation of a special function: to belong to God.[7]

In the Christian tradition, some things are normally dedicated only once, such as the dedication of children by their parents to be raised in the Christian tradition,[8] the dedication of church buildings and furnishings, and of public service agencies. At the same time, other rites, such as the washing of feet and the celebration of the Lord's Supper, can be repeated many times, for they encourage the participants to rededicate themselves to the covenant to which they were consecrated at baptism. No vows are professed in these rites, but an officiant or sponsor acts or speaks on behalf of

6. Some denominations have rewritten historic creeds to suit special emphases. But these are still the faith of the church, even if they are of a specific denomination at a specific point in time, rather than the catholic faith of the universal church.

7. Indeed, in Gen. 38:21-22 and Deut. 23:18, the word *qĕdēšâ* means a pagan cult prostitute, a woman dedicated to sexual service. The root, *qdš*, refers to any kind of setting aside for a special purpose, with no morally approving connotation.

8. In cases where parents read a personal statement of their intention to raise the child in the Christian tradition, there are no vows technically speaking, but there is an active participation more characteristic of confessional ceremonies.

the recipients of the dedication. The blessing of a home, a church meeting, or a pregnant woman all fall into this consecratory category without profession of vows.

Recently, in response to pastoral need and changing circumstances, an interesting twist on consecratory rituals has emerged: deconsecration of buildings and relationships previously consecrated. These include rites for the deconsecration of a church building, or for the dissolution of a marriage or a pastoral office. Such ceremonies can be psychologically helpful to preserve what has been accomplished, say farewell honorably, and free people to move on psychologically.

Covenantal Christian Consecration

Now we come to the most complex liturgical rites. In covenantal consecration, edification of the gathered body, confession by the principals (with the making of vows or promises), and consecration of a new relationship with God or the community — or both — happen all at once. These rites inaugurate new aspects of a person's identity, assign a new status, and impart authority. The institution and the witnesses require vows or other promises of faithfulness and diligence to the undertaking. The rite is usually symbolized by material symbols or gestures of office that are paralleled by appropriate gestures of gratitude and humility (kneeling or walking to the sites of the office — pulpit, font, and altar, for example) that indicate awareness of the challenges ahead. These covenantal ceremonies are all initiatory. They are baptism, marriage, and ordination (also known as "commissioning" or "installation").

In considering these rites, it is important to recall that they are increasingly being performed in a eucharistic setting. Celebration of the Lord's Supper does not fit neatly into any of our categories, though I previously touched on it in the discussion of consecratory rites. While the sacrament of the altar is edifying and proclaims the meaning of the practice, it does not impart a new status or authority to persons, nor does it consecrate them. Where the rite is a sacrament, it does consecrate the elements that enable the participants to relive their initial incorporation into Christ at baptism. Although there are no particular vows, when the creed is recited prior to the consecration of the elements, the participants do confess the faith of the church and, when they respond "Amen" when receiving communion, they are affirming their faithful reception of the elements. Thus there are covenantal elements here, but not as clearly as in the other cases considered in this section. As I noted above, communion is primarily for strengthening and rededication.

Perhaps it will be clarifying at this point to offer a note on preaching, since it often accompanies eucharistic celebration, as well as the rites discussed here when not performed in the context of the Eucharist. Some of the communions that emerged from the Reformation of the sixteenth century tended to replace the liturgy with preaching (Lutherans excluded) because at the time they deemed proclamation of the word more edifying. Today, however, with amplification systems and renewed liturgies, the proclamation function of preaching is included in the formal liturgy. This could be seen as making preaching redundant where the liturgy is well executed and well understood; but it does not, for the sermon provides the opportunity for the preacher to relate the day's lections to the liturgical event, and to apply both to the particular day and event for the congregation gathered.[9]

Be that as it may, locating the other covenantal rites within the Eucharist effectively carries what has been consecrated and inaugurated into the full worshiping life of the church at its most tangible movement. Embracing those newly consecrated in the eucharistic liturgy incorporates them into the body of Christ and propels them ahead, out into the world to do the work God has given them to do, to love and serve him as faithful witnesses of Christ.

For the most part — though not all denominational liturgies have included this — many newer covenantal liturgies add another element that is missing in all civic rituals and in the Christian rites discussed so far. After the verbal interaction between the officiant and the recipient, in which those officiating publicly state the appropriateness of the consecration and those being consecrated promise to uphold their duties, the consecration is verbally enacted, and there is a verbal role for the witnesses of the event. Here the congregation both confirms the consecration and vows to support these recipients in fulfilling their new responsibilities. In these cases the covenant is not between God and the individuals but among God, the individuals, and

---

9. Of course, Christian worshipers are accustomed to attending baptisms and celebrations of the Eucharist in which the sermon makes no reference to accompanying liturgical events and perhaps only barely to the Scripture readings, for something else has captured the preacher's attention. Be that as it may, the opportunity exists for integration of all of these for the edification of the congregation.

the church, which is represented universally by the administrator and locally by the witnesses.[10]

This is really quite remarkable. Although difficult to enforce, it places the baptizand, the newly consecrated minister, and the married couple under the care of the local congregation or parish. To paraphrase an African proverb, the church is effectively saying that it takes a village to have a successful Christian life, ministry (whether lay or ordained), and marriage. The Christian enterprise is a thoroughly social undertaking. This is why ministers are wary about baptizing or marrying those who are just passing through and have no ongoing relationship with the parish. These rites initiate relationships and nourish ways of life that are arduous to sustain and require nurture and guidance. Those who wander off afterward will need to fend for themselves, and that suggests lack of awareness of the seriousness and strenuousness of the undertaking inaugurated by these rites. The civic analogues, at least in the United States, have nothing like this recognition, nor the means to restore what has been lost. There the burden falls completely on the individuals to live up to the promises they have made and the standards set by the state.

Because covenantal rites have occupied such a prominent place in Christian sacramentology, pausing over each rite will be helpful in seeing the full effect of this kind of covenantal consecration.

Baptism

In renewed rites, the practices surrounding baptism cover a long process constituted by a cluster of liturgical events. Lengthy and gradual preparation appropriately recognizes the magnitude of what is taking place. Normatively speaking, initiation is into the company of all faithful people who lift their candle to the saving work of God, but far more importantly, it is initiation into the drama of salvation that God is effecting to restore his languishing creation.

---

10. Technically speaking, if the administrator is the consecrator, the covenant is between the church and the individuals, and God is called on to bless the persons but not consecrate them. Still, most churches that celebrate these nonsacramental consecrations would be sympathetic to the idea that the promises made are not only to the administrator and witnesses but also to God, and thus God is implicitly included in the covenant itself, apart from being invoked by the administrator to bless the undertaking.

In the case of infants, preparatory rites may include the blessing of a pregnant woman and prayers for a safe delivery; preparation of parents and godparents; thanksgiving for a healthy delivery; vows made by sponsors; confession of the baptismal covenant by all present, immediately followed by baptism itself; chrismation; reception of the light of Christ and welcoming through a final vow taken by the witnessing congregation to support the newly baptized in their life in God through engrafting into the death of Christ; and reception of first communion for strengthening toward the Christian life in hope of resurrection like Christ's. In the case of adults, the preparatory rites begin with admission to the catechumenate and formal enrollment as a catechumen. The baptismal rites themselves are the same. Ancient catechumenal rites include a full week of catechesis after the baptism as well. The point in both infant and adult sacraments of baptism is that becoming a Christian means both unification with God and the institutional church.

Christian Marriage

Christian marriage initiates a consecrated and holy relationship publicly. Most marriage rites contain all the elements of covenantal ceremonies discussed above. Such rites include proclamation, consecration, vows, usually the exchange of rings, the formal consecration, vows by the witnesses (some of whom also sign the marriage certificate), and concluding prayers and blessings. In the United States, the minister is authorized by the state to be the consecrator and does so in the first-person singular rather than invoking God to do so as in the case of sacraments. Still, Christian weddings normally assume that God is present with the assembly, blessing the proceedings and sanctifying the couple for joyous adventure in their life together.

Ordination/Commissioning/Installation

Ceremonies of ordination, commissioning, and installation are another form of consecratory initiation. Ranks of the ordained clergy are variously rendered as either bishop, priest, and deacon or bishop, elder, and deacon; or it may be presbyter, deacon, and elder. Some other interpretations of the scriptural and historic traditions recognize but two ranks. Although consecration to holy orders is traditionally a sacrament, meaning that God makes the person a cleric, many Protestant liturgies seek divine blessing on the minister, who is consecrated not by God but by designated ecclesiastical authorities. In this case, ordination is not a sacrament.

If the age of the church fathers was the age of the bishop, and the Middle Ages was the age of the monk, the modern age is the age of the laity. That we live in the age of the laity is clear from the great array of lay ministries within the church and increasingly the recognition of Christian ministries that carry the Christian witness into the world through missionaries, health workers, educators, and so forth. These ministries are now also consecrated by nonsacramental ceremonies that look very much like nonsacramental ordinations, though perhaps not as elaborate. Just as in the clerical offices, where a person is consecrated, professes vows of faithfulness and integrity, and assumes a special set of responsibilities, the laity now assume responsibilities for the proper performance of the liturgy, Christian education, and outreach ministries of the congregation in the community.

Healing

We have proposed consecration as a broad interpretive framework for understanding many liturgical ceremonies that sanctify persons, relationships, and places. Now we will turn to the healing power of these rites. The traditional healing sacraments of the church are the reconciliation of a penitent and the anointing of the dying, which are closely allied.[11] Since the liturgical renovation of the sacraments by the Second Vatican Council, the anointing of the dying has been the most elaborated. As a rite of spiritual healing, it has been extended and adapted to all kinds of settings and circumstances where the need for healing is manifest. At the same time, the rite for the reconciliation of a penitent, of which last rites or anointing was a variation, has all but vanished. This illustrates the modern turn from concern for life in the next world to life in this one.

To be more precise, here we recognize that even the most staunchly faithful Christian is constantly under stress. With knowledge that one has been sanctified for a dignified and uplifted life with God in the ecclesial setting, sanctification lays the foundation for restoration to that godly calling when it

---

11. This is the categorization of the Roman Catholic Church. See *Catechism of the Catholic Church* (Washington, DC: United States Catholic Conference, 1994), pp. 357-82.

is disrupted in various ways, as will inevitably be the case. Here, in addition to the two classic sacraments of healing, we suggest that all of the traditional sacraments, even if they now function nonsacramentally, may also heal.

Baptismal Initiation, Reconciliation, Anointing, Communion

BAPTISMAL INITIATION

Although traditionally recognizing but two sacraments of healing, penance and unction, the Western church has always, in truth, had another sacrament of healing: baptism. All of these sacraments work on several levels. Previously, we discussed baptism as engrafting into the drama of salvation. But classically, baptism is healing from original sin.[12] Ritual cleansing enables people to attend to actual sins committed, and not to be burdened with the paralyzing fear of an ineradicable flaw in one's nature against which one is helpless, for this implies that one is irrefragably and permanently a victim of oneself. As noted above, renewed baptismal liturgies may include a reclaimed catechumenate that attends to preparation for the Christian calling, while chrismation symbolizes the power of the Holy Spirit, and the candle symbolizes the light of Christ that will guide the baptized one for the rest of his/her life. Together these rites dramatize a break with the past and initiation into a new life with God and new friends with whom to live it. The dynamic here is repair and turning to a healed life.

RECONCILIATION

The rite of reconciliation picks up after baptismal rites. Knowing that the light of Christ will not always shine brightly from a person, confession of sin should give sinners an opportunity to express remorse, make amends where possible (or some substitute where not), and return to the lighted path with a cleaner heart. Auricular confession, now largely lost, can be psychologically cleansing in a way that the generic public confessions of sin that are now standard in modern eucharistic liturgies cannot be. Traditionally, auricular confession was of specific behaviors. But today we see in ourselves and one another character

---

12. There is no reason not to hold these together; 1 Cor. 6:11-17 seems to presuppose cleansing for incorporation as members of Christ.

flaws and unhealthy tendencies that recur regardless of the setting or temptation. Confession of sin should enable one to focus on the specific ways that
one's pet sins (e.g., anger, greed, jealousy, fear) may be ameliorated, since tem-
peraments and personalities differ so widely from one to the next. Forgiveness
is preliminary to insight and strength for the continued struggle. To paraphrase Paul, it is better to confess than have the sins fester. The traditional ad-
age regarding liturgical penitence is that all may, some should.[13]

ANOINTING

Reconciliation of penitents is related to ministry to the sick and dying, often
with anointing. Anointing of the dying classically functioned as the final opportunity for a person to prepare for death and what it might bring. The final confession of sin was an unburdening and formal absolution that provided reassurance that spiritual healing is possible, even at the last minute.
Further, the healing of damaged relationships is a great gift to the living,
who will continue to live with whatever has transpired between them and
the deceased with no further chance of repair. This writer is not aware of liturgies being written for families or other persons attending the dying who
have been estranged but now seek reconciliation through the ministrations
of the church. Such liturgies could be deeply healing for some people.

All three of these ceremonies are restorative liturgical actions whereby
the individual's relationships with God, the church, other people, and finally
with one's own self and one's past are repaired by the power of the Holy
Spirit, so that the person can rest from at least that sort of distress when facing death. Although they underwent significant transformations of meaning
and forms of administration over the centuries, the purpose of these three
rites has always been the care of the soul.

THE LORD'S SUPPER

Early on, communion was considered an agent of immortality and deification. Martin Luther also understood it to heal the soul. This may have been

---

13. The medieval penitential system neglected an important element of healing from
sin, and that is reconciliation on the horizontal plane, especially between those who have
harmed one another. Judaism, for example, dedicates a full month annually for this, prior to
the petitioning of God for forgiveness of sin on the Day of Atonement.

under pressure to retain the motif of healing after he eliminated penance, but his argument — that sacraments are not for solace only but also for strength — stands on its own. His 1527 treatise on the Eucharist, written against Zwingli, insisted on the real presence of Christ in the sacrament: "To give a simple illustration of what takes place in this eating: it is as if a wolf devoured a sheep and the sheep were so powerful a food that it transformed the wolf and turned him into a sheep. So, when we eat Christ's flesh physically and spiritually, the food is so powerful that it transforms us into itself and out of fleshly, sinful, mortal men makes spiritual, holy, living men."[14] For Luther, physically ingesting God is a powerful psychological means of keeping one pure and restoring Christian focus. Here the material shapes the spiritual. Just as very large athletes are not jockeys, and very short athletes cannot easily do slam dunks, Luther says that the spiritual life cannot proceed unless the very power of God enter the body materially, for it is literally nourishment for the Christian life.

There is another sense in which communion is healing, and that is *socially.* Outside the church, roles of power and status rule in very particular ways. So, too, within the church, hierarchical roles and status often control the institution. Yet those hierarchical relationships that rule the marketplace and those that rule the church are utterly different, for the very definition of the church is medicinal. Thus, regardless of education, economic power, sex, race, class, language, and so on, all are united to God and one another at the Lord's Table. Even if it is but an eschatological glimpse of heaven and after the service all reenter their worldly comfort zones, at least for one blink of an eye the unifying power of the saving work of God materializes. That is a great beacon of hope revealed nowhere else.

Confirmation, Marriage, Ordination

Confirmation, marriage, and ordination do not purport to be sacraments of healing as the other four traditional sacraments do. Yet, with changing demographics in several parts of the world, these rites also have therapeutic power.

---

14. Martin Luther, "That These Words of Christ, 'This Is My Body,' Etc., Still Stand Firm against the Fanatics, 1527," in Robert H. Fischer, ed., *Word and Sacrament III, Luther's Works* (Philadelphia: Fortress, 1961), p. 101.

CONFIRMATION

Confirmation is a sacrament, or sacramental rite, that lost its way once the liturgical renewal movement put chrismation back into initiatory rites and authorized infant communion. For churches with a catholic ecclesiology (Eastern Orthodox, Roman Catholic, Anglican) one does not make a decision to join a particular confession of the church, because there is only one universal church that an individual is joined to at baptism. For those with a radical Reformation ecclesiology, joining a local church may be of much greater significance, but in those churches that abjure sacraments, any analogues to confirmation may instead focus on the faith of the individual that has brought her to this decision. Where adult baptism — perhaps with infant dedication — is the norm, joining a local church is not the focus of attention; therefore, the rite loses its force here as well. In those churches that practice infant baptism and have a strong confessional rather than catholic orientation (Lutheran and Reformed), confirmation will come more to the fore.[15]

Despite these important differences — and sorting out the sacramentology (or antisacramentology) of each would be quite interesting — an emerging demographic reality is that churches practicing infant baptism are experiencing the loss of their adolescents, some of whom return or find their way to other churches later on. In these churches confirmation is thus not a rite in search of its theology but an opportunity to recraft an old rite to a new need. Some churches practice routine confirmation with adolescents who have stayed in the church, and then join to their number others who find their way to the church — or back to it — and who may have been confirmed as adolescents in other communions. Teen confirmation classes and adult seeker's groups are in the same business of helping people sort out their religious life and their theological identity. When this process is completed — and it may not be accomplished in the time allocated by formal classes — the proper public liturgical celebration should be the receiving of these persons as adults who are undertaking the Christian life in a particularly intentional way. Thus the appropriate ceremony, especially where confirmation as classically understood by the old-line denominations is no longer applicable, is perhaps a commissioning rite with vows and gestures demonstrating that these individuals are being embraced by the community.

---

15. For those confessional traditions that do not chrismate at all, confirmation, which is not a sacrament, may pose a different set of questions.

This whole process, if it is not limited to perfunctory instruction but attends to the person's history on an individual level, can very well be a healing experience, for such a decision may well mark a turn away from a worn-out lifestyle or set of attitudes and values and toward a fresh one. This may be especially true for refugees from communions where people were unhappy, but who steadfastly refused to leave the church altogether. These persons become pilgrims, seeking to live their life with God in what is for them a more wholesome setting.

MARRIAGE

As the age at which people are first married rises in the postindustrial world, more and more people getting married for the first time bring with them wells of loneliness or histories of mistakes to put behind them. In these cases, marriage is clearly a great moment of healing and hope. But it is also a rite overflowing with the taste and hope of healing for those remarrying after widowhood or divorce (in those communions that permit it). Perhaps those sobered by experience, as opposed to those in the first flush of youth, will be able to sustain one another better in their life together in God as a result of their struggles.

ORDINATION/COMMISSIONING/INSTALLATION

The final ceremony to consider from the perspective of healing is ordination and its lay analogues. The changing demographic that applies to confirmation and marriage, that of seeking refuge in the church not routinely but after having sustained some of life's bruises, also applies to ordination. The age of those being ordained is also rising, as more second-career persons seek ordained and lay ministry. For them, the path to ordination may be the result of more spiritual reflection and struggle than it was for those of previous generations. Here, too, it can be a deeply healing and hard-won moment in a person's life. This includes businesspeople and professionals who either seek holy orders or throw their energy into nonordained church service. For some, perhaps especially in the latter case, this may be after some unsettling turn of events in a person's life has sobered and reoriented him or her back toward the light of Christ. Here the new ministry is clearly undertaken to experience God's healing power. For some, it may even be penitential.

REFLECTION

Here we have focused on the power of ritual for those whom life has buffeted around somewhat. This might give the impression that confirmation, marriage, and ordination are more meaningful for older, more seasoned Christians. But this is probably not a warranted conclusion. Pain and suffering have been finding their way down the age scale since the 1960s in North America. The decline of long-term healthy marriages, the rise of divorce, the loss of even a pretext of permanent sexual and financial commitment, relaxation of sexual standards accompanied by adolescent and unwanted pregnancy and abortion, the prevalence of substance abuse, the exposure of domestic violence and abuse, the rise of adolescent suicide, and random outbreaks of unprovoked killings have exposed most youngsters to suffering and have caused anxiety from which many in earlier generations would have been protected. For example, though the carnage was horrendous in World Wars I and II, it was not televised, whereas now sexual scandals and violence are graphically replayed over and over, and children view them many times. Their exposure to violence and suffering recorded by broadcast journalism and simulated by the entertainment industry alone cannot but provoke anxiety. At increasingly tender ages, the young tell horrendous stories of suffering and pain that scar their souls. Those who have access to well-prepared, well-performed, and well-understood liturgical worship may perhaps find it helpful, especially if the adults recognize the potentially healing power of the liturgy as a safe place to take shelter in God.

What we are seeing here is that while baptism, Holy Communion, reconciliation, and anointing facilitate healing on the face of it, changing demographics — at least in the Western churches — are creating a context in which the healing power of other liturgical ceremonies is being revealed. This may be one reason why there is such an outcry for and openness to liturgical practices, even in communions that for centuries did not hold them in high esteem. Given the massive pain and suffering in which the church ministers, it is interesting to speculate whether the Holy Spirit as the agent of the church's rites (rather than the authority of the church in its own name) is not the more effective agent of healing.

In making these observations, we note in conclusion that those communions that deny sacraments altogether, as well as those that have limited the consecratory power of God to only two sacraments, may have inadvertently demoted the authority of God by enhancing the authority of ecclesiastical bodies to consecrate and make covenants on their own authority. It is my suspicion that people are more interested in the power of God to take them to himself, authorize them for a virtuous life, and heal them when they fall than they are in the power of the church to do so. Ironically, though they have intended to "lower" their ecclesiology, nonliturgical and weakly sacramental communions have done just the opposite. It is the "high" sacramental communions that have a "low" ecclesiology and the sacramentally "low" communions that have a "high" ecclesiology.

Conclusion

Let us survey the terrain we have traversed. I began with a broad definition of public ceremony that embraces both civic and Christian rituals. These edify those who actively participate in or witness them by preparing individuals for productive service in the society to which they belong for its flourishing and protection. And so it is on both civic and Christian sides, though the societies they serve may differ. By edifying, pledging loyalty to, being consecrated for special duties in, and being covenantally bound to relationships and moral responsibilities within a particular society, persons are ennobled for the common good as they become responsible for society's well-being. To be an agent of society's well-being is to advance one's own satisfaction with and enjoyment of one's life and work. This is true in both the civic and the Christian cases.

Now, while nonreligious people belong only to the civic sphere, Christians belong to both the civic and the Christian sphere, and so their identity is more complex: it has an additional layer of identity to negotiate. While nonreligious citizens have personal and national identities to navigate between, Christians have personal, national, and theological identities to negotiate, and that is trickier and perhaps costlier, for Christians will need to adjudicate among all three when pressed. There may be times when rising to the call of the national interest will prevail, as in national emergencies, and there will be times when one's Christian identity will prevail over both personal and national priorities. Being an adept Christian is a skill that must be honed over a long period of time.

Since unforeseen conflicts cannot be anticipated, most of our investigation here has been on the theological level, which is the broadest level of identity for the Christian. In order to avoid rehearsing unproductive Christian polemics of the past, I have tried to chart a path suggesting that in the inevitable tensions among personal, national, and theological narratives, Christians have a far more challenging time of it than do secular people, who only have to negotiate loyalty to their homeland against personal self-interest. Christians, on the other hand, must reassess personal self-interest in light of God's claim on their life as well as those claims made by national citizenship.

Of course, there will be many instances in which no conflict exists between upholding the national welfare and the modern baptismal vow to serve Christ in all persons. Yet Christianity's cosmic framework of meaning provides a palpable Christian bulwark against both personal and national self-interest. Christians live in God's redemptive plan working itself out in the cosmos, and that is grander than any personal or even national calling. Christian identity claims persons for God, and in him they participate in his redeeming work at whatever level. It is not a realm that highlights personal accomplishment, for God has accomplished all. This is both a nobler and humbler self-concept than what popular culture offers through personal narrative alone.

But above and beyond that, Christian rites, be they sacraments in which the Holy Spirit empowers or nonsacramental rites in which the community exercises its proper authority, are instruments that repair damaged souls struggling to negotiate their way between personal narrative, with its civic calling, and life in God, with its theological calling. This is the real point of Christian rites and ceremonial commemorations.

The Healing Practice of Ecclesial Reconciliation

Douglas M. Koskela

In 1968, a group of ministers and laypeople who had recently departed from the Evangelical United Brethren Church (EUB) met in Portland, Oregon. At that organizing conference, they established a new denomination to be known as the Evangelical Church in North America. The reason for the secession of this group from the EUB Church was, ironically, an ecclesial merger. Just months earlier, the EUB Church and the Methodist Church had joined together to form the United Methodist Church; this was a union that those who would gather in Portland steadfastly resisted. Thus a celebrated (if limited) movement toward ecclesial unity was immediately followed by an occasion of division.

This is but one of many examples that could be cited to indicate the challenges to ecclesial communion in a context of "denominationalism." The feeling of taking one step forward only to take one step backward became well known to committed ecumenists toward the end of the twentieth century. Many have recently expressed their sense that the ecumenical movement — and the churches' commitment to it — are "stalled in place."[1] Yet the theological and practical problem of disunity in the church remains. In what follows I wish to reflect on the category of "ecclesial reconciliation" as healing practice.[2]

---

1. Carl E. Braaten and Robert W. Jenson, *In One Body through the Cross: The Princeton Proposal for Christian Unity* (Grand Rapids: Eerdmans, 2003), p. 6 (preface).

2. The language of "ecclesial reconciliation" is drawing increasing attention in con-

So long as division persists at multiple levels of the church's life, practices of reconciliation are essential to the renewal and flourishing of the church.

Ecclesial Reconciliation and Ecumenism

While it might be natural to assume that ecclesial reconciliation is synonymous with ecumenism, I would suggest that they are overlapping but not identical concepts. The notion of ecclesial reconciliation is both narrower (in some respects) and broader (in other respects) than "ecumenism," at least as that term has been used by the modern ecumenical movement. Ecclesial reconciliation is a narrower concept in that it is limited to practices of and in the Christian church *qua* church. Doubtless, there is great value in ecumenical institutional structures (such as the World Council of Churches) and theological work groups (such as the 2003 Princeton Project sponsored by the Center for Catholic and Evangelical Theology).[3] The work of such bodies is often indispensable for churches as they engage in practices of reconciliation, particularly at the inter-ecclesial level. Those practices, however, are ultimately undertaken by and within the church. Therefore, there is a great deal of ecumenical labor that supports, but is distinct from, the work of reconciliation within Christ's church. Ecclesial reconciliation is also narrower than ecumenism in that the former implies a degree of repentance.[4] For reconciliation of any kind to occur, all parties must acknowledge their respective roles in division and estrangement. In a climate of sincere optimism, the ecumenical movement of the twentieth century was occasionally prone to forget the importance of confessing wrongs and seeking forgiveness.[5] Any attempt to

---

temporary theology. For instance, see Stefanos Alexopoulos, "An Example of Ecclesial Reconciliation in the Early Church: Three Homilies by Paul of Emesa and Cyril of Alexandria," *St. Vladimir's Theological Quarterly* 45, no. 4 (2001): 339-58; see also John W. Wright and J. Douglas Harrison, "The Ecclesial Practice of Reconciliation and the End of the Wesleyan," *Wesleyan Theological Journal* 37, no. 2 (2002): 194-214.

3. The *Princeton Proposal* made clear that its framers were not appointed by their churches and did not attempt to speak for them.

4. It should be obvious that the corporate practices of ecclesial reconciliation that are the subject of this chapter are distinct from the sacrament of reconciliation/confession. Nonetheless, an element of repentance is crucial to both.

5. This point is captured nicely by Wright and Harrison in "The Ecclesial Practice of Reconciliation," p. 200.

force ecclesial unity while bypassing repentance and forgiveness would not constitute a practice of ecclesial reconciliation.

There is also a sense in which reconciliation is a broader term than ecumenism. Ecumenism is appropriately focused on the reunion of separated ecclesial communities toward the goal of full visible communion. Ecclesial reconciliation would certainly include such inter-ecclesial practices, but it would also include *intra*-ecclesial (and even intra-congregational) reconciliation. Recent disputes over ordination in the Episcopal Church and the United Methodist Church, for example, have pointed up the need for reconciliatory practices within particular Christian traditions. Division has long been a problem at the congregational level as well.[6] Practices of reconciliation within the local church have not generally been considered under the rubric of ecumenism, but they clearly fall within the category under present consideration. The experience of disunity in the church is also marked by various kinds of social division, particularly along the lines of race, gender, and class. There is increasing interest in theological reflection on reconciliation that can account adequately for these socioeconomic dimensions.[7] The work of ecclesial reconciliation is not complete so long as these divisions persist. Thus the healing practice of reconciliation must attend to such categories even more than has been the case in the ecumenical movement.

It is common for the term "ecclesial reconciliation" to be used as a rough equivalent of visible communion.[8] There is something intuitively correct about this, since reconciliation implies a relationship fully restored. A merely "spiritual" or "invisible" communion does not adequately capture the concrete and complete quality of being reconciled. The vision of unity expressed by the New Delhi Assembly of the World Council of Churches has become the standard account of this goal:

---

6. 1 Cor. 1:10-13; 3:1-9.

7. One might point to the John Perkins Center for Reconciliation, Leadership Training, and Community Development at my own institution, Seattle Pacific University, or the Center for Reconciliation at Duke Divinity School. Much as the various ecumenical institutions and work groups support the work of inter-ecclesial reconciliation, these centers offer tremendous resources that can and should be embraced by Christian churches in addressing socioeconomic division.

8. For just one example, see Richard John Neuhaus, "A Closed Question and Ecumenism Now," *First Things* 26, no. 1 (Oct. 1992): 65.

> We believe that the unity which is both God's will and his gift to his Church is being made visible as all in each place who are baptized into Jesus Christ and confess him as Lord and Saviour are brought by the Holy Spirit into one fully committed fellowship, holding the one apostolic faith, preaching the one Gospel, breaking the one bread, joining in common prayer, and having a corporate life reaching out in witness and service to all and who at the same time are united with the whole Christian fellowship in all places and all ages in such wise that ministry and members are accepted by all, and that all can act and speak together as occasion requires for the tasks to which God calls his people.[9]

This expression of "the unity we seek" has given the ecumenical movement its bearings since that New Delhi Assembly. Even if its doctrinal minimalism may not be agreeable to every communion, this is a very illuminating portrait of ecclesial reconciliation on a global scale, and it marks the goal toward which all reconciliatory practices are directed. Yet I would also regard partial and more limited acts of reconciliation to be "healing practices." It would not be inappropriate to consider the recovery of some *degree* of visible communion — at the global, congregational, and/or social levels — to be representative of ecclesial reconciliation.

The Call to Reconciliation

To a great extent, the impulse behind the practice of ecclesial reconciliation has been the scandal of disunity in the church. Indeed, this is entirely appropriate. It is no accident that the modern ecumenical movement emerged in the context of global ministry. In the nineteenth and early twentieth centuries, missionaries in Africa and Asia recognized that their efforts were being undermined by the evident disunity between various churches and missionary societies.[10] What we might call a "negative impulse" toward reconciliation found expression, then, in the movement that would emerge formally in

---

9. New Delhi Statement on Unity, Third Assembly of the World Council of Churches, 1961, I.2.

10. William G. Rusch, "A Survey of Ecumenical Reflection about Unity," in Carl E. Braaten and Robert W. Jenson, eds., *The Ecumenical Future* (Grand Rapids: Eerdmans, 2004), p. 2.

1910.[11] The experience of missionaries working at cross-purposes with fellow Christians was not merely regarded as a *practical* problem. It illuminated a failure of the church to live into the reality for which Jesus prayed in John 17:

> I ask not only on behalf of these, but also on behalf of those who will believe in me through their word, that they may all be one. As you, Father, are in me and I am in you, may they also be in us, so that the world may believe that you have sent me. The glory that you have given me I have given them, so that they may be one, as we are one, I in them and you in me, that they may become completely one, so that the world may know that you have sent me and have loved them even as you have loved me.[12]

The call to ecumenism, then, was not driven strictly by a sense of competition among missionaries, but also by a growing recognition that the church had failed to exhibit the unity it was graciously given by God. This was rightly seen as a scandal.

More recently, Bruce Marshall has aptly characterized disunity as a threat to the credibility of the gospel: "The credibility of the gospel . . . depends upon the unity of the church by which that life is exhibited to the world. Jesus prays that the church may be one, 'in order that the world may believe.' Jesus' prayer clearly seems to be that the oneness of his followers may draw the unbelieving world to the fullness of saving faith in him."[13] The concern that ecclesial division would undermine the mission of the church has been a crucial motivating factor for the ecumenical movement. As we have already seen, disunity is not only a problem between Christian communities; it is also a problem within them. In that light, the scandal of division and its impact on the church's proclamation is also a driving concern for the broader practices of ecclesial reconciliation. Reconciliatory acts within congregations, denominations, and across social boundaries are clearly necessary if the church is adequately to fulfill its evangelistic vocation.

However, it is important to recognize that ecclesial reconciliation is not only motivated by this negative impulse; there is a clear positive impulse that impels this healing practice as well. Not only does the pursuit of re-

11. The World Missionary Conference at Edinburgh, held in 1910, is generally identified as the origin of the modern ecumenical movement.

12. John 17:20-23 (NRSV).

13. Bruce D. Marshall, "The Disunity of the Church and the Credibility of the Gospel," *Theology Today* 50, no. 1 (1993): 82.

stored communion at multiple levels address the scandal of division, but it also aims to foster renewal in the church. Focusing again on the modern ecumenical movement, we see that ecclesial renewal was central to the agenda of those involved. In fact, William J. Abraham has called the ecumenical movement "a paradigm case of a renewal movement in twentieth-century Christianity."[14] Echoing this judgment is Michael Kinnamon, who notes that the movement was not always in agreement on how best to proceed:

> Renewal of the church has been at the top of the ecumenical agenda, inseparable from unity, almost from the beginning of the modern ecumenical movement. Faith and Order and Life and Work . . . had different recipes for how renewal happens — one emphasizing a new commitment to shared service, the other a common recovery of the full apostolic faith — but both spoke explicitly of renewal in their early conferences.[15]

The aims of early ecumenists (and many recent ones) were geared toward the health, vitality, and faithfulness of the church. The pursuit of visible unity was hailed as a new moment for the global community of faith.

As both Abraham and Kinnamon recognize, however, the connection between ecumenism and renewal eventually eroded for a variety of reasons.[16] In considering ecclesial reconciliation as healing practice, we must bring the notion of renewal back to the center of focus. This is true not only for ecumenical conversations but also for the other contexts of reconciliation within the church that have been identified. At every level of disunity, Christian communities are called to reconciliation both because of the practical-theological costs of division and because of the promise of spiritual revitalization within the body of Christ. Practices aimed at restoring communion offer both a cure for ecclesial and spiritual maladies and a fresh experience of health and well-being. Thus the church is both driven by and drawn to various dimensions of ecclesial reconciliation.

---

14. William J. Abraham, "Ecumenism and the Rocky Road to Renewal," in Braaten and Jenson, *The Ecumenical Future*, p. 177.

15. Michael Kinnamon, *The Vision of the Ecumenical Movement and How It Has Been Impoverished by Its Friends* (St. Louis: Chalice Press, 2003), p. 23.

16. Abraham, "Ecumenism and the Rocky Road to Renewal," pp. 177-78; see also Kinnamon, *The Vision of the Ecumenical Movement*, p. 25. Kinnamon seems to mark this erosion fairly recently, while Abraham describes a long and complex process over the course of many decades.

Acts of Reconciliation

What are the practices of ecclesial reconciliation? What concrete things are Christian communities to *do* when they are stirred by the positive and negative vocation to restored relationship? I would identify six categories of such practices: dialogue, recognition of areas of agreement and disagreement, confession, forgiveness, commitment, and communion (to whatever degree currently possible). To some extent, there is a logical progression in the order of these dimensions of reconciliation. One follows naturally after the other, from entrance into dialogue to restored communion. But this does not mean that the order is necessary. It is certainly conceivable that confession might precede recognition of agreement and disagreement or that commitment might precede forgiveness. What is most significant at this point is the recognition that all such practices can be reconciliatory, but that the fullness of reconciliation only emerges when each of these dimensions occurs. Again, it is wise to emphasize the value and necessity of partial gains toward reconciliation, as well as the ultimate aim of full reconciliation and visible communion.

Entering into dialogue is an initial and necessary act of reconciliation. Whatever the nature of estrangement within or between churches, healing cannot emerge out of isolation. Only within the context of genuine dialogical engagement can the possibility of reconciliation arise. Quite clearly, just coming to the table can be a significant challenge for a variety of reasons, one of which is hidden — or even manifest — distrust. A history of misunderstanding, injustice, or fundamental disagreement can leave divided Christians deeply pessimistic about the possibility of reconciliation. There is skepticism — often justifiable — about whether all parties will have a voice in the conversation or that power will be exercised appropriately.[17] In that light, initiating or engaging in dialogue might seem pointless at best and dangerous at worst.

Another reason for resisting dialogue is the belief that areas of disagreement are already clear. It is often the case that divided Christians assume that they fully recognize the fundamental positions, arguments, and criteria at issue. They regard dialogue as nothing more than a venue for re-

---

17. See the insightful account of reconciliatory practices in Chris P. Rice, *Grace Matters: A Memoir of Faith, Friendship, and Hope in the Heart of the South* (San Francisco: Jossey-Bass, 2003).

hashing well-worn arguments, so they focus time and energy elsewhere. Another kind of challenge to dialogue stems from positive theological conviction rather than ill will or weariness. Particularly in ecumenical engagement, specific ecclesiological commitments can preempt even the possibility of dialogue. A classic case of this is the preconciliar Roman Catholic Church: despite the crucial work of many individual Catholic theologians on the problem of Christian disunity,[18] the Catholic Church formally abstained from ecumenical engagement for much of the twentieth century. This abstention did not signal a lack of desire for unity; rather, it signaled certain reservations about the *way* that unity could be sought given the ecclesiological orientation of Catholicism.[19] Despite these reservations, the Second Vatican Council (particularly the Decree on Ecumenism) marked the entrance of the Roman Catholic Church into formal ecumenical dialogue.[20] This case provides reason for hope that genuine dialogue can and does commence even in the most surprising contexts. It is important to recognize the preparatory work of many Roman Catholic ecclesiologists in supplying the theological resources to justify formal ecumenical engagement. Their labor serves as an example for others facing similar barriers to various kinds of ecclesial dialogue.

One desired outcome of dialogue is an articulation of points of agreement and points of disagreement between the estranged parties. Such articulations represent a second category of reconciliatory practices. At first glance, the recognition of areas of agreement and disagreement might seem out of place or irrelevant in cases of social division within the church, because the causes of disunity in such cases seem to be something very different from cognitive disagreement over propositions. Yet the areas of agreement and disagreement that are identified need not be propositions. They might address desired terminology, articulations of mission, criteria for

18. Yves Congar, *Chrétiens désunis: Principes d'un "oecuménisme" catholique* (Paris: Éditions du Cerf, 1937) is a seminal work in this respect.

19. In particular, the primary avenue to unity before the Second Vatican Council was framed as a return of dissident Christians to the one true church. See a helpful summary of the road to Catholic ecumenism in Jeffrey Gros, F.S.C., Eamon McManus, and Ann Riggs, *Introduction to Ecumenism* (New York/Mahwah, NJ: Paulist Press, 1998), pp. 28-32.

20. The utter surprise of veteran Protestant ecumenists at this development — and the direction of Vatican II in general — is nicely captured by Robert McAfee Brown in *The Ecumenical Revolution: An Interpretation of the Catholic-Protestant Dialogue* (Garden City, NY: Doubleday, 1967; rev. and exp. ed., 1969).

moral discourse, responsibility for past wrongdoing, and the like. Understood along these lines, this practice can serve as a stimulus toward better understanding and further degrees of reconciliation.

The process of identifying points of agreement often provides the opportunity to clarify misunderstanding or overcome caricatures. It can also yield surprising instances of agreement — or at least of compatibility. A remarkable example of the success of this practice is the *Joint Declaration on the Doctrine of Justification* affirmed by the Lutheran World Federation and the Roman Catholic Church in 1999.[21] This document has been appropriately lauded as a model for future bilateral dialogues and an indicator of the potential for ecclesial reconciliation.[22] It represents what Ola Tjrhom calls a "differentiated consensus" that "embraces both a basic agreement and remaining differences."[23] To be sure, not every dialogue toward ecclesial reconciliation will yield such consensus. It might well happen that agreement cannot even be reached on *where* agreement and disagreement exists. This might indicate a failure of understanding, which is always a possibility, given human finitude and the epistemic consequences of sin. Yet if reconciliation is to mean anything more than empty sentimentalism, as it must, partners in ecclesial dialogue must not give up or bypass this practice.

It is not surprising that the process of articulating points of agreement and disagreement often calls attention to wounds within and between churches — some fresh and some longstanding. In order to move forward toward greater degrees of reconciliation, a confession of and a repentance for responsibility for these wounds are necessary. It was noted earlier that the term "ecclesial reconciliation" implies an element of repentance, and thus emerges a third category of reconciliatory practice. The act of confes-

21. For a fine set of essays assessing the *Joint Declaration* from a variety of ecclesial traditions, see William G. Rusch, editor, *Justification and the Future of the Ecumenical Movement: The Joint Declaration on the Doctrine of Justification* (Collegeville, MN: Liturgical Press, 2003).

22. The negative response to the document among a number of prominent Protestant theologians in Germany reflects another example of ecumenical gains generating fresh cases of dissent (like the example offered at the outset of this essay). While such reactions temper the ecumenical enthusiasm somewhat, they should not undermine the reconciliatory potential signaled in this agreement.

23. Ola Tjrhom, *Visible Church — Visible Unity: Ecumenical Ecclesiology and "The Great Tradition of the Church"* (Collegeville, MN: Liturgical Press, 2004), p. 85.

sion certainly does not imply the abandonment of conviction, and no one should be asked to repent for disagreement.

However, disunity is much deeper than mere disagreement. In the sixteenth century alone, one finds myriad examples of ecclesial division that constituted moral and spiritual failure beyond the theological disagreements. In that light, reconciliation must involve more than theological consensus. The practice of confession and repentance acknowledges culpability for breaches of unity and the continuation of disunity. The Decree on Ecumenism from the Second Vatican Council abounds with references to this theme. One particularly striking passage in the Decree serves as a model for the practice at hand:

> The words of St. John hold good about sins against unity: "If we say we have not sinned, we make him a liar, and his word is not in us." So we humbly beg pardon of God and of our separated brethren, just as we forgive them that trespass against us. All the faithful should remember that the more effort they make to live holier lives according to the Gospel, the better will they further Christian unity and put it into practice. For the closer their union with the Father, the Word, and the Spirit, the more deeply and easily will they be able to grow in mutual brotherly love.[24]

By engaging the category of sin, the Decree acknowledges the depth of ecclesial division and places reconciliation in the context of God's redemptive work. In other words, confession is directed both to God and to those from whom one is separated. Ecclesial reconciliation in its fullest sense is thus more than a mere merger or doctrinal agreement. It is at root the restoration of communion in every dimension of ecclesial life, and it depends fundamentally on the redemptive grace of God.

The Decree on Ecumenism not only offers a confession of sins against unity, but it also offers forgiveness to other ecclesial communities for similar iniquities. This action typifies a fourth category of reconciliatory action: forgiveness. The challenge and complexity of practicing genuine forgiveness has been well documented. The work that has emerged as something of a standard in this area is Gregory Jones's *Embodying Forgiveness*.[25] Jones pre-

---

24. *Unitatis Redintegratio*, p. 7.
25. L. Gregory Jones, *Embodying Forgiveness: A Theological Analysis* (Grand Rapids:

sents an account of forgiveness as a craft that is grounded in a robust Trinitarian vision. He challenges psychological or "therapeutic" notions of forgiveness and insists that forgiveness is best understood as a movement toward reconciliation. In this light, reconciliatory practice must not underestimate the reality of sin, nor can it be regarded as a merely verbal exchange. Reconciliation involves the recovery of shared life.

The challenge of forgiveness is particularly acute in cases of ecclesial division where the identity of communities or congregations is integrally connected to the initial cause of division. That is, some ecclesial communities have framed their self-understanding in contrast to another ecclesial community from whom they are separated at some level. It is precisely here that forgiveness emerges as a practice that is distinct from repentance. For a particular church might welcome confession and repentance offered by another while remaining closed to the possibility of restored communion. Forgiveness involves the acknowledgment and healing of wounds that have served as barriers to reconciliation — even those that have been essential to the identity of a given community.

The act of commitment represents a fifth category of ecclesial reconciliation. In a sense, commitment is the most difficult to place in the progression of reconciliatory acts precisely because it is involved at many stages. Each of the categories addressed to this point requires some level of commitment. But by marking out a distinct category, I have in mind the commitment to seeking the fullness of reconciliation. This is not a step to be taken lightly, and it naturally implies that other practices of reconciliation have been at least initiated.[26] It also implies that there is more work to be done before the fullness of reconciliation is realized.

An interesting and promising expression of this practice is Pope John Paul II's encyclical *Ut Unum Sint*. At one level, the letter reaffirms the "irrevocable" commitment to the pursuit of unity that was made at the Second Vatican Council.[27] Yet John Paul II also outlines the specific issues that will require ongoing prayer, reflection, and creative dialogue if full communion is to be restored. Even as he invoked his specific duty as the Bishop of Rome

---

Eerdmans, 1995). In light of the previous paragraph, it is worth noting that Jones does not regard repentance as a prerequisite for forgiveness.

26. Though, again, Jones would not be inclined to distinguish forgiveness from the commitment to full reconciliation.

27. *Ut Unum Sint*, p. 3.

to encourage all Christians toward reconciliation, he invited "patient and fraternal" dialogue from ecclesial leaders and theologians of other traditions regarding the nature of the Petrine ministry.[28] The overall tone of the letter signals a deep commitment to full reconciliation, and it does so with a clear recognition of persistent impediments to that goal. It gives voice, that is, to the kind of honest and realistic commitment that will be essential to any genuine and complete restoration.

A sixth and final category of ecclesial reconciliation involves practices of communion. While full visible communion (of the nature articulated in the New Delhi Statement on Unity) represents the ultimate goal of reconciliation, more measured practices of communion are part of the church's vocation in the meantime. Such acts can take a variety of forms and are often delimited by the ecclesiological judgments of one's community of faith. For example, sharing in the celebration of the Eucharist is the act of communion *par excellence*. While this can be a powerful reconciliatory act in cases of social or congregational disunity, it is not an option in many cases of inter-ecclesial division. To whatever degree possible, as one remains faithful to his or her tradition, practices of communion manifest the fruit of all of the reconciliatory acts we have explored. Other examples might include joint worship, mutual recognition of ministries and sacraments, teaching theological subjects with ecumenical sensitivity, cooperation in shared acts of service, Moravian-style love feasts, and the like. Even if such practices are partial or limited in scope, they serve as visible indicators of the power of God's reconciling grace and thus are indeed healing practices.

The Posture of Ecclesial Reconciliation

The affirmation of the divine initiative and power at the heart of reconciliation leads us naturally to a final consideration: What is the posture of those who engage in genuine reconciliatory acts? Here we must recognize the es-

---

28. *Ut Unum Sint*, p. 96. This invitation inspired a variety of ecumenical responses, including Carl E. Braaten and Robert W. Jenson, eds., *Church Unity and the Papal Office: An Ecumenical Dialogue on John Paul II's Encyclical* Ut Unum Sint (Grand Rapids: Eerdmans, 2001); see also James F. Puglisi, ed., *Petrine Ministry and the Unity of the Church: "Toward a Patient and Fraternal Dialogue"* (Collegeville, MN: Liturgical Press, 1999).

sential priority of the Holy Spirit in the work of reconciliation. William J. Abraham has described the ultimate agency of the Holy Spirit as follows:

> [Ecumenism] is driven by a vision of God's people as one people throughout the earth, abiding in one body, sharing one faith, blessed by common sacraments, preaching one gospel, and so on. Mere human schemes, institutions, and practices can never achieve such unity; it is a precious gift of the Holy Spirit that can be resisted as well as implemented. Thus the current instruments may fall by the wayside and even become the enemy of ecumenism. Mature ecumenists will be on the lookout for such negative possibilities. They can do so while remaining persistent in their ecumenical passion and unrelenting in embracing whatever new instrumentalities the Holy Spirit may create to achieve what is imperative in renewal as a whole.[29]

The moment that we take the achievement of full reconciliation into our own hands — apart from the gracious movement of God — is the moment we assure failure. Abraham reminds us that practices of ecclesial reconciliation are always responses to God's gracious priority. The movement toward manifesting unity in the church is always gift and task. As Michael Kinnamon suggests, our task "is not to create unity, but to address divisions of human origin in order that the unity God has given may be visible to the world."[30] The posture of reconciliation, then, is one of faithful response to God's redemptive grace.

A second aspect of our approach to ecclesial reconciliation demands that we be immersed in the canonical heritage of the church.[31] Reconciliation simply cannot be marked by doctrinal indifference. Rather, the full resources of the church's canons can and must be utilized to draw us toward further healing and fuller communion. In this light, Abraham calls our attention to "the classical faith of the church, a faith that [doctrinal renewalists] see as integral to the full healing and renewal of the denominations in which they serve their risen Lord."[32] Elsewhere he reminds us that

29. Abraham, "Ecumenism and the Rocky Road to Renewal," p. 186.

30. Kinnamon, *The Vision of the Ecumenical Movement*, p. 9.

31. For a vision of the contemporary import of the canonical heritage, see William J. Abraham, Jason E. Vickers, and Natalie B. Van Kirk, eds., *Canonical Theism: A Proposal for Theology and the Church* (Grand Rapids: Eerdmans, 2008).

32. Abraham, "Ecumenism and the Rocky Road to Renewal," p. 182.

the resources of the canonical heritage must be approached "in a spirit of repentance and humility" for genuine healing to occur.[33] Attempting reconciliation by circumventing doctrinal substance or ignoring past and present sins against unity can bring at best only shallow and temporary healing. With a humble openness to fresh possibilities that lie in the riches of the Christian heritage, however, churches facing various forms of division can find hope for ecclesial renewal.

Ultimately, the practices of reconciliation require a shared commitment. The fullness of restored life together can introduce each of us to treasures that we lack or neglect in a condition of disunity. Terence L. Nichols offers this analysis:

> Each of the major denominational groupings possesses some aspects of communion necessary for fullness and lacks others. Given the natural tendency to define oneself by stressing what one's competitors lack, it seems unlikely that any of the denominations can recover the fullness of communion alone without the cooperation of the others. In a sense, the body of Christ is like a body in which each part is growing in isolation from the others. Ecumenical reunion, guided by the Spirit, which integrates the whole, is essential to restore the health and fullness of the body.[34]

The reconciliatory acts we have explored hold promise not only as remedies for distrust, exclusion, and misunderstanding within Christ's church, but also as pathways to revitalization. Restored communion — to whatever degree — makes manifest the unity that holds together the body of Christ. Empowered by God's grace and guided by the Holy Spirit, we can face even the most tenacious marks of division and engage in the difficult work of restoration. When we engage such practices, we hold out hope that God will bring healing to broken individuals and communities and shower new life on the church.

---

33. Abraham, *Canon and Criterion in Christian Theology* (Oxford: Oxford University Press, 1998), p. 54.

34. Terence L. Nichols, *That All May Be One: Hierarchy and Participation in the Church* (Collegeville, MN: Liturgical Press, 1997), pp. 315-16.

The Healing of Cognition in Deification: Toward a Patristic Virtue Epistemology

Frederick D. Aquino

Lars Thunberg has aptly observed that rereading the church fathers never entails merely copying them. Rather, assessing this different world philosophically involves ongoing "dialogue — learning, reacting, and sharing their wisdom in our hearts."[1] One strategy, for example, may require rigorous historical investigation complemented by nuanced hermeneutical insights. Another may try to deconstruct the "modern project," and reclaim faith in the aftermath of the leveled epistemic playing field. Still another may appeal to resources such as reason, tradition, experience, an infallible text, and an infallible agent as criteria of religious knowledge. However, as the work of William Abraham has shown, canonizing theories, processes, materials, persons, and texts is not the answer to our crisis of authority. The "canonical heritage of the church" (an expression coined by Abraham) functions primarily as a means of grace, not as a formal theory of knowledge, truth, justification, warrant, and rationality.[2] It includes a set of practices, materials, and persons that initiate people into the life of God. The last item here also targets requisite dispositions, intellectual virtues, processes, and properties of human agents for regulating inquiry about God.

---

1. Lars Thunberg, *Man and the Cosmos: The Vision of St. Maximus the Confessor* (Crestwood, NY: St. Vladimir's, 1985), p. 11.

2. See William J. Abraham, *Canon and Criterion in Christian Theology: From the Fathers to Feminism* (Oxford: Clarendon Press, 1998); Abraham, *Crossing the Threshold of Divine Revelation* (Grand Rapids: Eerdmans, 2006).

Frederick D. Aquino

Epistemic Evaluation: From Neglect to Regulative Practice

Distinguishing the canonical heritage of the church from epistemology proper does not rule out rigorous epistemological reflection and theorizing. In other words, a robust version of canonical theism does not prohibit attempts to flesh out its ontology in different epistemic clothing; in fact, it demands such efforts.

> The canonical heritage generates rigorous epistemological reflection and theorizing. Such work needs to be pursued at the highest intellectual level. There is no drawing back from the epistemology of theology into some kind of naive credulity or a shutting down of the question of meaning and justification rightly raised by philosophers in the twentieth century. Canonical theists are interested in pursuing the implications of epistemologies compatible with canonical theism for the understanding of the history of the church and the study of Scripture. Canonical theism may lead to the development of epistemological insights that have overtones for all of human thought and existence that are as yet unidentified and unexplored.[3]

Nevertheless, the key is not to confuse formal theories of knowledge, justification, truth, rationality, and warrant with the ontology of the canonical heritage and its set of practices, materials, and persons.

With this distinction in mind, I use recent work in virtue epistemology to show briefly how Maximus the Confessor's (c. 580-662) conception of deification fits within the category of epistemic evaluation. The link between his world and ours may come through expanding the desiderata of religious epistemology. Such a connection explores how paradigmatic properties of evaluators — agents of deification — contribute toward shaping a patristic virtue epistemology. The long-term goal will be to identify and unpack indispensable virtues of the mind for forming excellent cognitive agents of deification.

Maximus grounds properly formed evaluation in the natural state of the intellect: progress towards divine likeness. Such movement entails healing or transforming the cognitive faculties through the three-stage process

---

3. William Abraham, "Canonical Theism: Thirty Theses," in William J. Abraham, Jason E. Vickers, and Natalie Van Kirk, eds., *Canonical Theism: A Proposal for Theology and the Church* (Grand Rapids: Eerdmans, 2008), Thesis XXII.

of deification: the practice of the virtues (πρακτική), the contemplation of nature (φυσική), and the contemplation of God (θεολογία). The vision here is the reconstitution of the intellect in which the cognitive agent experiences and actualizes various aspects of deification potentially in human nature. Maturation of the human is not simply a return to a pristine world or to a pre-fallen state. Rather, cultivating properly formed dispositions, habits, contemplative practices, and so on enables humans to realize and develop divine likeness.

A virtue-based account of deification includes the much-neglected regulative practice of evaluation. A clarification of terms may help. Robert Roberts and Jay Wood have recently distinguished "analytic epistemology" from "regulative epistemology." The former seeks to furnish theories of knowledge, truth, justification, warrant, and rationality, and restricts most of its analysis to beliefs. The latter focuses primarily on the question of how epistemic agents ought to regulate their cognitive lives, thereby highlighting how evaluation guides epistemic practices. As a result, "regulative epistemology is a response to perceived deficiencies in people's epistemic conduct," and is "particularly attentive to the character traits of the excellent epistemic agent."[4]

Such an approach, however, does not envision success as a necessary condition for forming intellectual virtue. A person can embody openmindedness, love of knowledge, humility, intellectual honesty, desire to attain truth and avoid falsehood, rigorous concern for details and key arguments, and still fall short of arriving at a full understanding of truth. Regardless of the outcome, such traits are fundamental to one's intellectual character and to healthy exchange among radically different intellectual traditions. The fact that we readily ascribe epistemic virtue to intellectual giants such as Plato, Aristotle, Gregory of Nyssa, Augustine, Aquinas, Descartes, Newton, Galileo, Einstein, and so on, though they all fall short of epistemic perfection, "is eloquent testimony to the fact that success at accomplishing the immediate targets of cognition or inquiry, true belief, is not necessary for intellectual virtue."[5]

---

4. Robert C. Roberts and W. Jay Wood, *Intellectual Virtues: An Essay in Regulative Epistemology* (Oxford: Clarendon Press, 2007), pp. 21, 27. Roberts and Wood actually draw this distinction from Nicholas Wolterstorff's work on Locke. See N. Wolterstorff, *John Locke and The Ethics of Belief* (Cambridge: Cambridge University Press, 1996).

5. Wayne D. Riggs, "Understanding 'Virtue' and the Virtue of Understanding," in Michael DePaul and Linda Zagzebski, eds., *Intellectual Virtue: Perspectives from Ethics and Epistemology* (Oxford: Oxford University Press, 2003), p. 214.

Though both options have a proper place in religious epistemology, the regulative approach is closer to what I have in mind in this essay. This is not to suggest that my proposal severs conceptual analysis from regulative inquiry. I certainly care about conceptual issues, especially since logically sound analysis may contribute to the formation of excellent agents. However, my focus on epistemic evaluation warrants a regulative lens, monitoring the three-stage process that forms agents of deification. More specifically, a robust patristic virtue epistemology must do justice to the actual process of coming to know, love, and understand God as witnessed, for example, in the lives of the saints. Such a move unearths epistemic evaluation in Maximus's notion of the natural state of the intellect, focusing on the requisite habits, practices, and dispositions that guide both human inquiry about God and the path toward actualizing the logic of divine likeness. Maximus is one illustration of how to go about constructing a patristic virtue epistemology along the lines suggested by William Abraham's work.

Expanding the Desiderata:
A Matter of Location and Connection

The pluralistic enterprise of contemporary epistemology warrants a broader net of desiderata. Such a move explores a richer set of conditions and properties for examining the actual processes, faculties, agents, and communal contexts of belief-formation and epistemic evaluation. The regulative features of evaluation easily fit the list, and a saint such as Maximus seems especially relevant to fleshing out this task within the current setting of religious epistemology. His discussion of the natural state of the intellect paves a way for reconceiving the connection between the formation of the mind and the path of deification.

Locating relevant sources, materials, aims, and goals of recent work in epistemology is important for constructing a robust account of cognitive agency. In its varied expressions, virtue epistemology gives primacy more to evaluative qualities of the human agent than to properties of beliefs. Its vast terrain includes claims that reliable belief-forming faculties, abilities, processes, properly formed dispositions, character traits, and human agents of wisdom form a cognitively viable way of being in the world.[6] Such a list em-

6. See Linda T. Zagzebski, *Virtues of the Mind: An Inquiry into the Nature of Virtue and*

phasizes the normative features of cognitive agents themselves, not simply the foundational status of beliefs or the logical coherence of beliefs. For example, an epistemic agent's (EA) knowledge and understanding of p includes properties other than those of beliefs. It is one thing to focus on the content of propositional knowledge and to explore whether what a person believes to be true is actually the case; it is another to explore how cognitive behaviors, practices, and habits that lead to knowledge and understanding of p in EA are epistemically responsible and thereby intellectually virtuous. As a result, epistemic responsibility and intellectual virtue are not simply properties of a belief; they are the actual practices, habits, and dispositions of epistemic evaluation. These are certainly integral to belief-formation, but the focus here is on the properties of the evaluator.[7] A patristic virtue epistemology thus comprises practices of religious inquiry, but such a focus is not restricted to the evaluation of beliefs.[8]

Epistemic evaluation happens on at least three levels: description of actual practices, materials, and forms of inquiry (Level 1), normative ap-

---

the Ethical Foundations of Knowledge (Cambridge, UK: Cambridge University Press, 1996); Ernest Sosa, *Knowledge in Perspective: Selected Essays in Epistemology* (Cambridge, UK: Cambridge University Press, 1991); John Greco, *Putting Skeptics in Their Place* (New York: Cambridge University Press, 2000); Michael Brady and Duncan Pritchard, eds., *Moral and Epistemic Virtues* (Oxford: Blackwell, 2003); Guy Axtell, ed., *Knowledge, Belief, and Character: Readings in Virtue Epistemology* (Lanham, MD: Rowman & Littlefield, 2000); Jonathan Kvanvig, *The Intellectual Virtues and the Life of the Mind* (Lanham, MD: Rowman & Littlefield, 1992) and *The Value of Knowledge and the Pursuit of Understanding* (New York: Cambridge University Press, 2003); James A. Montmarquet, *Epistemic Virtue and Doxastic Responsibility* (Lanham, MD: Rowman & Littlefield, 1993); Lorraine Code, *Epistemic Responsibility* (Hanover, NH: University Press of New England for Brown University Press, 1987), and Jason S. Baehr, "Character, Reliability and Virtue Epistemology," *The Philosophical Quarterly* 56 (2006): 193-212, and "Character in Epistemology," *Philosophical Studies* 128 (2006): 479-514.

7. Wayne Riggs, "The Value Turn in Epistemology," in Duncan Pritchard and Vincent Hendricks, eds., *New Waves in Epistemology* (New York: Palgrave Macmillan, 2008), pp. 300-323, provides the basic framework for my argument here.

8. William Alston, *Beyond Justification: Dimensions of Epistemic Evaluation* (Ithaca, NY: Cornell University Press, 2005), p. 5, favors a "pluralistic epistemic desiderata approach," but restricts the focus to "the epistemic evaluation of belief." However, Kristoffer Ahlström, "The Desiderata of Epistemology," unpublished paper (www.phil.gu.se/kristoffer/), pp. 1-15, includes both properties of beliefs and properties of agents as dimensions of epistemic evaluation. Roberts and Wood, *Intellectual Virtues*, p. 115, prefer "epistemic" practices to "doxastic" practices, especially since the goods that the former promotes "are not limited to beliefs."

praisal and improvement of these practices, materials, and forms of inquiry (Level 2), and the meta-epistemological task of deciphering the most relevant desiderata for making progress on the path to deification (Level 3). Level 1 involves phenomenological analysis of theological practices; Level 2 inquires whether one ought to adopt or recommend these practices; and Level 3 keeps the other levels in its purview while regulating the process of epistemic evaluation. More specifically, Level 3 highlights "the relation between central questions" on Levels 1 and 2, and identifies what we want our processes of evaluation (or epistemological theories) to accomplish and what goals we intend to achieve through such processes.[9] For example, the process of deification clearly involves evaluating everyday practices and beliefs (Level 1), thereby identifying misguided desires/beliefs while offering correctives about how one ought to proceed (Level 2). However, Level 2 neither regulates the order of the formation process nor does it unpack how select virtues achieve the goal of deification. Rather, Level 3 determines what virtuous and contemplative practices enable the agent to actualize the appropriate interior and exterior habits on the path of deification.

These levels include not only features of beliefs (e.g., justified true beliefs) but also "features of persons" (e.g., watchfulness, discernment, humility, dispassion, and wisdom). "The reason for this is that, from a more general perspective, we not only want our beliefs to have this or that valuable quality, but also intellectual agents to be among other things, *thorough, insightful, open-minded, fair-minded.*"[10] Hence, epistemic evaluation expands the net of desiderata. Such a diverse terrain perhaps reflects a plurality of aims, goals, and virtues; the use of each enterprise gives "rise to a plurality of epistemic goods."[11] For example, the conditions for knowledge are different from those for wisdom, understanding, and humility; all are legitimate endeavors, but they tackle different concerns and questions. Determining what matters calls for the intersection and filtering of these levels of epistemic evaluation.

---

9. Ahlström, "The Desiderata of Epistemology," p. 5. Ahlström's threefold distinction shapes my focus on epistemic evaluation, though the connection to theosis is entirely my concern.

10. Ahlström, "The Desiderata of Epistemology," p. 3.

11. John Greco, "Virtues in Epistemology," in *The Oxford Handbook of Epistemology* (Oxford: Oxford University Press, 2002), p. 302. Greco recognizes here an important distinction between "knowledge per se and some epistemic value of a higher grade. This allows us to weaken the requirements on knowledge so as to make it generally attainable, and at the same time to recognize" other intellectual virtues (p. 301).

Four Versions of Virtue Epistemology

Such variety is certainly evident in recent versions of virtue epistemology. I illustrate the point briefly with four accounts. Differences aside, the common factor among these versions is greater emphasis on the normative features of inquiry. All versions agree on shifting the focus from properties of beliefs to evaluative qualities of human agents, but they disagree on the aim and scope of epistemic evaluation. Versions 1 and 2, for example, tackle traditional issues such as externalism and internalism, coherentism and foundationalism, and the Gettier problem through the lens of virtue epistemology. Version 1 targets truth-conduciveness as the outcome of reliable belief-forming faculties and processes: it falls under the label of "virtue reliabilism" and essentially functions as a form of externalism. Belief-forming processes such as memory, sense perception, introspection, and reason are intellectually virtuous (reliable) to the extent that they produce true rather than false beliefs.[12] Version 2 combines properly formed dispositions (motivation criterion as a form of internalism) and reliable-belief-forming processes (success condition as a form of externalism). It traces the subjective and objective conditions of knowledge back to the human agent, departing from version 1 in conceiving intellectual virtues more as traits of a responsible agent than simply as reliable faculties of an agent. Therefore, a belief is justified if it is properly formed and acquired through reliable processes, and all of this arises from the intellectual virtues of a responsible agent. This version falls under the label "virtue responsibilism," though its concern with showing how an account of intellectual virtues resolves problems in traditional epistemology distinguishes it from other responsibilist versions.[13]

---

12. Alvin I. Goldman, *Pathways to Knowledge: Private and Public* (Oxford: Oxford University Press, 2002), p. 52.

13. Zagzebski, *Virtues of the Mind,* is a major representative of this version. Code, *Epistemic Responsibility,* falls within the responsibilist version, though she argues for the pursuit of intellectual virtues in their own right without including the success condition (reliabilism). Baehr, "Character in Epistemology," *Philosophical Studies* 128 (2006): 480, argues convincingly that the intellectual virtues fail to meet the necessary and sufficient conditions of knowledge and therefore "*any* attempt to give the intellectual virtues a central role in an analysis of knowledge seems bound to fail." Alternatively, Baehr hints at a preliminary version of responsibilist epistemology that pursues the contours of intellectual flourishing in their own right.

Versions 3 and 4 differ over the relationship between the intellectual virtues and traditional epistemology. Version 3 argues that an account of the intellectual virtues tackles "new and different questions" independently of the standard issues in traditional epistemology. Moreover, it contends that "this new focus should *supplant* the old focus," thereby reorienting epistemology toward a more robust understanding of the nature, scope, and aims of the intellectual virtues.[14] Version 4 (perhaps a different form of virtue responsibilism) does not claim to supplant traditional epistemology with a new focus on the intellectual virtues. Its call for expanded desiderata does not reorient traditional issues around the intellectual virtues (unlike versions 1 and 2). Rather, it deciphers whether the formation of intellectual virtues contributes to the flourishing of the human agent, though this focus does not fit the typical procedure of determining whether this approach meets the necessary and sufficient conditions of knowledge. The goal is to clarify the regulation of intellectual conduct for forming excellent cognitive agents.[15] Though such a focus expands the scope of epistemic inquiry, it does not imply replacement.

Obviously, these versions do not exhaust the enterprise of virtue epistemology; they simply illustrate the pluralistic nature of the terrain and the importance of further reflection. Such diversity challenges the assumption that these positions are mutually exclusive or that one version exhausts all possibilities. Rather, my overview here recognizes the relevance of using virtue epistemology to address traditional problems while also seeing the need to expand the horizons of the desiderata in new directions. As we shall see, both interior and exterior habits appear in Maximus's account, which makes strict loyalty to categories and camps problematic in the end.

Maximus's notion of the natural state of the intellect fits nicely within such a discussion. His proposal unpacks formative practices, people, and habits that contribute to the transformation of the self from image to likeness. Though excellent historical accounts of Maximus exist, rarely has there been a connection made between his focus on virtue and the process of

14. Jason S. Baehr, "Three Varieties of Character-Based Virtue Epistemology," unpublished paper (www. myweb.lmu.edu/jbaehr/publications.htm), p. 5. Baehr categorizes the terrain of virtue epistemology as conservative (my versions 1 and 2), radical (my version 3), and moderate (my version 4). He argues that Kvanvig, *The Value of Knowledge,* fits the radical version.

15. For example, Roberts and Wood, *Intellectual Virtues,* and Baehr, "Character in Epistemology," 479-514, seem to fit version 4.

epistemic evaluation. This essay thus rereads and unearths a possible link between Maximus's thought and contemporary versions of virtue epistemology. More importantly, it explores the therapeutic power of the materials, persons, and practices constitutive of initiation and formation in the Christian faith.

The Deified State of the Intellect

Maximus grounds his claims about the intellect in soteriology, showing how the three-stage process of deification materializes its true nature, dignity, and nobility. This involves cultivating a properly disposed mind and fostering a noetic space as "the place of divine wisdom."[16] Thus the reconstituting of the intellect unfolds a fuller experience than simply returning to a pre-fallen state. Receiving Christ's intellect "does not come to us through the loss of our intellectual power; nor does it come to us as a supplementary part added to our intellect; nor does it pass essentially and hypostatically into our own intellect. Rather, it illumines the power of our intellect with its own quality and conforms the activity of our intellect to its own."[17] The rigid distinction between nature and grace does not apply here. Our humanity is neither absorbed nor overcome; the economy of God's salvation infuses within the intellect an ever-growing desire for union with God, from whom it, according to another ascetic writer, "had its origin, by whom it is activated, and towards whom it ascends by means of its natural capabilities."[18] Therefore, God's gift of shared life is an invitation to be fully human.

The natural state of the intellect entails movement of rational human beings toward their "proper end" in accordance with the logos. The problem occurs "when the intellect fails to cultivate its natural powers."[19] So the focus here involves redirecting misguided desire and integrating the whole person into the natural state of affairs. The term "natural" does not simply mean the biological or physical minimum. Rather, it connotes the mediation of cosmic realities through an agent in the process of reintegrating the whole self. A true philosopher embodies ascetic virtues of the mind, and "studies how

---

16. Maximus, *Ambigua*, 71, in Andrew Louth, *Maximus the Confessor* (New York: Routledge, 1996), p. 165.

17. Maximus, *Capita theologica et oeconomica*, II. 83, in *The Philokalia*, vol. 2, p. 158.

18. Nikitas Stithatos, *Kephalaia gnostika*, 12, in *The Philokalia*, vol. 4, p. 143.

19. Maximus, *Capita de caritate*, III.4, in *The Philokalia*, vol. 2, p. 83.

to rectify such impulses [misguided desires]."[20] Reintegrating the self presupposes maturation of select intellectual virtues, thereby moving the deiform agent from potential (image of God) to actual (divine likeness). Evaluation, then, involves reflexive appraisal of daily practices, and the inclusion of healthy interior and exterior habits.

The agent of deification learns to embody the virtues of Christ, and so in practicing them, he or she participates in the reality of God. For example, love endows the deiform person with "a holy state of the soul, disposing it to value knowledge of God above all created things."[21] Cultivating the right state of heart is undergirded by love for God and propels this search beyond any other good. EA (epistemic agent) values *p* because *p* precipitates such a value. The person "who loves God values knowledge of God more than anything created by God, and pursues such knowledge ardently and ceaselessly."[22] Other things may have value, but they are ultimately derivative of this knowledge and understanding. Hence, the basis for such a pursuit of God is love initiated by the triune God — the subject and object of human inquiry. If God is the origin of all things, then it seems incoherent to place the inferior over the superior. "Since the light of spiritual knowledge is the intellect's life, and since this light is engendered by love for God, it is rightly said that nothing is greater than divine love."[23]

The three-stage process of deification, however, requires something more than properly functioning belief-forming abilities, powers, or processes. Deflating cognitive agency to "an input-output machine,"[24] as many epistemologists tend to do, obscures its reflective dimension, and essentially ignores the task of forming the deiform person as an exemplar of epistemic evaluation. The natural state of the intellect includes belief-forming processes such as memory, sense perception, reason, and introspection, but it also demands a well-formed character to continue on the road to deification — assimilation to the triune God. Forming intellectual excellences or reflective virtues such as watchfulness, discernment, humility, dispassion, and

20. Maximus, *Capita de caritate*, II.56, in *The Philokalia*, vol. 2, p. 75.
21. Maximus, *Capita de caritate*, I.1, in *The Philokalia*, vol. 2, p. 53.
22. Maximus, *Capita de caritate*, I.4, in *The Philokalia*, vol. 2, p. 53.
23. Maximus, *Capita de caritate*, I.9, in *The Philokalia*, vol. 2, p. 54.
24. Guy Axtell, "Blind Man's Bluff: The Basic Belief Apologetic as Anti-skeptical Stratagem," *Philosophical Studies* 130 (2006): 143. Axtell provides here a clear and accessible discussion of the connection between the reflective virtues and human agency. However, the relevance of such a link for developing an epistemology of theosis is entirely my concern.

wisdom presupposes that properly focused desire and motivation are integral to a robust conception of cognitive agency. The interior focus here certainly includes reliable practices external to the agent's ken of awareness (e.g., memory, sense perception, intuition). It is true that without these basic belief-forming processes people would be incapable of cultivating reflective virtues. At the same time, without reflective virtues we are left with no way to trace the maturation process of cognitive excellence,[25] and such a process seems central to deification. When people constantly "strain toward God," they are "called 'a portion of God' because [they have become] fit to participate in God. By drawing on wisdom and reason and by appropriate movement [they lay] hold of [their] proper beginning and cause."[26] The image is the initial endowment in creation, a potentiality pointing forward, and likeness indicates the final aim, the realization of the eschatological hope. As Norman Russell points out, deification "is the final end of salvation, the attainment of the destiny originally intended for humankind that Adam had in his grasp and threw away. It may be anticipated in this life, but it reaches its fulfillment in the next in the fullest possible union with the incarnate Word."[27]

However, some of these reflective virtues (e.g., the inclusion of watchfulness and dispassion) do not follow for people in all domains of thought. Thus, a patristic virtue epistemology operates from a particularist standpoint, emphasizing the conditions and properties under which human agents integrate the cognitive, affective, and moral dimensions of human selfhood. Deciphering divine things certainly requires truth-conduciveness as an important goal, but not as the only goal of epistemic evaluation. Certainly, the exercise of these intellectual virtues combines a properly disposed mind and processes such as memory, perception, and so on. The aim is to link basic belief-forming processes and reflective virtues. In some situations, perceiving God may not necessitate intellectual virtues; one may perceive what is obvious or noninferential. Nevertheless, the route to perceiving or knowing God generally involves the cultivation of certain habits of mind. Haste or inattentiveness certainly hinders progress on the road to theosis,

25. Axtell, "Blind Man's Bluff," p. 138. See also Wood and Roberts, *Intellectual Virtues,* pp. 3-149.

26. Maximus, *Ambigua,* 7, in *On the Cosmic Mystery of Jesus Christ,* trans. Paul M. Blowers and Robert Louis Wilken (Crestwood, NY: St Vladimir's, 2003), p. 56.

27. Norman Russell, *The Doctrine of Deification in the Greek Patristic Tradition* (Oxford: Oxford University Press, 2004), 262.

crippling the deiform person from focusing on the moment at hand and internalizing the right state of mind.

As a result, a patristic virtue epistemology may not be best suited for meeting the necessary and sufficient conditions of knowledge. Rather, it focuses more on the regulative question of how one ought to inquire about God. The intellectual virtues are not necessary for low-grade processes of belief-formation. For example, intellectual courage is not necessary for recognizing that a bird is sitting on the fence in one's backyard. Conversely, reducing intellectual virtues to properly functioning faculties is not sufficient for forming excellent epistemic agents. Historical analysis, scientific investigation, moral decision-making, and the three-stage process of deification involve more than the capacity to see, hear, reason, intuit, and so on.[28] Such activities require honed interpretive and regulative practices. In other words, the "mature functioning of the epistemic agent depends on and makes use of the faculties, but the dispositions that are needed for high-level functioning are not the faculties alone, but the epistemic skills and virtues that are built on them."[29] Faculties alone are not sufficient for making nuanced judgments about various pieces of data and thereby rendering a synthetic understanding of the issue at hand.

In this regard, Maximus couples Christian practices and rigorous noetic reflection, spelling out how the journey of deification links moral discernment, praiseworthy dispositions, rigorous contemplative exercises with immersing the self into the life of God. Underlying his understanding of deification is a particular conception of the nature, function, and focus of the intellect. The highest function of the intellect is not discursive, conceptual, and explicitly logical modes of reasoning. Rather, the proper state of the intellect secures understanding of theological truths through affective knowledge, immediate experience, or intuition. Such a process may include discursive reasoning *(dianoia)*, but its more fundamental modality, or at least its ultimate goal, is apprehending *(nous)*, or perceiving the deeper realities of created things and of God. Knowledge of God ultimately fits under the category of "knowledge by acquaintance," an immediate awareness (noninferential perceptual knowledge) of objects and people.[30] The net-

---

28. For an extended discussion of this point, see Baehr, "Character, Reliability and Virtue Epistemology," pp. 194-212, and Roberts and Wood, *Intellectual Virtues,* pp. 85-112.

29. Roberts and Wood, *Intellectual Virtues,* p. 111.

30. For good philosophical treatments of religious experience and the epistemic contours of perception, see William Alston, *Perceiving God: The Epistemology of Religious Expe-*

work of practices that facilitate this process includes Scripture, liturgy, tradition, moral exercises, and one's own immediate experience of the divine. Essentially, a patristic virtue epistemology depicts deification as an ongoing immersion into the life of God, thus creating growth of awareness within the deiform person and transforming the agent's perception of things. The logic here is that "those who are united to something or participate in something are said to *know* that to which they are united or in which they participate."[31] Continual participation in the life of God illuminates the nature of things and empowers the deiform person to see "things clearly in their true nature."[32]

The deified state of the intellect reconnects human beings to their intended noetic function. Maximus implicitly links epistemology and select loci of Christian theology (e.g., creation, anthropology, and soteriology) by way of virtuous dispositions and practices. The task is to realize the union of the human and divine not only in Christ but also in the new humanity envisioned in the creation. Cultivating the natural state of the intellect enables humans to function as the miniature microcosms, unifying fractures in the world (e.g., body and soul). The result is the reconstitution of the whole person as a mediation of the unity of all things.[33] Such a move highlights the conditions under which "the body is deified along with the soul through its own corresponding participation in the process of deification."[34] All in the ascetic tradition affirm the indispensability of virtue for the process of spiritual formation, but not all articulate a microcosmic theology of human

---

rience (Ithaca, NY: Cornell University Press, 1991); Caroline Franks Davis, *The Evidential Force of Religious Experience* (Oxford: Clarendon Press, 1989); Jerome Gellman, *Mystical Experience of God: A Philosophical Inquiry* (Burlington, VT: Ashgate, 2001) and *Experience of God and the Rationality of Theistic Belief* (Ithaca, NY: Cornell University Press, 1997); Bill Brewer, *Perception and Reason* (Oxford: Clarendon, 1999); and Mark R. Wynn, *Emotional Experience and Religious Understanding: Integrating Perception, Conception and Feeling* (Cambridge, UK: Cambridge University Press, 2005).

31. Robert Wilken, *The Spirit of Early Christianity: Seeking the Face of God* (New Haven: Yale University Press, 2003), p. 308.

32. Maximus, *Capita de caritate*, I.92, in *The Philokalia*, vol. 2, p. 63.

33. See Maximus, *Ambigua*, 41, in Andrew Louth, *Maximus the Confessor*, pp. 156-62.

34. Maximus, *Capita theologica et oeconomica*, II.88, in *The Philokalia*, vol. 2, p. 160. See Kallistos Ware, "The Soul in Greek Christianity," in M. Lames and C. Crabbe, eds., *From Soul to Self* (London: Routledge, 1999), pp. 49-69; Panayiotis Nellas, *Deification in Christ: Orthodox Perspectives on the Nature of the Human Person* (Crestwood, NY: St. Vladimir's, 1987).

personhood. Maximus offers some important clues for constructing an epistemology of deification.

An agent of deification follows a three-stage process of formation. Such a person strives to internalize the virtues of Christ that advance in moral understanding, follows contemplative practices that engender spiritual knowledge, and desires to experience directly the qualities of God. Appropriate motivation and virtuous practices link people to their proper end — assimilation to God. Knowledge implies immersion in the life of God, "not only intellectual knowledge, but a state of the entire human being, transformed by grace, and freely cooperating with it by the efforts of both will and mind."[35]

Participation also presupposes gradual levels of awareness of one's spiritual life and of one's knowledge and understanding of God. Moreover, virtuous and contemplative practices are not the end but the means for achieving assimilation to God. Virtue furnishes intellectual stability, enabling the deiform person to pursue the path of deification. Consequently, virtuous and contemplative practices are truth-conducive to the extent that they are appropriately motivated and function as regulative processes in leading the deiform person to union with God. Perhaps this is one instance where contemporary versions and categories of virtue epistemology are not hermetically sealed and thereby strict categories cannot be easily applied to ancient thinkers. Maximus seems committed to both interior and exterior processes, though such a move does not apply to all domains of knowledge. Consequently, I want to restrict the focus here to the regulative practice of epistemic evaluation, especially as it relates to the process of inquiring about and being transformed into the likeness of God.

The synthetic dimension of deification correlates ascetic virtues and stages of cognitive development. The argument here is that all the virtues, like a chain, are bound together, and when this occurs, as one ancient ascetic writer puts it, "they lead [the deiform person] to the summit of his desire."[36] As a result, an exemplar of deification combines all the virtues, perceives divine causality in created things, and experiences the realities beyond the realm of discourse. St. Gregory of Sinai nicely summarizes the threefold process of *theosis:*

---

35. John Meyendorff, *Byzantine Theology: Historical Trends and Doctrinal Themes* (New York: Fordham University Press, 1974), p. 8.

36. Pseudo-Macarius, *Epistola Magna,* trans. George A. Maloney, *The Fifty Spiritual Homilies and the Great Letter* (Mahwah, NJ: Paulist Press, 1992), p. 266.

A true philosopher is one who perceives in created things their spiritual Cause. He does not simply learn about divine things, but actually experiences them. Or again, a true philosopher is one whose intellect is conversant equally with ascetic practice and contemplative wisdom. Thus the perfect philosopher or lover of wisdom is one whose intellect has attained — alike on the moral, natural, and theological levels — love of wisdom or, rather, love of God. . . . A divine philosopher is one who through ascetic purification and noetic contemplation has achieved a direct union with God.[37]

It is through the threefold process that the deiform agent learns about the reconfiguration of things, thereby showing him or her what the natural state of the intellect means for developing a robust epistemology of deification. Such a process implicitly connects epistemology and soteriology, without confusing them, by way of virtuous dispositions and practices. An epistemically virtuous lifestyle solidifies dispositions and forms an intellect that intensely longs for and ceaselessly pursues God. Moreover, acquiring virtue and spiritual knowledge enables the epistemic agent to view things correctly and according to their true nature: "A pure intellect sees things correctly. A trained intelligence puts them in order. A keen hearing takes in what is said."[38]

Underlying the entire process is the triune activity of God. It is only when the intellect is deeply immersed in the life of God that, according to Peter of Damascus, "it is granted direct vision of what pertains to God and, through the indwelling of the Holy Spirit, becomes in a true sense a theologian."[39] A properly disposed mind "apprehends, through the grace and wisdom of the Holy Spirit, the knowledge of things both human and divine."[40]

Toward a Patristic Virtue Epistemology

Maximus's insights about cognitive agency are profoundly microcosmic. We are called to become a "second cosmos," thereby "reflecting in ourselves the

37. Gregory of Sinai, *Capita valde utilia per acrostichidem*, 127, in *The Philokalia*, vol. 4, p. 246.

38. Maximus, *Capita de caritate*, 2.92, in *The Philokalia*, vol. 2, p. 82.

39. Peter of Damascus, "A Treasury of Divine Knowledge," in *The Philokalia*, vol. 3, p. 143.

40. Peter of Damascus, "A Treasury of Divine Knowledge," in *The Philokalia*, vol. 3, p. 100.

complexity of the whole universe." Our vocation, in this sense, is "to mediate between all the divided extremes in the created order. Within ourselves we are to draw all things to unity, overcoming the divorce between matter and spirit, between earth and heaven."[41] This is precisely what a patristic virtue epistemology entails. The focus is not simply on assessing the logical validity of propositional beliefs, though this is important, but it covers the formation of properly disposed levels of inquiry. Thus evaluation does not avoid the connection between the subjective and the objective dimensions of knowledge but simply recognizes the insufficiency of ignoring the actual conditions under which human agents form virtues of the mind.

Deification is unattainable without internalizing Christian practices and virtues, and it refuses to divorce epistemology from formation. Properly focused desire has a transformative dimension. It does not merely attempt to satisfy the objective conditions of knowledge, but regulates how the knower inquires about the triune God. In this sense, knowledge entails immersion in the reality that one seeks to understand. This move resembles ancient philosophical traditions and the early Christian focus on contemplative participation. The human agent of deification engages in an "intellectual ascesis," empowering "self-centered beings" to live out "a discipline of God-centered contemplation."[42]

A patristic virtue epistemology entails a set of practices, habits, materials, and people that enable the intellect to be conformed to the life of God. It involves the whole person, not simply one facet of human personhood. In fact, without the body, cultivating epistemic virtues seems incoherent and, at least, incomplete. Moreover, deflated accounts of cognitive agency render the relevance of the Incarnation problematic. By contrast, my proposal reaffirms the importance of the Incarnation as a basis for a more holistic cognitive agency. The meta-epistemological task is to make explicit how practices, processes, and habits form epistemic agents and enable them to achieve deification. However, such a proposal does not focus primarily on the question of whether intellectual virtues are necessary and sufficient for every kind of knowledge. Rather, it explores how these virtues, as a synthetic web of dispositions, habits, and practices, contribute to the formation of an agent of deification.

41. Kallistos Ware, "'My Helper and My Enemy': The Body in Greek Christianity," in Sarah Coakley, ed., *Religion and the Body* (Cambridge, UK: Cambridge University Press, 1997), p. 98.

42. Fergus Kerr, "Tradition and Reason: Two Uses of Reason, Critical and Contemplative," *International Journal of Systematic Theology* 6 (2004): 38.

If a person is motivated to pursue deification, it follows that such an endeavor would presuppose the internalization of intellectual virtues requisite for its commensurate character. Also, since the desiderata of epistemology are varied, this focus on intellectual character should not be relegated to a secondary or less important status. Both traditional questions and our current expansion of the epistemic toolbox care about the processes under which cognitive agents flourish. Of course, knowledge is one element; but it is not the only one. As Jason Baehr rightly points out, the "quality of one's intellectual character also plays a crucial role — both as a means and (arguably) as a constituent — determining the quality of one's intellectual life."[43] In other words, intellectual virtues here may be important for deciphering the contours of evaluation without necessarily being reduced to effective strategies for resolving traditional problems in epistemology. Evaluating the process of deification, then, may be one of the tasks of religious epistemology.

Such an account, for example, would identify the kinds of cognitive activities, practices, habits, processes, and states required for obtaining a deeper understanding of deification. This would certainly include, but not be limited to, knowledge. An epistemology of deification also includes discernment, humility, love, dispassion, and so on. With this in mind, perhaps we can get on to the business of exploring different areas of religious epistemology in their own right. Such a conclusion neither supports a fideistic approach to Christian belief in which the terrain has its own integrity and is not subject to the broader discussion, nor does it operate from a conception of religious epistemology in which the secured methodology then leads to the adjudication of particular claims. Different domains of theological enquiry note the varied terrain and proceed from there. Hence, my proposal calls for an expansion of the desiderata, not a replacement of the standard narrative of religious epistemology. This move would constitute a character-based religious epistemology that focuses on the role of virtues of the mind in the process of deification.

Some describe this move as "value pluralism," especially since it claims that varied epistemic goods and related concepts such as wisdom, understanding, humility, and love, have distinct aims and goals. The standard ac-

43. Baehr, "Character in Epistemology," p. 507. In this article Baehr addresses the relevance of a character-based approach in the broader world of epistemology proper. My argument here focuses more on the connection between this broader arena and the world of patristic theology.

count of justified true belief does not exhaust the range and scope of epistemology. Wayne Riggs observes:

> For one thing, it is not hard to imagine someone who has a head full of knowledge, but who would not be what anyone would consider an 'epistemic exemplar.' Here we can imagine phone-book memorizers and the like. Such (typically imaginary) people can lay claim to huge amounts of knowledge, yet their cognitive life seems to lack much epistemic value. This, I take it, is one indication that offering an account of knowledge is not all there is to do in epistemology.[44]

As this example shows, there is a fundamental distinction between basic propositional knowledge (*A* knows *p*) and discernment, insight, or wisdom (*A* connects various pieces of data through a synthetic judgment). This seems to hold for deification: it is not merely about an infinite search for intricate details (e.g., memorizing everything in the Bible or in the history of the Christian tradition). Rather, cognitive agents try to decipher the relevant details, people, and questions about the process of deification — what it entails, the kind of person it forms, and the object of its pursuit. We do not pursue the truth of deification for its own sake. Rather, we pursue God as the primary goal of deification, and the truth of deification results from such a search.

Consequently, one can know many unrelated pieces of information, but "understanding is achieved only when informational items are pieced together by the subject in question."[45] We blur the distinction between knowledge and discernment. Yet this conflation is counter-intuitive and, more importantly, it hinders the cognitive, emotional, and moral growth envisioned by an epistemology of deification. As a reflective virtue, discernment plays a role in forming epistemic agents of deification, distinguishing cultivated judgment from a minimalist definition of knowledge. The process of reasoning in discernment is not strictly rule-governed, and in this regard it seems analogous to what the ancient Greeks called *phronēsis*. This virtue requires mastery of the domain-specific stages of deification, materialized in a vibrant set of practices, habits, and exemplars of cultivated judgment. Discernment also calls for the convergence of various pieces of data, practice, and experi-

---

44. Riggs, "The Value Turn in Epistemology," p. 306.
45. Kvanvig, *The Value of Knowledge and the Pursuit of Understanding*, p. 192.

ence into a synthetic judgment and skilful application of this knowledge to particular situations (e.g., helping others navigate the path of deification). Such discernment "involves an aspect of knowing-how that is partially learned by imitation and practice."[46] Thus the rationale for a more robust epistemology of cognitive agency seems ripe for further consideration.

Maximus's discussion of the natural function of the intellect paves the way for reconceiving the link between religious epistemology and deification. This would not have been a strange conversation in the ancient world, but it seems out of step with our modern sensitivities. Yet, the recent conversation among some epistemologists suggests that it is time to expand the terrain of epistemology. The connection between virtue and epistemology is a fairly recent project. As I have noted, single-minded focus on the question of justification of true beliefs has sidelined other epistemic goods such as wisdom, understanding, and so forth. I think that this also follows in theology, especially with the ongoing crisis in finding the correct theological method. Furthermore, the areas of virtue epistemology and patristics seem to form a proper fit, though from the vantage point of a particularist religious epistemology. Self-understanding, mediated through key texts, can be captured through the identification of paradigmatic persons, refined habits, and robust practices. In other words, a patristic virtue epistemology envisions integrating the "human person as a practice, as the act, or series of acts, of living in accordance with the true essence of personhood, in an ascending fashion."[47] I hope that this essay will stir greater conversation about fleshing out a virtue-based account of deification along these lines.

Epistemology and Deification: Rethinking Nature

If we have learned anything from William Abraham, it is the church's historic temptation to confuse the ontology into which its members have been initiated with the various attempts to understand and explain it. Given Maximus's take on deification, inquiry about our ontological commitments is natural, assuming that it is undergirded by proper disposition and practices. What we see in Maximus is a deconstruction of a facile distinction be-

46. Zagzebski, *Virtues of the Mind*, p. 21.
47. John Chryssavgis, *John Climacus: From the Egyptian Desert to the Sinaite Mountain* (Burlington, VT: Ashgate, 2004), p. 11.

tween nature and grace, provoking us to reconsider our awkward stance toward the former. In this regard, intellectual dishonesty, quick answers, or canonizing a particular epistemic scheme will not suffice. Rather, the task is to see how the natural function of intellect is laden with the potential to be God-like. The term "natural" has its many supporters and advocates, though rarely has it been couched in the context of formation and epistemology.

Maximus's thought is ripe for a more expansive understanding of the requisite skills, practices, virtues, judgments, and properties for advancing in the life of God. The current epistemic options make such a project more than an illusory grasp for a premodern embarrassment or another example of a religious wish fulfillment. They furnish helpful insights for rethinking the nature of epistemic evaluation, and, more specifically, its role both in the noetic structure of religious beliefs and in the formation of intellectual agents of deification.[48]

---

48. I recognize but do not take on the complex issues surrounding the contours of cognitive agency. In this regard, my essay is preliminary in nature, and I simply try to provide a rationale for constructing a patristic virtue epistemology of deification. I want to thank my colleague, Dr. Paul Morris (professor of physics, Abilene Christian University), for his invaluable insights, challenging questions, and provocative inquiries about the possibility of getting the notion of human agency off the ground, considering what seem to be some intractable problems (e.g., the problem of free will and determinism, the dilemma of moral luck) and some ongoing problems (e.g., the problem of agential authority, the problem of subjective normative authority). See Michael Bratman, *The Structures of Agency: Essays* (Oxford: Oxford University Press, 2007); R. Jay Wallace, *Normativity and the Will: Selected Essays on Moral Psychology and Practical Reason* (Oxford: Clarendon Press, 2006); John Martin Fischer, *My Way: Essays on Moral Responsibility* (Oxford: Oxford University Press, 2006); Richard Moran, *Authority and Estrangement: An Essay on Self-Knowledge* (Princeton, NJ: Princeton University Press, 2001).

Confession as Self-Culture:
Nietzsche and the Demands of Faith

R. R. Reno

Credo, I believe: confession of faith is a statement of fundamental loyalty. Whether words of ancient creeds or extemporaneous confessions of faith in Christ's saving sacrifice, we seek to become "slaves of God" (Titus 1:1; James 1:1; cf. Rom. 6:22). Our lips and minds are given over to "the power and wisdom of God" (1 Cor. 1:24). In confession divine truth invades the crumbling ruins of our illusion-filled minds. We take no refuge in the wisdom of this world, which is doomed to pass away (1 Cor. 2:6). We trust not in our futile thinking and our darkened, senseless minds (Rom. 1:21). Confession gives us over to "Christ Jesus, whom God has made our wisdom, our righteousness and sanctification and redemption" (1 Cor. 1:30). He becomes our light and life.

The existential dynamics of confession are as simple as the many rightful roles of reason, conscience, and judgment in the life of faith are complex. Confession is a handing over of our lives to the Lord, a handing over that is given full and final form in Christ's passion. Our death to sinful self and new life in Christ cannot be too complete. His command over our lives knows no limits, no discrete or modest reserve, no boundaries carefully drawn to give us room for a personal sphere free from the demands of faith. The goal of confession is to become so captive to the will of God that we can say, with St. Paul, "If we live, we live to the Lord, and if we die, we die to the Lord; so then, whether we live or whether we die, we are the Lord's" (Rom. 14:8). An engine of servitude, confession coils Christ around us, binding our minds and wills to him.

The modern world has long litigated against the confessional logic of Christianity. In the aftermath of the religious wars that defined European politics in the sixteenth and seventeenth centuries, Spinoza wrote, "Religion is no longer identified with charity, but with spreading discord and propagating insensate hatred disguised under the name of zeal for the Lord."[1] He urged his readers to apply the cooling power of critical reason to the hot passions of faith. Later Enlightenment figures attacked "priestcraft" and "superstition." The power of faith to subjugate souls was, they implied, a tool by which the powerful maintained their grip. In order to liberate minds and wills, they dismissed the miraculous. They overthrew the historical accuracy of the Bible. They juxtaposed the supposed "three-tiered universe" of ancient faith to what they claimed were the beliefs and needs of "modern man."

The brief for modernity is multifaceted, but at root it amounts to an objection to the various ways in which Christianity has encouraged submission to Christ. Modernity wishes to protect and promote the rights of the individual. The long Enlightenment defense of the prerogatives and powers of reason is but one dimension of a broad modern effort to identify a properly independent zone of human existence. These days we are less confident about reason, but our postmodern culture retains the basic existential agenda of the Enlightenment. If anything, we want a deeper and more fundamental freedom. Voltaire wished to strangle the priests so that modern men and women could be freed to obey reason. With our present, soft skepticism, we just want to be free to live. As a result, it is no longer the content of faith, no longer Christianity's institutional forms, no longer claims about the inspired accuracy of Scripture that grate. It is simply confession that offends: we are to serve nothing other than ourselves.

"Let it be with me according to your word" (Luke 1:38): I cannot remove from the gospel the stumbling block of submission; nor can I spin a fine web of argument in which I hold modern commitments to self-regard and self-possession aloft in a fine gossamer of Christian truth. We must gird up our minds, be sober, and put our hope completely in the revelation of Jesus Christ (1 Pet. 1:13).

Yet faith, however exclusively it draws its truth from Christ alone, can seek understanding. In this instance, an engagement with Friedrich Nietz-

---

1. *A Theologico-Political Treatise,* vol. I, trans. R. H. M. Elwes (New York, Dover, 1951), p. 99.

sche may illuminate our investigation. Nietzsche provides us with a rich understanding of the relationship of the soul to power — the power to judge, the power to command, the power to control. By way of a close rereading of his apparently anti-Christian polemic *On the Genealogy of Morals*, I plan to show that Nietzsche turns the modern anticonfessional presumption on its head. He knows very well the deepest concern of his free-thinking readers: If I hand over my mind, my life, and my soul to God, how can I retain my uniquely valuable individuality? What is so remarkable, however, is that Nietzsche does not give a conventionally modern, reassuring answer. Over the course of his rhetorically vertiginous analysis of the sources of morality, he slowly reshapes the expectations of his readers and guides them toward a deeper question, perhaps the deepest existential question of all: Is it possible to have a distinct individuality, a soul to which I might be loyal, if I do not finally say with Christ in the garden of Gethsemane, "Not my will but thine"?

*   *   *

At the beginning of *On the Genealogy of Morals*, Nietzsche reports that his polemical book of pseudo-history, pseudo-anthropology, and pseudo-psychology shall be an exercise in knowing ourselves.[2] We cannot simply investigate morality and Christianity, as if these were subjects that we could entertain with dispassionate detachment as we do biological specimens or mathematical equations. Nietzsche is not a modern social scientist who believes that morality rests superficially on the surface of human life, a taboo system or artifact of cultural history that can be isolated and analyzed. No, according to Nietzsche, our commitment to a moral frame of reference penetrates to the depths of our soul. We are invested in the value of values, the moral significance of morality, and as participants in a culture profoundly shaped by Christian ideals of self-denial and self-sacrifice, what we think and decide about these ideals entails a judgment and decision about ourselves. To inquire into the origin and value of morality is to peer into the hidden recesses of our ambitions and fears, our longings and loathings — to know ourselves.

Here, then, at the very outset, we encounter the eccentric — even para-

2. *On the Genealogy of Morals*, trans. Walter Kaufmann (New York: Random House, 1967). Throughout I will provide citations by essay (Preface, I, II, III) and section, in this case from the first section of the Preface, thus P.1.

doxical — trajectory of Nietzsche's polemical ambition, a strange and paradoxical arc of rhetoric and logic that causes many commentators to misread *The Genealogy*, and the entire modern critical project.

At first glance, Nietzsche's tract is clearly a brief against Christianity. Its ethic of "pity, self-abnegation, self-sacrifice," he insists again and again, deforms if it does not destroy the human spirit. Under the spell of self-denial, we view natural exuberance and its impulse toward positive achievement as evil desires to be cut out of our souls by the harsh demands of Christ-like, cruciform righteousness. In the place of a noble strength, the Christian logic of confession encourages weakness, sickness, and ugliness. The overall effect, Nietzsche claims, has been disastrous. A denial of strength and self-expression, and the affirmation of weakness and self-denial, are profoundly unnatural. This unnatural moral system, which has bewitched Western culture for so long, leads to the spiritual exhaustion and despair that he labels "nihilism."

But there is hope. We need not consider ourselves helpless before the dehumanizing forms of our inherited Christian morality. We can attain an intellectual self-mastery through "a critique of moral values," and in so doing we can call "the value of values themselves into question . . ." (P.6). The critical project requires "a knowledge of the conditions and circumstances" under which Christian morality and its self-sacrificing imperatives came to dominance — the genealogical project (P.6). From this perspective, then, Nietzsche seems to outline the characteristic form of modern intellectual life. We are to step back and undertake a sober, objective inquiry into the real origins of Christian morality, and in this way we can arrive at a proper, rational assessment of its self-denying logic. Then, with this critical self-knowledge, we will make a genuinely free decision about how we want to live.

It all seems quite familiar. We are to "think critically." Yet — and here we find ourselves suddenly and violently thrown out of our conventional posture as objective inquirers — Nietzsche immediately suggests that our commonplace assumptions about critical inquiry are complacent and self-serving. He turns to accuse his readers of naïve illusions. Getting to the bottom of the moral impulse will not be a simple matter of clear thinking, something one can reserve for the lecture hall. Instead, Nietzsche warns that his inquiry traverses "quite novel questions" that will take him (alone and without comrades) to a distant and hidden land (P.7). Following his analysis will require remarkable courage and fearlessness. Questioning the value of values, especially the value of self-denying moral and religious commitments, is an all-involving existential project.

In a deep sense, then, critical thinking about morality is itself a moral commitment, and, paradoxically, it is one that seems to require its own forms of self-denial. As Nietzsche warns his readers, we are to go with him across the high mountain ranges of inquiry only if we are willing to endure pain and suffering. We must have the inner strength to bring to the altars of sacrifice our most cherished beliefs. In order to think fearlessly about the value of values, we must deny our weak impulse to live amidst the platitudes of our age. We need to discipline ourselves and renounce comfortable conclusions, not the least of which are the easy beliefs that critique liberates rather than limits, that seeing the truth about the human condition ennobles rather than impoverishes. A genuine act of self-knowledge will be extraordinarily difficult, Nietzsche warns, perhaps impossible for most.

Nietzsche is so convinced that his readers will lack the power of self-denial necessary to follow his penetrating analysis that he digresses to defend himself against readers who, he is sure, will be offended and outraged by his inquiry. Any troubles that readers might have understanding *The Genealogy,* claims Nietzsche, are simply signs of weakness. We do not follow his logic to the end, Nietzsche warns, because we recoil from the pain that accepting the conclusions will entail. Like Christ at Gethsemane, Nietzsche should be read as hectoring his readers: "Are you still sleeping and taking your rest?" (Matt. 26:45). Only a reader with a capacity for self-denial has strength necessary for a genealogy of morals designed to overcome the ideal of self-denial. Only an ascetic such as Zarathustra can go far enough and deep enough into the inner springs of our moral nature to escape from the bewitching power of ascetic ideals.

The paradox is puzzling. On the one hand, Nietzsche seems to provide a genealogical critique of self-denying morality that is very much in accord with the modern rebellion against the logic of confession. On the other hand, he seems to warn his readers that only those with the courage and desire to embrace self-denial will have the powers of the soul necessary to follow his analysis and accept his conclusions. This paradox should guide our reading of *The Genealogy* as a whole, because working it out will illuminate both the logic of confession that Nietzsche understood so well and the slack Nietzscheanism of the present that seeks to live without confession.

*   *   *

Essay One is the most famous part of *The Genealogy,* the section most likely to be read in an undergraduate survey course. This is no accident: Essay One is structured with narrative simplicity. It reads like the usual sort of historical critique of tradition that fills bookstores these days, and it seems to issue a rather clear and negative assessment of the life-denying consequences of Christian morality. But even Essay One defeats the simplistic notion that we can escape from self-denial in an easy, life-affirming way.

Nietzsche begins by describing what he imagines to have been the moral ambiance of antiquity. (Or perhaps he begins by describing what he wants his readers to imagine was the moral ambiance of antiquity. Nietzsche is always playing rhetorical tricks.) Two moralities operate. An aristocratic morality affirms as "good" the achievements of powerful men and the excellence of superior human beings. "Badness" is just an afterthought; it is simply the absence of strength, power, and excellence. For this reason, Nietzsche sees aristocratic morality as essentially active and life-enhancing. The strong are free to give expression to their superior qualities, and they do not worry themselves about the badness of the weak, except as a condition to be avoided.

The opposite of aristocratic morality is what Nietzsche calls slave morality. Unable to be excellent, the mediocre reverse the values of life. Slaves turn the natural domination of the strong over the weak into wickedness; success becomes a form of sin, and creative achievement indicates prideful selfishness. The slaves are motivated to effect this transvaluation of values because it allows them to celebrate their fates as spiritual achievements. Craven submission to the stronger, greater man becomes humble obedience — or it even gets transformed into "love of one's enemies" (I.14). Slave morality turns weakness into a virtue: "Blessed are the meek."[3] Therefore, instead of an aristocratic love of human excellence and our potential for creative achievement, Nietzsche observes that the slave morality inculcates a perverse self-hatred: Not my will but thine.

Although Nietzsche makes no effort to hide his disdain for slave morality, he is well aware that history has already formed us to accept and affirm its life-denying precepts. Men and women of the nineteenth century may or may not affirm explicitly Christian principles, but according to Nietzsche's reckoning, almost everybody endorses some form of slave morality. He is surely right, both of his own time and today. We presume that a

---

3. See *The Genealogy* I.7, for Nietzsche's direct reference to the Beatitudes.

good person subordinates self-interest to the demands of the common good. We think that we should pity the weak and make sacrifices to care for those less capable, accomplished, and powerful. Our egalitarian ethos requires us to denounce claims to superiority. But how could this have happened? How could this deliberate self-weakening have become such a powerful moral ideal? To answer this question, Nietzsche posits a moral revolution perpetrated by a cabal of conniving priestly conspirators. "With the Jews," he writes, "there begins *the slave revolt in morality:* that revolt which has a history of two thousand years behind it and which we no longer see because it has been victorious" (I.7).

The revolution refers, of course, to the spread and eventual triumph of Christianity in the ancient Mediterranean world. By Nietzsche's analysis, Christianity did not succeed on the basis of its martyrs or its doctrines. Instead, Christianity expressed a subtle psychological dynamic that has bewitching power: *ressentiment.* Perhaps Nietzsche used the French term for resentment as a way to signal the extraordinary social creativity and artificial self-display that effects the transformation of gnawing and painful resentment into a joyful sense of spiritual superiority. Or perhaps Nietzsche was amused that Rousseau had failed to see how Christian morality succeeded in turning a debilitating *amour propre* into a self-affirming *amour de soi,* and the French term was a natural way to assert his superiority over the earlier Enlightenment figure's earnest sincerity and childish moralism.

Whether or not we can determine Nietzsche's motives for using the term, the psychological process of *ressentiment* should be familiar. I have certainly felt myself making its basic moves. As I walk past row after row of expensive cars in the parking lot at the university on my way to my twelve-year-old pickup truck, I burn with resentment. "Why," I ask myself with bitterness, "can't I have a nice car like my students, children of so many well-to-do parents?" I hate my meager circumstances, and I regret my choice of genteel professorial poverty. But a lasting recognition of my fate is unbearable. How can I allow that I am a failure? So, in a heartbeat, I suddenly reverse my situation. Now I look at the expensive cars with a smug sense of superiority. "Look at all the grotesque materialism," I say to myself. I remind myself of the careerism that dominates student culture. My mood brightens, and by the time I get to my car I am congratulating myself for having the "right values." I pat myself on the back. I have chosen the dignity and nobility of the intellectual life rather than "selling out" — as the rich parents of those students have, and no doubt as the students themselves will as well. The reversal is now complete. As I drive home, my failure has been transformed into my accomplishment. The strengths and benefits that others enjoy are not goods at all. They are signs of moral weakness and spiritual deformity. In this way, reports Nietzsche, "the venomous eye of *ressentiment*" destroys strength, excellence, beauty, achievement, and nobility with its transvaluing lie: strength is weakness and weakness is strength (I.11).

As Nietzsche tells the story, the dynamics of *ressentiment* define the life-denying trajectory of slave morality. The noble man is purely active and creative. He meets obstacles and adversaries, and he tries to overcome or defeat them, but always for the sake of the good sought and never out of a reactive bitterness. In contrast, according to Nietzsche, the child of *ressentiment* is reactive, derivative, and full of anxious denials and accusations. He is "ill-constituted, dwarfed, atrophied and poisoned" (I.11). The world of slave morality is created by the power of hatred, Nietzsche's rhetoric implies, the hatred of all that is strong, well constituted, and living. Within the logic of slave morality, goodness has no substantial reality; it is pure negation, that is, "not evil," which really means "not strong" or "not powerful."

But more importantly, *ressentiment* sets up an impossible situation. "To demand of strength," says Nietzsche, "that it should not be a desire to overcome, a desire to throw down, a desire to become master, a thirst for enemies and resistances and triumphs, is just as absurd as to demand of weakness that it should express itself as strength" (I.13). This absurd demand, thinks Nietzsche, is the germ of nihilism. Slave morality trains us to hate the natural exuberance and creativity of the human animal. Our instincts, drives, and urges, all of which press us outward to act on and find our satisfactions in the world, become powers to be denied, suppressed, and tamed. As a result, Nietzsche suggests, we become disgusted with our own human condition. Under the influence of slave morality and its demand that strength become weakness, Nietzsche observes, "the sight of man makes us weary — what is nihilism today if not *that?* — We are weary *of man*" (I.12). Christian morality wishes to emasculate the potency of the human will. This great project of redefining strength as weakness ends in an enervated, paralyzed moral exhaustion: "If only I could be . . . not me."

At this point Nietzsche has reached a rhetorical apex. The aristocratic morality leads to human excellence and creativity, while the slave morality based on hatred exhausts itself with its impossible program of self-denial that collapses into nihilism. But the astute reader must pause. It would seem odd that Nietzsche should build to such a stark and decisive dichotomy so quickly and so early in his book. Did he really intend the subsequent pages simply to clean up the details and fill in some blanks? Furthermore, as Nietzsche himself admits, the subtle psychological dynamic of *ressentiment* is profoundly creative: it recasts strength as weakness and weakness as strength! The historical influence of this moral creativity has been remarkable. The aristocratic desires of well-born Romans gave way to a desire for an ascetic heroism. Christianity triumphed. To be able to move so many, indeed, to be able to move the strong themselves, surely these historical facts indicate that slave morality has its own kind of conquering strength, its own kind of power, however unnatural.

Nietzsche knows that the historical dominance of Christianity contradicts his assessment of slave morality as mere weakness. In order to address this difficulty, he spins a tale of conspiracy. Christian morality did not win in a fair fight against the aristocratic morality of Greco-Roman culture. Christian victory was the result of a Jewish conspiracy, a secret, priestly plot to displace the noble morality of the strong with the slave morality of the weak. I cannot detail Nietzsche's caricatured depiction of this conspiracy (*"three Jews,* as is known, and one *Jewess"* [I.16]), and his evocation of its dark and secret workshop of values (I.14). And the details are unnecessary in any event, because Nietzsche is mocking his readers rather than enlightening them. His basic commitment to power and the primacy of the "deed" ("the deed is everything," I.13) overwhelms any attempt to explain away the victory of Christianity. "Consider," he says, "to whom one bows down in Rome itself today" (I.16). Victory reveals strength, and "Rome has been defeated beyond all doubt" (I.16).

Ultimately, we are wrong to read Essay One as a straightforward attempt to unmask the "real" history of morality so that we can throw off the shackles of hate-infected Christian morality and recommit ourselves to the "good," life-affirming Greeks, whom Nietzsche admired. Nietzsche could never be so naïve. A few well-chosen metaphors, a dash of historical analysis, some appeals to neutral scientific ("instinct") and medical terms ("health") cannot transport us to enlightenment like a comfortable express train taking commuters home after a long and difficult day at the office. Nietzsche was not a contemporary college professor retailing fifty-minute lectures on the genealogy of morals to young students as so many stops on the itinerary of intellectual and moral self-possession. Nietzsche did not think we could simply adopt critical poses and thus fancy ourselves to be free to think independently about a moral tradition that has dominated Western culture for two thousand years.

To be sure, Nietzsche takes the basic dichotomy developed in Essay One very seriously: "Rome against Judea, Judea against Rome" (I.16). He certainly thinks that the deepest question we face as a culture is the structure of our moral imaginations, or, as he puts it, the value of our values. Shall we live confessionally (Judea) or shall we live simply for the sake of what we can do and impose on the world (Rome)? But as the preface to *The Genealogy* foreshadows, and the final sections of Essay One make clear, Nietzsche wants to destroy our illusions concerning how we can go about answering this kind of question, which is, after all, a question about who we are and want to be. He wants to puncture our modern illusions of objectivity, our reassuring assumption that cultural and moral sickness can be shed like a snake's skin, our easy optimism that we have the capacity to choose and redirect our lives and our culture on the basis of rational analysis and well-intentioned judgment. All these applications of "critical thinking," itself an emasculating assault on the strength of convictions that energize the will, are epiphenomena of slave morality. Thus, Nietzsche ends Essay One by recounting the whiggish history of our supposed triumphs over superstition, priest craft, and tyranny — the Renaissance, the Reformation, the French Revolution. He labels them moments of redoubled *ressentiment* (I.16). They were not heroic and noble achievements of the human spirit; they were further, deeper Judean triumphs.

Nietzsche taunts because he wants to warn. We cannot think our way out of a confessional life, as his concluding note to Essay One indicates with its tone of false, mockingly scientific urgency. All forms of modern critique and rebellion, he suggests, have simply transformed our service of the God of Israel into a service of truth or humanity or scientific understanding or conscience or some other surrogate deity. The basic structure remains the same: "Not my will but thine."

*   *   *

Only in Essay Two does Nietzsche provide his readers with a patient, theoretically cogent account of how and why we ever came to imagine that we should live for the sake of something other than ourselves. The answer he gives functions as a naturalized form of Augustinian anthropology. Our impulse toward self-denying moral effort, however alienating and life-denying Nietzsche might judge it, arises out of our instinctual lives. Our hearts are restless. Our lives are not governed by the need for survival; instead, human personality is most deeply formed by a creative desire to be and do something *more*. We cannot honestly know ourselves unless we acknowledge that we live as creatures of ambition.

Nietzsche does not advance his anthropological theory in the modern, scientific sense of the term. Instead, like Hobbes, Locke, and Rousseau, he pictures a state of nature that allows him to describe what he takes to be the inner springs of human personality. In our original condition, we are happy, and our happiness stems from a capacity for forgetfulness, what Nietzsche calls a "positive repression" of time and the burdens of finitude. However, Nietzsche presumes that a competitive environment puts pressure on lives. Only the strong can afford the luxury of forgetfulness, for they can ward off the blows of others at every turn. The weak, in contrast, require memory: they need to prudently navigate through life, and to do so they must carefully fix the signs of danger in their memories.

Nietzsche's account of the transition from forgetfulness to memory involves lurid descriptions of brutal punishments. He observes: "Man could never do without blood, torture, and sacrifices when he felt the need to create a memory for himself" (II.3). When the powerful demand the services of the weak, their commands must be burned into our bodies so that they will be remembered. "Pain," says Nietzsche, "is the most powerful aid to mnemonics" (II.3). As human societies become more complex and hierarchical, the need for memory increases. This need gives rise to a ritualized economy of pain, punishment, and suffering that Michel Foucault has suggested lay underneath the moralizing and rationalizing projects of modernity as its true source.[4]

In contrast to classical thinkers who saw human nature as intrinsically ordered toward higher goods, modern theorists (Foucault included) tend to treat human beings as fundamentally motivated by a desire for pleasure and a fear of pain. Although Nietzsche does not echo the traditional consensus that man is a rational animal, neither does he join the modern consensus. "The actual effect of punishment," he writes, "must beyond question be sought above all in the heightening of prudence, in an extending of mem-

---

4. See *Discipline and Punish: The Birth of the Modern Prison*, trans. Alan Sheridan (New York: Vintage Books, 1979).

ory" (II.15). But as every moralist knows, the calculations of prudence are not the same as the spurs of conscience. "Punishment *tames* men," says Nietzsche, "but it does not make them 'better' . . ." (II.15). In short, the logic of confession, the giving over of one's life and will to the service of a higher good, cannot be explained by the external pressure of social practices and the manipulation of Pavlovian pleasure and pain responses.

Freud was another modern figure who did not view the human animal as a simple compound of pleasure-seeking and pain-avoiding instincts. He saw that our lives are characterized by an oversupply of moral energy. His patients exhibited forms of compulsive self-discipline that seemed to create suffering without any positive payoff. This clinical experience led Freud to conclude that moral demands have far more force than can be explained by normal impulses to seek pleasure and avoid pain. In order to explain the sources of the heightened force of inner-directed expectation, Freud posited the existence of the love and death instincts, two limitless and mysterious sources of psychic energy that push us far beyond the limited economy of survival.

Nietzsche's observations about the victory of slave morality parallel Freud's clinical experience. The over-supply of moral energy that turns inward and acts upon the instinctual life of the human creature must be explained, and in anticipation of Freud's mythic instincts of *eros* and *thanatos*, Nietzsche also posits a limitless source of psychic energy. Nietzsche famously calls this source our will-to-power. It is this creative, dominating impulse that drives "the strong" toward the self-exaltations of "goodness." However, punishment and the consequent personality of memory and prudence restrict the instinct for creative freedom. Caged by fear of punishment, creative freedom turns inward. "Those fearful bulwarks," writes Nietzsche, "with which the political organization protected itself against the old instincts of freedom — punishments belong among those bulwarks — brought about that all those instincts of will, free, prowling man turned backward *against man himself*" (II.16). Conscience and its self-limiting, self-sacrificing dynamics are, paradoxically, the inwardly turned expressions of the instinct of will-to-power. Slave morality expresses inwardly all the outward, aristocratic qualities that Nietzsche champions in Book One.

Contemporary readers should be able to recognize Nietzsche's basic insight in Freud's psychoanalytic theory of the superego. Conscience is not an internalization of social norms, or at least not merely so. The felt power of moral demands goes far beyond the power of society to discipline and punish. Moral idealism drives individuals to a fevered pitch of self-motivated and self-administered discipline. According to Freud's theory, this occurs because our mental images of good and evil are energized by the repressed erotic potency of the id. The very sources of transgression are redirected toward the self-denying project of moral perfection.

Freud was a cool rationalist. He regretted the intensity of Christian morality, and he thought its self-denying project unnecessarily harsh. In its place, he advocated a temperate management of the circulation of transgressive desire and repressive discipline. In order to support this therapeutic project, Freud avoids the deeper question: what triggers and sustains the dominance of the superego? Freud backslides into a medical evasion at this point, describing imprudent moral idealism and religious zeal as a form of collective psychosis, explaining the origins of personality by recourse to his own carefully tailored myths (see *Totem and Taboo* and its fantastical scene of primal Oedipal violence). In contrast, Nietzsche pushes forward. According to his principles, the engines of history and culture are necessarily the desires, actions, and personalities of the strong. This includes the reality of moral and religious zealotry, especially the embrace of self-denial. Thus, at the crucial point in Book Two, Nietzsche clearly formulates what he takes to be the deep paradox of culture — that strength should choose self-limiting weakness, and call it glory.

Not only does Nietzsche formulate the paradox; he resolves it. Our animal natures encourage us to seek pleasure and avoid pain. In the pressurized environment of external threat and the internal need to negotiate conflict, the human animal learns to carefully and prudently negotiate threat and exploit opportunities. Life evolves in precisely the way that sociobiologists might predict. Yet a problem emerges. According to Nietzsche's account of the human animal, we possess a drive that transcends the limited ambitions of pleasure and survival. The will-to-power wants to create and dominate, not pursue pleasure and avoid pain by way of craft and calculation. The soul, like radioactive material driven inward by the pressures of survival, reaches critical mass, and the human animal becomes a moral agent. Homesick for the wild, the instinctual zest for life that characterizes the will-to-power turns to the soul itself as an unexplored territory to be conquered. We declare war on our instincts (II.16). As our carnal selves fight back against the project of carving up the psyche into good desires and wicked desires, we become for ourselves a dangerous place of adventure (II.16). We live an outward life dedicated to survival, but our inward lives are a mysterious wilderness. In this way the will-to-power fills its creative needs by creating the distinction between good and evil, and by applying it with relentless force to itself.

The inner struggle, the agonistic formation of the soul, allows Nietzsche to explain the positive allure of slave morality. We conquer ourselves with an artistic cruelty and "secret self-ravishment" (II.18) that would make any Greek warrior proud. As the creative freedom of the will-to-power reaches its goal — which is domination of instinct itself! — we give ourselves the greatest gift of strength, which Nietzsche identifies as forgetfulness. We wear the hair shirts of spiritual discipline to defeat our bodies, and in so doing we forget that we are animals with physical needs and desires. We live with indifference toward our weak flesh, ignoring its demands just as the noble strongmen of Nietzsche's imagination were indifferent toward their weak slaves, indulging them now and again in gestures of magnanimity but never counting them or their needs as relevant to the ideal life. Instead of conquering others, we conquer our souls.

Nietzsche views the inward turn as inevitable. No slave revolt or Jewish conspiracy was necessary, or if it was, then the conspiracy was formulated and executed by the strong themselves in a creative act of self-deception. Rome defeated herself. Surrounded by glorious achievements and dominating the known world, the greatest soldiers and statesmen were slaves to the glory of past heroes. Under these conditions, should we be surprised that the great souls of late antiquity felt the attractions of *ressentiment*? Nietzsche helps us picture Marcus Aurelius, the Stoic emperor, saying, "My forefathers may have conquered the world, but *I* have conquered my humanity!" He exercises the ultimate prerogative of the strong by forgetting his worldly past and glorious legacy so that he can concern himself with — *himself.* Outward success drove the Roman aristocrat toward the inner adventure of self-discipline in the service of a divine truth. Thus does the morality of self-denial emerge out of the breasts of the strong, not as an inexplicable capitulation to the weak, but as a creative and heroic form of life. We need the logic of confession — "Not my will but thine" — in order to live more fully, more deeply, more courageously, and more ambitiously.

*　　*　　*

No doubt Nietzsche regards our bondage to self-denial, our lives in the thrall of a desire to love and serve God, as a "bad fate." In this sense, we can properly read Nietzsche as a patron of our postmodern rebellion against the domineering demands of truth. But unlike so much contemporary pious posturing about "difference" and "diversity," Nietzsche will not countenance any easy, self-deluding alternatives. For this reason, Essay Three involves an extended demonstration of what Nietzsche correctly anticipates will be the one truth that his readers cannot bear: the inescapable power of self-denying moral ideals. Nietzsche surveys the standard modern methods of self-liberation from Christian confession: art, philosophy, humanistic and cultural studies, politics, and even atheism. In each instance, he shatters illusions. All the standard routes of escape lead us back into the logic of confession. Covert forms of Christianity, they are all the more unappealing because of their self-protective blindness and uncreative mendacity.

The coda for Essay Three is straightforward: the human will needs a goal. Is this so difficult to understand? asks Nietzsche. We want to make something out of our lives; we want to add up to something. But do we really understand what it means to "make something of our lives," to achieve something "worthwhile," to choose something "meaningful," to create something "beautiful"? Do we realize how difficult it is to have an ambition or a goal that does not require us to sacrifice our individuality, our polymorphous instincts, our spontaneous freedom? Do we really know how hard it is to make something of ourselves without cutting into ourselves, carving and sculpting with disciplinary strategies of self-denial? Do we not see that wanting to be something — anything — other than our present selves involves obedience to an ideal? These sorts of questions express Nietzsche's deepest exasperation with modern culture. Modern fantasies about post-Christian ways of life make men and women into the most deformed of all possible creatures: ignorant slaves of slave morality.

Nietzsche's two digressions into the spiritual dynamics of art and philosophy help us understand the larger purpose of Essay Three. Both art and philosophy have served as modern alternatives to Christianity, and both promise to provide their followers with purpose, absent the degrading necessities of obedience. However, as Nietzsche shows, neither can deliver.

How many young university students have taken up the cry "Art for art's sake"! Devotion to form, discipline of voice, clarity of vision — all defined and redefined in endless discussions of artistic integrity and purpose — this and more define the artistic vocation. As Nietzsche observes, the atmosphere of urgency gives art its ascetic character. Our painting must render what is real. Our poetry must serve the muse. With music, Nietzsche provides a vivid image that captures the ambitions of late Romantic composers. "The *musician* himself" must become "a kind of mouthpiece of the 'in itself' of things, a telephone from beyond." The composer is a "ventriloquist of God" (III.5), and the listener is no less subservient. We must put ourselves entirely at the disposal of the music. "Not my will but thine" remains as the covert imperative.

Nietzsche finds Wagner emblematic. One can hardly accuse Wagnerian opera of cold formalism and constrained expressive range. Yet Wagner turned toward Christianity in his final years. According to Nietzsche, Wagner's embrace of Christianity was entirely in keeping with the logic of all art, which is characterized by a will-to-power expressing itself as self-denial. We can build new temples to art (museums, concert halls), found new monasteries of art (conservatories, artist colonies, studios), fund new programs (writer's workshops, endowments for the arts, musical competitions), we can even refashion artist funding, education, and practice to serve moral and political ideals (urban art projects, AIDS tapestries, agitprop theater); but we cannot escape from the self-denying trajectory of art. The artist serves his or her art. Wagner only followed his vocation back to its explicit source, betraying humanity but not art.

Nietzsche's treatment of philosophy follows the same pattern as his analysis of art. Philosophy is, at root, a project of purification, and philosophers are punctilious priests enforcing codes for mental cleanliness. Indeed, Nietzsche links philosophers to the clergy when he observes that all philosophers criticize fame, princes, and women (III.8). This teasing equation reflects Nietzsche's insight into the disposition toward truth that philosophy encourages. We are to obey her severe demands. Not surprisingly, Plato sought to root out temptations by eliminating poetry, sublimating sexual love, rejecting the comforting myths of traditional religion, and encouraging a steely resistance to the blandishments of wealth and the threats of political power. We need a capacity for self-denial and a willingness to serve the truth in order to become philosophers.

In his analysis of the spiritual project of philosophy, Nietzsche helps clarify the difference between material conflict of modern ideals with the older dogmas of Christianity, and the deeper continuity of modernity with Christendom. Just because modern philosophy has detached itself from Christianity, has even placed itself as Christianity's most implacable opponent, it remains ascetic in structure. The high and mighty philosopher demands objectivity. The same holds for the larger project of modern critical education. We must question our dearly held pieties. We need to discipline ourselves to step back and coolly examine our presuppositions.

Nietzsche sees the spiritual effect. Guided by the modern critical project, "we violate ourselves nowadays, no doubt of it, we nutcrackers of the soul, ever questioning and questionable . . ." (III.9). All the conclusions may contradict Christian doctrine, but the underlying knife of self-denial cuts as deep as ever. "We experiment with ourselves," Nietzsche observes of the modern atmosphere of critique that contemporary professors continue confidently to impose on credulous college freshman "in a way we would never permit ourselves to experiment with animals and, carried away by curiosity, we cheerfully vivisect our souls . . ." (III.9). With the severe application of reason, philosophy is proud of its courage, its insights, its honesty. Truth is divine, and it is truth that the philosopher nobly serves. Max Weber's famous lecture on the rigors of the modern intellectual, "Science as Vocation," clearly reminds us that the confessional form of life endures, even as it is evacuated of all faith.

As Essay Three concludes, Nietzsche's rhetoric gains momentum. On the one hand, he wants his readers to see the awesome power of Christianity. "Where is the match of this closed system of will, goal and interpretation? Why has it not found a match? — Where is the *other* goal?" (III.23). In contrast to the modern alternatives, one practically feels Nietzsche's relief when he comments on the stratagems of his deadly adversary, the "ascetic priest." With self-consciously confessional Christians, Nietzsche feels as though he has at last come "face to face with the actual *representative of seriousness*" (III.11). At least they know what they are about. On the other hand, he utters shrill denunciations to convince his readers that self-denial is demonic and destructive. "The ascetic ideal has not only ruined health and taste, it has also ruined a third, fourth, fifth, sixth thing as well — I beware of enumerating everything (I'd never finish)" (III.23). Christianity has had "monstrous and calamitous effects" (III.23). And yet — and yet, all the supposed alternatives fail to escape the gravitational pull of the cross.

Nietzsche impatiently races through still other modern alternatives to Christianity: science, cultural study, historical analysis, social activism, even atheism itself. These are simply further pale echoes of Christianity, comical when not pathetic. Science is a busy world of conferences and publications, career advancement and technological gadgets. When science puts on airs and claims to defend intellectual integrity and experimental rigor, it reveals its religious character as a strict disciplinarian. "This 'modern science' — let us face the fact! — is the best ally the ascetic ideal has at present" (III.25). A similar parallel holds for the human sciences: sociology, modern history, anthropology, psychology. They are characterized by an "insistence on intellectual cleanliness," and these disciplines "still have faith in truth" (III.24). For the same reason, even a self-conscious atheism reinforces rather than overcomes the logic of confessional submission. "Unconditional honest atheism (and it is the only air we breathe, we more spiritual men of this age!), is therefore *not* the antithesis of [the ascetic] ideal, as it appears to be," says Nietzsche. "It is rather only one of the latest phases of its evolution, one of its terminal forms and inner consequences . . ." (III.27). In fact, atheism may be the most extreme form of self-denial. It is a frenzied perfectionism of the intellect that "forbids itself the *lie involved in belief in God*" (III.27). Saying no to dogma in obedience to pure reason still involves saying yes to the logic of confession.

The wild swings of passion and intense rhetoric of the final pages of *The Genealogy of Morals* drive home the lesson in self-knowledge that Nietzsche promised to deliver — and warned that we would resist. Modernity has not lived up to its ambitions: the logic of confession endures. In the final section he even suggests that the cold facts of our fragile humanity make self-denial the only real alternative for a human life that does not simply give up in despair. As the author of Ecclesiastes tells us so eloquently, all the worldly things we struggle to achieve are swept away by decay and death. Under these conditions — the human condition — we are all enslaved by our finitude, as the ancients knew and taught. Against the meaninglessness of life in which the human is as an animal who merely lives and dies, Nietzsche observes that the creative impulse that drives our lives and makes us human presses us toward self-denying projects of obedience to an otherworldly ideal. "To repeat in conclusion what I said in the beginning," writes Nietzsche in his final line, "man would rather will nothingness than not will" (III.28). We would rather live for an otherworldly ideal than abandon ourselves to enslavement to the fickle instincts of our decaying bodies.

*   *   *

Nietzsche was a strange and complicated thinker. He clearly despised Christianity, and yearned for a form of human life that is creative, free, and fully developed. Yet his most lucid and disciplined investigation into the dynamics of faith ends with a mockery of modern alternatives and a grudging affirmation of the logic of confession as what seems to be (much to his dismay) the only real possibility for human life. For if we leave our lives simply as we find them, he suggests, then we are doomed to live a nihilism deeper and more threatening than the most unworldly and aggressive asceticism — life without will.

I am not convinced that any reader of Nietzsche can fully and finally parse his loyalties and make a coherent system out of his explosive insights. However, it is possible to draw our own cultural analysis from *The Genealogy of Morals,* an analysis that helps us make sense out of our equally strange and complicated postmodern culture. Here I can only offer halting gestures.

We tend to think that modern scientific and secular culture marks the great break in Western spiritual life. But this turns out to be an illusion created by the clash of dogmas. As Nietzsche shows, the hard-nosed atheist continues in the mode of slave morality: such a person wishes to serve reason, and however many mistakes he or she makes in logic, judgment, and epistemology, escape from the confessional form of life is not the upshot. Men and women can dissent from Christian orthodoxy and maintain rigorous lives of moral and rational commitment. One can serve the larger, greater, universal master of reason or truth or some other transcendent reality independent of a specifically Christian confession of faith. The content of Jeremy Bentham's utilitarianism collides with Christian morality, but the young John Stuart Mill followed in the footsteps of the apostles when he pledged himself to the greatest good of the greatest number as his Lord and God.

Nietzsche helps us see that a rejection of a disciplining obedience, whether to apostolic Christianity, the dictates of reason, or the commands of conscience, involves the deepest possible transformation of human life. Philip Rieff famously described this break as the therapeutic revolution in modern consciousness.[5] Richard Rorty, one of the most eloquent and perceptive representatives of postmodern philosophy endorses this transformation with characteristic clarity:

> In its ideal form, the culture of liberalism would be one which is enlightened, secular, through and through. It would be one in which no trace of divinity remains, even in the form of a divinized world or divinized self. Such a culture would have no room for the notion that there are nonhu-

5. See *The Triumph of the Therapeutic: Uses of Faith after Freud* (New York: Harper & Row, 1966).

man forces to which human beings should be responsible. It would drop or drastically reinterpret, not only the idea of holiness, but those of "devotion to truth" and of "fulfillment of the deepest needs of the spirit."[6]

Whether or not Rorty characterizes modern liberalism rightly (indeed, whether or not his characterization is self-consistent in light of his rather pious devotion to American democracy), his vision is a straightforward instance of our broader cultural efforts to untangle ourselves from the confessional form of life. Rorty does not want a creed of reason to supplant the canonical witness of Christian revelation. He does not want new, scientific, or humanistic dogmas to take the place of the old dogmas of Christendom. Instead, he wants what Nietzsche seems to have both desired in his anti-Christian polemics and feared in his own concluding evocation of the deep nihilism of life that no longer wills: a world without creeds. Rorty seeks a postconfessional form of life, a soul unformed by the ascetic impulse to give one's life over to a higher truth.

What Richard Rorty wants is not eccentric. The central feature of postmodern culture is a multifaceted cultural project designed to free us from the logic of confession and return us to full possession of our humanity, untroubled and undisturbed by aspiration. Deconstruction is a technical method of interpretation, but it is also a broad habit of mind that seeks to atomize inherited culture into uninspiring bits of social power and will-to-domination that are too base to command loyalty. Irony is a disposition that insulates the soul from commitment. Multicultural education requires no actual knowledge of the confessional systems that animate all traditional societies. Instead, exposure to diversity is meant to inculcate a nonjudgmental attitude of acceptance. Thus does Rorty's ideal society come into existence. We are left alone to simply live our human lives — or so we are promised.

But can we simply live? Is the spiritual quiescence of willing small and manageable and unambitious things possible? Can we rest in our humanity, as Rorty wishes? Can we set aside ideals and leave ourselves alone? Nietzsche suggests that the answer is no. His strange concluding affirmation of the ascetic impulse — humans would rather will nothingness than will nothing at all — echoes St. Augustine's basic insight into the human condition. Our hearts are restless. The human animal wishes to give itself to something

---

6. *Contingency, Irony, and Solidarity* (Cambridge, UK: Cambridge University Press, 1989), p. 45.

higher. We want a life of confession; it is a need more basic than our instinc-tual urges.

Perhaps, then, the real dangers of the present age are not to be found in a listless, empty nihilism, an open-ended nonjudgmentalism that encour-ages us to imagine our world devoid of compelling truths. Instead, if Nietz-sche is right in his contorted final concession to the deep human need for confession, the danger we face may be idolatry. Our future challenge may well be a secular fervor nourished by finite but genuine human needs and goods made absolute. Deprived of a God worth worshiping, we will find substitutes, even to the point of prostrating ourselves before birds or animals or reptiles that our modern minds have transformed from graven images into moral imperatives and political causes. The last century's graveyards testify to the reality of this danger. Deprived of something truly greater than ourselves, we will not come to rest in a modest loyalty to humanity. Instead, as the insights of Nietzsche and Augustine into the human condition warn us, we will fall into a devotion to subhuman, primal powers ("Blood and Soil," "The Cunning of History") that reward our service with debasement.

The Insufficiency of Any Secular Case for Absolute Human Rights, and the Resources of Divine Revelation: The Suicide Argument

Thomas D. Sullivan and Sandra Menssen

Can a purely secular case — a case that does not refer to the divine — be made out for fundamental absolute human rights? No, we maintain. In Section I we present and defend our basic argument, "the suicide argument," for this thesis, and in Section II we discuss objections to our argument.

We do not take the moral of our investigation to be that people should give up on fundamental absolute human rights. Rather, the possibility that a nonsecular defense of such rights is available should be taken very seriously. Here we can do no more than gesture in the direction of such a possibility. But that possibility is what inspires this essay — that, and the conviction that there are myriad facts about the world, including the breadth and depth of commitment to absolute rights, that can best be explained by appeal to the truth of Christian revelation. Thus, through a process of inference to the best explanation, through a process of arguing that, time and again, the best explanation for some fact about the world is that Christianity is true, one may develop a *philosophical case* for the truth of the revelation.[1] Our friend William J. Abraham, who has led the way in shining a light on the concept of revelation found "in the cracks and tensions between philosophy and theology," as he puts it, wrote at the outset of *Crossing the Threshold of Divine Rev-*

---

1. We discuss the strategy of this sort of inference to the best explanation in Sandra Menssen and Thomas D. Sullivan, *The Agnostic Inquirer: Revelation from a Philosophical Standpoint* (Grand Rapids: Eerdmans, 2007).

elation: "If there is anything I want to lift up at the beginning, it is that revelation is a fascinating epistemic concept; it deserves attention in its own right; and it makes a deep difference in how we think about the rationality of Christian belief and related topics."[2] We could not agree more.

I

Here are the bones of our "suicide argument":

1. A secular case can be made out for fundamental, absolute human rights only if a secular case can be made out that it is necessarily impermissible intentionally to kill innocents against their will.
2. There are times when nonexistence is rationally preferable to existence unless there is a God (i.e., leaving God out of the picture).
3. If there are times when nonexistence is rationally preferable to existence unless there is a God, then suicide — that is, intentionally killing one's innocent self — is sometimes morally permissible unless there is a God.
4. If suicide is sometimes morally permissible unless there is a God, then it is also sometimes permissible intentionally to kill an innocent person unless there is a God.
5. If it is sometimes permissible intentionally to kill an innocent person unless there is a God, then it is sometimes permissible intentionally to kill an innocent person when it is against that person's will, unless there is a God.
6. If it is sometimes permissible intentionally to kill an innocent person against that person's will unless there is a God, then a secular case that it is necessarily impermissible cannot be made out.
7. Therefore, a secular case cannot be made out for fundamental absolute human rights.

PREMISE 1: A secular case can be made out for fundamental, absolute human rights only if a secular case can be made out that it is necessarily impermissible intentionally to kill innocents against their will.

2. William J. Abraham, *Crossing the Threshold of Divine Revelation* (Grand Rapids: Eerdmans, 2006), pp. xi, xii.

A number of terms here require explanation.

When we consider whether a "case" can be made for a particular claim, we are considering whether an *argument,* perhaps a collection of arguments, can be constructed that adequately justifies the claim. If there is a collection of arguments, it may or may not be unified (through interlocking of premises and conclusions). The collection may include responses to serious objections. The argument will adequately justify the claim if it renders the conclusion more worthy of credence than any and all possible cases against the claim.

A justification will not necessarily take the form of an argument. An attempted justification may simply declare that some truth is obvious, as in Thomas Jefferson's "We hold these truths to be self-evident. . . ." In this instance we do not have a *case* for the assertion. Our interest in this chapter is in attempted justifications that constitute arguments — cases — for the claim at issue.

We are interested in whether a *secular* case can be made for fundamental, absolute human rights. In our view, an adequate case for such rights is going to have to include two sorts of nonsecular layers: first, it will include nonnatural properties; second, it will include reference to Providence. However, though we do think that the concept of human freedom involves nonnatural properties, and hence is not purely secular, we are going to leave the first of these layers aside, since we do not want to get sidetracked by debate about the nature of free will. We will work here with a thinner notion of a secular case, and we will simply stipulate that, for present purposes, a secular case is any case that does not include reference to a divine creator or a providential deity.

Fundamental absolute human rights are binding absolute prohibitions of a certain sort. The prohibitions may literally be such, of the form "Do not do x"; or they may be prohibitions in a looser sense, of the form "It is impermissible to do x." We abstract from questions concerning the vehicle of expression, such as whether an authority is issuing the prohibition. To say that a prohibition is absolute is to say that it is exceptionless: in no circumstances under the sun, whatever the consequences, may the prohibited action be undertaken. We do pin the absoluteness of the prohibition to this world (the prohibited action may be performed "in no circumstances under the sun" — our sun). That is, we do not include worlds where, for instance, decapitating a person does not result in the person's death, but instead induces in the beheaded person a thrilling hyperconsciousness. To say that an absolute prohibition is binding is to say that it is correct, that it actually holds: a person who acts in a way that does not accord with the prohibition acts wrongly. Absolute rights are not merely rights that a group of people agree to respect; they hold regardless of the existence of social contracts.[3]

A human being enjoys a fundamental absolute right only if it is always wrong to secure the death of an innocent person (that is, attempt to kill an innocent) against that person's will. "Innocent" does not mean morally unblemished. The idea, rather, is that persons are innocent if and only if they are not assailants in the relevant context. An adult soldier running toward you with a fixed bayonet counts as an assailant in the relevant context. A person justly convicted of murder and justly sentenced to be executed counts as well.[4]

There are cases in which it is difficult to say whether an individual who poses a threat is an assailant in the relevant context. Does a ten-year old "soldier" about to throw a grenade at you count as an "assailant"? How about a frightened child running toward you with a bomb strapped to his back, knowing that he poses some sort of threat, but helpless to defuse the situation? How about a child running toward you, oblivious to the fact that she is about to trip a wire that will detonate a bomb? How about a fetus in an ectopic pregnancy, whose continued growth will cause the mother's death?

Fortunately, for our purposes it will be unnecessary to resolve these difficulties. It will suffice to recognize that all of these hard cases differ from a situation in which an individual becomes an assailant by the *choice* of another. In the cases just mentioned, it is a fact that the subjects pose threats, independently of choice. Even the child unknowingly about to trip a detonating wire, even the fetus growing in the fallopian tube, are in fact threats by virtue of what they are doing, though the subjects do not know they pose threats and thus are in one important sense innocent. All these cases differ from the situation in which a terrorist threatens to blow up a city unless you kill the next person who walks in front of the window. In this new case, the subject (the person walking in front of the window) becomes a threat only

---

3. We do not take our thesis to have any immediate implications concerning what it would be reasonable or rational to *enforce:* the question of what rights should be protected using the machinery of government is well beyond the scope of our discussion. And we also set aside issues concerning what role, if any, appeals to divine revelation should have in the public square.

4. In this case the individual *has been* an assailant, and that is the relevant context. We leave open the question of whether individuals ever are justly sentenced to be executed.

by choice of another. But the walker does not become a genuine assailant by virtue of being *deemed* such, by virtue of the terrorist's decision to victimize the next person who walks by the window. The walker is an innocent person, in our sense of the term.

PREMISE 2: There are times when nonexistence is rationally preferable to existence unless there is a God (i.e., leaving God out of the picture).

Suffering and grief may so burden a person — a friend, a loved one, or maybe a stranger — that we find ourselves saying, "That person would be better off dead."[5]

We must be cautious in making such a pronouncement, of course. Commentators rightly observe that in some mouths the phrase "better off dead" betrays contempt for persons whose afflictions are seen as somehow diminishing their value as persons. Other discussants, also urging caution, point to the fact that it is relatively rare that nothing whatever can be done for somebody in great pain, and that science and medicine (in wealthy areas) offer far more palliation than even some professionals might imagine. Furthermore, it should be emphasized that some terribly afflicted people heroically endure their suffering with amazing joy. Nevertheless, despite all these useful reminders that we must be exceedingly careful in judging that any individual would be "better off dead," the judgment is *sometimes* appropriate: in certain circumstances, certain individuals might, in fact, be better off dead.

Some commentators suggest that there is a logical problem with the judgment that a person would be better off dead: how could a person be better off dead if that person no longer exists? But consider a parallel case, a case meant to bring out a point not touching on whether a person is better off dead, but on the invocation of an underlying logico-metaphysical assumption of the argument. That assumption is that one can be in a state or perform an action only if one exists. The assumption is true enough. But it is misleadingly invoked in connection with the claim "one can't be better off dead," just as it is misleadingly invoked in connection with an old puzzle about dying. The puzzle goes: "How can one die? Dying is doing something. So one would have to exist at the time one dies. But for as long as one exists,

5. Some of the points we make in defense of premises 2, 3, and 5 can be found in Thomas D. Sullivan's "Assisted Suicide and Assisted Torture," *Logos: A Journal of Catholic Thought and Culture* 2, no. 3 (1999): 77-95.

one has not died. So it is not possible to die." In both cases — the case of being better off dead, and the case of dying — the invocation of the logico-metaphysical assumption is the source of the puzzle. But the puzzle is dissolved by merely redescribing each situation. In the case of dying, one notes that dying is ceasing to be, and ceasing to be is not a state of the thing that ceases, let alone an action of the thing that ceases. It is, rather, the end of all states and actions for a particular subject. And likewise, the loose way of talking about being better off dead can be replaced by stricter discourse that more accurately depicts the situation. What is to be asserted is not that one exists and is in a certain state, a state of being dead that is superior to the state of living, but rather that not existing at all is preferable to existing in the burdensome condition that grounds the judgment.

In any event, if there were a logical problem with the judgment that a person would be better off dead, it could be circumvented by reformulating the question: instead of asking whether a person might be better off dead, we could ask whether there are situations in which life might not be choice-worthy. Might it be rationally preferable for you not to exist than to exist in certain situations of extreme suffering (assuming there is no God)? Here is a particular circumstance to consider: you are trapped in a burning building, pinned under a fallen girder, at the top of a tower that the fire fighters cannot reach. Who would want to live ten minutes longer if the ten minutes are to be spent roasting to death amidst flames? Why do firefighters hope that if they die in a fire it will be not by flames, but by asphyxiation? And why is it sometimes so reassuring to be told that an accident victim "died instantly"? We may simply stipulate that to say an individual would be "better off dead" is to say that for that individual, in the given circumstances, nonexistence would be preferable to existence.

Of course, one who believes in a revelation of a providential God has some basis for thinking that human lives at every moment retain significance, and perhaps the greatest significance in the most trying circumstances. As portrayed in the *Phaedo*, Socrates thought that he would be better off dead, since his soul would then be free of the body weighing it down. Nonetheless, since he was the property of superior beings, the gods, he was not free to decide to terminate his earthly life.[6] Religious believers in the great monotheistic traditions may dare hope for more than Socrates expected from an afterlife, and may have deeper objections than his to suicide.

6. Plato, *Phaedo*, 62C.

But Premise 2 says that we are to leave God out of the picture in judging whether there are individuals and circumstances such that nonexistence is rationally preferable to existence. And when we take God out, it seems clear: in certain situations life is not choice-worthy.[7]

PREMISE 3: If there are times when nonexistence is rationally preferable to existence unless there is a God, then suicide, that is, intentionally killing one's innocent self, is sometimes morally permissible unless there is a God.

Like Premise 2, Premise 3 seems plausible after just brief reflection on the possibility of being trapped in desperate circumstances, where death will inescapably follow on unimaginable suffering. With Premise 3, like Premise 2, the burden of proof is on one who would reject the premise.

On what basis might Premise 3 be rejected?

It is relatively easy to find counterexamples to the claim that suicide is always permissible in situations where an individual is suffering gravely (i.e., relatively easy to find counterexamples when we leave God out of the picture). Suicide may not be an option because self-destruction may be unjust to others, family members whose livelihood depends on your not doing yourself in, for instance. But that possibility does not show Premise 3 to be false. For there are surely circumstances in which suicide does no one else an injustice and in which life is not choice-worthy. It is only in these circumstances that we properly say nonexistence is rationally preferable to existence (unless there is a God).

There are, of course, philosophers who have held that suicide is always wrong, no matter what horrendous suffering must be borne in the alternative. But it is sometimes far from evident how the arguments for the position are supposed to go, much less that the arguments are sound, much less that they successfully avoid appeal to a supernatural order. In Section II we will comment on some of these arguments. For now we reiterate that the burden of proof appears to be on the party that *rejects* Premise 3.

---

7. The list of objections to pronouncing that someone would be better off dead could be extended. Jorge Garcia offers a particularly interesting objection. See J. L. A. Garcia, "Are Some People Better Off Dead? A Reflection," *Logos: A Journal of Catholic Thought and Culture* 2, no. 1 (1999): 68-81. But we need to stop somewhere. We would only emphasize what we have referred to above, that the existential reality here is that there are circumstances where people think nobody in his right mind would want to remain alive: standing in flames and burning to a crisp. That is a definition of hell.

PREMISE 4: If suicide is sometimes morally permissible unless there is a God, then it is also sometimes permissible intentionally to kill an innocent person unless there is a God.

This we understand to be true in virtue of the definitions of the terms involved: the person committing suicide intentionally kills himself or herself, and (barring exceptional circumstances) is innocent, in the sense in which we use that term.

PREMISE 5: If it is sometimes permissible intentionally to kill an innocent person unless there is a God, then it is sometimes permissible intentionally to kill an innocent person when it is against that person's will, unless there is a God.

There is no good reason why people must actually go through great suffering before they have a right to kill themselves. If it is permissible for you to kill yourself while, and because, you are undergoing great suffering, on the grounds that in these circumstances nonexistence is rationally preferable to existence, then the prospect of great and unavoidable suffering should be enough. The focus once again must be on what is rational. If you do nothing wrong by taking a suicide pill when you are trapped in a burning tower and have nearly passed out from the pain of the fire, why is it wrong to take the pill when the pain is beginning, before it becomes horrendous, given that all available evidence suggests there can be no rescue? It is rational and permissible to take your own life, assuming your suicide treats nobody else unjustly (and assuming there is no God).

Furthermore, if it is sometimes permissible to kill yourself to avoid *your* going through great agony (followed by death), why is it not also acceptable to kill yourself to prevent *others* from suffering greatly and dying? Again, the focus should be on what is rational. People have killed themselves for altruistic reasons when they are part of a stranded group without sufficient food for all. And sometimes individuals fleeing a brutal enemy have committed suicide when their age or infirmity impedes their companions' escape. In these cases it might even be argued that there is a *duty* to take one's life. That is, it's the reasonable thing to do: it's what serves the common good. Notice that in such cases it is typically far from certain that without the suicides the remaining group members will suffer agony and death; it is enough, in the eyes of those who sacrifice themselves, that death by starvation, or death by hand of a brutal enemy, is a real possibility.

And if it is rational and hence acceptable to kill yourself in these situations, acceptable, that is, to save others in grave peril, can we not imagine instances where it is rational, and hence permissible, to take the life of an unwilling innocent to spare others, perhaps many others, death — or some other horrendous fate? Men and women who volunteer for military service may be expected to undertake missions that almost certainly will lead to their death. At the time the mission comes up, they may change their minds. Maybe they have just developed a carefully worked-out argument that the war they are fighting is unjust; maybe they are simply, and understandably, filled with panic at the thought of the assigned mission. They are unwilling to go, but we force them to go anyway. Is there not a rational case behind our insistence that they obey the order to march? Countries that conscript military service *also* force the nonvolunteer soldiers to put themselves in the way of great harm and death. In the name of the common good, we ask the ultimate sacrifice. When the terrorists require it, why may we not draw lots to pick an innocent individual, and hand that person over to be executed?

Take one final example illustrating the point that it may sometimes be rational to set aside any expectation of *consent* to destruction. Imagine that a group of terrorists hold hostage a city's children (perhaps the terrorists have taken control of all the schools). The terrorists have a record of doing exactly what they say they will: they make good on their threats; they keep their promises. They have promised to release the children if one parent shoots himself, commits suicide in front of a TV camera. Otherwise, the terrorists will incinerate the schools and the children. A parent volunteers. To assure his compliance, the terrorists require that several more individuals hand themselves over; they are to be released once the voluntary sacrifice has been effected. At the last minute, the volunteer panics. He agrees it is right and rational for him to proceed with the suicide, but he cannot bring himself to do it, and he doesn't want anyone else to kill him either. The terrorists say, "Either the rest of you shoot the parent who volunteered, or we will douse the adult hostages with gasoline and burn them along with all the schoolchildren." Would it really be wrong to shoot the parent who initially volunteered, but who has now changed his mind and no longer consents?

But are there not classic arguments against intentionally killing an innocent person against that person's will? There are some historically important arguments here, Thomistic arguments, for instance, and Kantian arguments.[8] For our present purposes, the point to note about the arguments is

8. See, for instance, Aquinas, *Summa Theologiae,* II. II q. 64. Kantian arguments often

this: if they succeed, they not only rule out intentionally killing an innocent against that individual's will; they *also* rule out suicide.

PREMISE 6: If it is sometimes permissible intentionally to kill an innocent person against that person's will unless there is a God, then a secular case that it is necessarily impermissible cannot be made out.

The truth of premise 6, we assume, is obvious, given that we have stipulated that a "case" is an argument that adequately justifies the claim at issue. The overall conclusion of our "suicide argument" then follows: A secular case cannot be made out for fundamental absolute rights.

II

OBJECTION: There are time-honored and perfectly adequate secular arguments for the conclusion that it is never permissible intentionally to kill the innocent.

As we see it, neither Kantian ethics nor the "new natural law theory" popularized by Joseph Boyle, John Finnis, Germain Grisez, and others can provide an acceptable secular argument for the claim that murder, intentional killing of the innocent, is always impermissible. As we have elsewhere argued, it is not even clear exactly how the arguments are supposed to run, and the premises require defense that is often not forthcoming.[9] And one cannot go very far in an exploration of these theories without recognizing what the proponents of the theories fairly straightforwardly acknowledge (though strangely, the admissions drop out of the popular picture): these classic ethical theories are *not* purely secular. "Morality," Kant says, "thus inevitably leads to religion."[10] And Grisez, Boyle, and Finnis are very explicit

---

take as their ground some form of the categorical imperative, but Kant also offers this consideration: "Man can only dispose of things; beasts are things in this sense; but man is not a thing, not a beast." It certainly follows that murder is wrong. But then it also follows, just as Kant says: "If he disposes of himself, he treats his value as that of a beast. He who so behaves, who has no respect for human nature makes a thing of himself." Immanuel Kant, *Lectures on Ethics*, trans. L. Infield (London: Methuen, 1930), p. 151.

9. Menssen and Sullivan, *The Agnostic Inquirer,* chap. 5, sec. 5.4.

10. Immanuel Kant, *Religion within the Boundaries of Mere Reason,* trans. and ed. Allen Wood and George di Giovanni (Cambridge, UK: Cambridge University Press, 1998), p. 35.

about the point in their summary statement of twenty-five years of work together on natural-law theory:

> As a theory of some of the principles of human action, what we offer here presupposes many theses of metaphysics and philosophical anthropology — for example, that human intelligence is irreducible to material realities . . . that human persons and their actions are caused by an uncaused cause, and so on.[11]

It is a puzzling thing that it is commonly assumed that the Christian tradition is foursquare behind the notion that absolute rights are grounded in nature. In fact, the tradition is anything but crystal clear on that point. Grisez, Boyle, and Finnis represent what gets called the "new" natural-law theory. What about the "old" natural-law theory? Where does Aquinas stand on the point? Aquinas defines natural law as a participation in the eternal law: his entire discussion of natural law indicates a theistic backdrop. This hardly puts us in the realm of secular ethics. There is a large body of literature that attempts to show that this reference to the divine in Aquinas need not or should not be seen as a commitment to the proposition that the natural law is unintelligible without reference to God. Whether or not this kind of bracketing of God can be made out for Aquinas's position when he is talking about natural law, it appears to be impossible to read him in that key when taking into account his discourse on the "old law," which he construes as a representation of the natural law. For at the bottom of the old law lie the two interconnected foundational principles: "love God" and "love your neighbor."[12]

Someone may object that our "old" natural-law theory isn't old enough; someone may object that we need to go back to Aristotle, who lays a foundation on which Aquinas and other natural-law theorists build, a framework that does not invoke the Judaeo-Christian theistic tradition. Let us consider whether Aristotelian concepts might generate a secular argument that it is always wrong to intentionally kill the innocent.

11. Germain Grisez, Joseph Boyle, and John Finnis, "Practical Principles, Moral Truth, and Ultimate Ends," *The American Journal of Jurisprudence* 32 (1987): 100 (this definitive statement of their position is found on pp. 99-151).

12. Because Aquinas asserts that these principles are self-evident, either to reason or to faith, the principles are quite clearly functioning as axioms, in the old sense of *evident, justifiable justifiers.* See Aquinas, *Summa Theologiae* I, II q. 100, a. 3 corpus.

Inspired by Aristotle's comments in the *Nicomachean Ethics* that the very names of certain kinds of actions imply wrongdoing, some maintain that there clearly are universal prohibitions known to hold or obtain — that is, to be valid. Aristotle speaks here of murder (among other things). Some might think that by definition murder just is wrongful killing: therefore, murder is always wrong. We concede of course that if that is the view adopted, then there are universal prohibitions that are knowable. It is knowable that murder (defined as wrongful killing) is always wrong. But what is not knowable is whether anything falls under the concept of murder. That is to say, it would not automatically follow from (a) murder is always wrong, that (b) undertaking to bring it about that an innocent person be dead will always count as murder in the defined sense. And so this does nothing to take care of the substantive problem with regard to killing, which can be worded without reference to murder by asking: Is it always wrong to intentionally bring it about that an innocent person be dead? Is *this* always wrongful killing, and thus murder in the specified sense?

Here an analogy may help. Consider two groups that have for centuries been at each other's throats, the A's and the B's. The A's have come to think that the B's are by definition ***, or *!*, or !!!. They have no language except epithets for the B's. So one of the A's could argue, "Don't you see, the words we use to denigrate the B's condemn them?" But of course the outsider says: "Look, *we* can identify the B's without using your epithets. They live *here,* come from *there,* have such-and-such associations, have been at war with you for centuries, and so on." And the outsider can follow up with the question, "Are these epithets really deserved?" This is certainly a question that the A's cannot avoid by hurling epithets at the outsider, the inquirer, and saying, "This is how we talk."

There's a more sophisticated objection along the same direction that can be made to our position. It's not by definition of terms, the objection goes — not by reason of the surface definition of the expressions "murder" or "adultery" — that the actions of murder and adultery are condemned. Our above reply to that view is correct. What really should be said, according to this objection, is that if you understand the underlying, the "real" definition of the action of murder (let us say), then you'll see that it carries this property of being wrong. It's inferable somehow from the combination of universals involved. For example, consider the properties of gold. It is not by definition that the outer electrons of atoms of gold are tightly bound to the nuclei (making gold highly resistant to corrosion): that isn't what people *mean* by "gold." But if you understand what protons and neutrons are, you have the requisite concepts. You'll see that the electrons *must* be held tight to the nucleus of an atom of gold, given that an atom of gold has as many protons as it does. So, to put it a little more abstractly and technically, if you grasp the *essence* of gold, you'll have grasped that it has to have the consequent property of having tightly bound electrons, and you'll have grasped this through an immediate intuition into the connection between the properties of having a massive nucleus of protons, and binding the electrons.

Enlarging this point, some offer a sophisticated Aristotelian idea that is drawn this time not from his *Ethics* but from his logical works, in particular his *Posterior Analytics,* where Aristotle talks about possible interconnections between the universals in a proposition where both subject and predicate are universals. In one way, technically referred to as "the first mode of perseity" (*per se* = through itself), the predicate is contained in the essence designated by the subject. To illustrate, we might say that in the case of gold, it would mean that, not by surface definition but by scientific "real" definition, gold has the property of having electrons in its orbits. So one might say, "Of course gold has electrons in its orbits," and if you know what gold is, you can say that it obviously does have electrons in its orbits, not obviously because you can say that's what the word means as people use it when they are shopping for jewelry, but having electrons in its orbit is a constituent of the essence of the thing articulated by such expressions as "having the atomic mass 196.96655 amu."[13]

But Aristotle discusses a second mode of perseity, which forms the basis of the sophisticated objection we are now considering.[14] We introduce it

13. The Aristotelian notion of perseity in the first mode has kinship here with the Kantian idea of analytic definition, where the predicate is contained in the subject. In both cases the idea is that, should the subject of the proposition be understood properly, it will be understood that it includes the predicate, as in the case of the proposition "A cube is an extended object." Obscurities attend both the Aristotelian and Kantian formulations, though Aristotle appears to see more clearly that the first mode of perseity can be understood in two ways. As he notes, it is often the case that the trait indicated by the predicate expression belongs to the essence of what is pointed to by the subject expression, but that the connection is not understood. For example, "Gold is composed of protons" is *per se* in the first mode, even though centuries ago nobody knew this. Still, the connection is there, and so the proposition is said to be *per se* (in the first mode) *in itself.* If, however, we can readily determine the connection between the subject and predicate, the proposition is said to be *per se* (in the first mode) in relationship to us. That is how it is with the example of a cube.

14. This objection has been pressed by our colleague Gary M. Atkinson.

with one of Aristotle's examples. He points out that it is evident that every integer is either odd or even. The proposition is necessary, and perspicuously so. However, and this is what distinguishes it from propositions in the first mode, the definition of "integer" — not just the surface definition but the real definition that penetrates to its essence — falls short of including anything about odd or even. The fact that every integer is odd or even follows from the definition; it's not packed into it. However, if you shift your glance from the subject to the predicate, and think about being odd or even, you see that, in the relevant sense of "odd" or "even," only integers can be such. This is to say, then, what the predicate expression designates — the property of being odd or even — by definition includes the subject. For you won't understand the requisite sense of odd or even unless you see that it is tied to integers (after all, you could think we were talking about odd people if you didn't refer oddness to numbers). So, more generally, the idea of the second mode of perseity is, in contrast to the first, that while you work from the interconnection of the universals expressed in the subject and predicate, the guarantee of a necessary connection comes not from the inclusion of the predicate in the definition of the subject, but the other way around.

To return to our ethical objection, the idea here would be that if you think about something such as murder or adultery, you can *see* that the action is always wrong, you can intuit it, not because wrongness is included in the definition of murder or adultery, but because wrongness by definition can only be understood as attached to a certain kind of subject, such as murder or adultery, just as "odd" and "even" can only be attached to a certain kind of subject — integers. When we say "murder is wrong," there is a necessary definitional connection running from predicate to subject; thus it's not analytic in Kant's sense, but necessary and perspicuous nonetheless, at least to those who can penetrate to the essence of the acts (murder and adultery) in a fashion analogous to penetrating to the essence of gold. And this is the best understanding of Aristotle on these topics, the objector will say (and might actually be right). Aristotle is not saying that adultery, by surface definition of the term, is wrongful sexual congress by a married person with somebody else's spouse; rather, he's saying that sexual congress between a married person and somebody else's spouse is definitionally connected in the second mode, and that's why the name picks up the connotation of wrongfulness.

In response to this objection, we'd say first that it's easy to supply a decisive counterexample to the main claim underpinning the objection, if the claim is that the definition of the predicate guarantees the necessary truth of the proposition and perspicuous access to it by those in possession of the relevant concepts. We don't deny that in some cases there are such a necessity and such access. The very example that Aristotle offers about odd and even is such. However, it's a special case, and carefully chosen. Notice, for one thing, that it is a disjunctive predicate, which carries you right back to the principle of non-contradiction. Given that you're dealing with integers, it's quite clear that a particular integer is either divisible by two or not: even if so, odd if not. So for anybody who understands "integer," "divisible," and "two," the proposition is immediately evident, and in the second mode. But it's clearly a special case, and you can see that it is by considering a counterexample. Consider the assertion: "Every curve has two tangents at any arbitrarily selected point on the curve." This is false, and necessarily false. Nonetheless, the definition of the predicate makes mention of the subject: "tangent at every point of the curve" mentions "curve." So it does not follow from the fact that a proposition is *per se* in the second mode that it is even true, let alone necessarily true, let alone perspicuously so. Anyone who has doubts about the universal properties of certain acts, such as adultery and murder, can say, "Maybe there is some second mode of connection here, but the mere possibility doesn't secure what you need to secure."

There's another point to be made here, a very important point. If you look more carefully at the claim that the wrongfulness of these actions is *per se* in the second mode, you see that that simply is not correct. For the definition of "wrong," or "impermissible," or whatever condemnatory expression one wishes to use, does not mention specific acts such as adultery and murder. Someone (maybe a child) can grasp the concept "wrong," its very essence, without having any conception whatever of adultery. So it's not the case that the definition runs backwards from "wrong" to "adultery" the way it runs backwards from the concept "odd" or "even" to "integer."

What it runs backwards to is open to philosophic dispute. One can say that the wrongness by definition attaches to, in Aristotelian terms, deviation from a mean, as suggested in the context of the earlier cited text in the *Nicomachean Ethics* (the names "adultery" and "murder" by definition imply wrongfulness). One could also say, and this comports with some things Aristotle and Kant say, that wrongfulness attaches to irrationality in the conduct of one's agency. Or again, one could say, invoking Kant's second formulation of the categorical imperative, that wrongfulness attaches to any action that fails to take into account the special character of rational beings.

What, then, of the business of adultery and murder? They can be condemned as universally wrong only because they are seen to fall under the proper subject, whatever it is, that wrongfulness attaches to in the second mode of perseity: for example, murder could be seen to be wrong if and only if murder in all circumstances intrinsically fails to respect the demands of human nature. So the point about murder and adultery is derivative: in other words, you need an argument to show that the actions in question fall under the requisite concept in the subject. The issue then becomes: Is it in fact the case that these actions always offend human dignity when one takes into account the prospect of calamity for the entire race if something injurious to one member isn't done? Again, it takes an argument. And the argument cannot simply be that the proposition is in the second mode of perseity. That gets us exactly nowhere.

It may be said that the proper subject, the subject wrongfulness attaches to in the second mode of perseity, is "disgusting and degrading acts," and that a reasonable person of good will and proper philosophical formation will simply see, unaided by argument, that those who are willing intentionally to kill an innocent person are, *eo ipso,* willing to perform disgusting, degrading acts. And, the line continues, it is possible to set out considerations (an argument, in fact) that should be sufficient to persuade a reasonable person of good will who lacks the proper philosophical formation. The argument is an argument against consequentialism: a resolve to maximize the greatest good for the greatest number may result in a situation where you must kill and eat your close relatives (to avoid some catastrophe).[15] If you don't see that you shouldn't be the kind of person who eats his or her relatives, then so much the worse for you.

In response, we can offer two points. First, our position does not commit us to consequentialism (even if there is no God), not directly, not without other assumptions that we are not prepared to make. It is perfectly intelligible to put family and tribe before the common good; that is simply what most of the race has done through history. Second, suppose one admits that he or she will have to do disgusting things. Many disgusting things are such that everyone acknowledges they need to be done: changing diapers, manuring the farm field, cutting open a person's stomach to remove a tumor. It

15. Atkinson develops such an argument in "What Else Could I Do? The Self-Definition of Consequentialists," *Logos: A Journal of Catholic Thought and Culture* 4, no. 3 (2001): 204-14.

may be replied that these things are not disgusting in the relevant sense, that is, they are not *morally* disgusting. But then the question is being begged. "Don't do morally disgusting things" can hardly be a premise of an argument, when the very issue is whether, without appeal to God, such-and-such would be wrong.

Let us summarize by reiterating key points, this time with Jefferson rather than Aristotle in mind. Notice what Jefferson has to be maintaining when he claims, "We hold these truths to be self-evident," if by "self-evident" he means anything like "obvious to most rational adults": that by surface definition of a human being, there is a notion of some sense of created equality of each. This is manifestly false. Certainly one can understand what a human being is, how to use the term, without even thinking of a creator, let alone endowment with equality by a creator. If Jefferson had in mind a more penetrating sense of "human being," where you grasp its essence, it is still not the case that the definition would refer to equality, any more than the real definition of "integer" would refer to "odd" or "even." Or, to bring the example closer to what we are talking about, any more than the definition of "two" would include "equality with the cubed root of eight."

Therefore, we are left with the idea that Jefferson's dictum is *per se* in the second mode, where the definition of "created equality" refers to rational being. And we are left with the problem brought up in connection with tangents. Created equality, in the relevant sense, only refers to rational beings (though it might be said that members of a certain species of minnows have a kind of created equality). But there's no guarantee that every member of the human species would share in this created equality just by reason of the fact that the Jeffersonian principle is *per se* in the second mode. That is the moral of the story about tangents. Let it be stipulated that every member is in fact created equal. Suppose this is true by virtue of members sharing the property of being a human being, however defined — for example, "rational animal." Of course, this would require that the overarching proposition "all rational animals are created equal" be true, and necessarily so — and, for the immediate purposes, perspicuously necessary. But of course it is not, despite Jefferson's table-thumping. The great majority of human beings have thought other humans were not equal. At a minimum, one needs to penetrate to the essence of human beings, as one must penetrate to the essence of gold, to see what ensues. And it is by no means obvious without argument that the essence connotes some foundational equality, let alone the conferral of fundamental rights by a creator on members of the species.

In fact, mention of a conferral of the right implies that the possession of absolute rights comes about through an extrinsic cause. The rights spring not from the human essence alone, but from a contingent endowment by a creator. And to this extent we can agree with Jefferson that absolute rights depend on an endowment, while disagreeing with Jefferson — and the proponents of the objection we have been examining — that somehow the status of these rights turns out to be perspicuously necessary.

OBJECTION: Assuming non-consequentialist secular arguments for an absolute prohibition against intentionally killing the innocent fail, the suicide argument points in a very different direction than the one imagined, for there are serious problems with the "divine-command" theories that constitute the alternative to secular ethical theories: consequentialism is the only real choice left (which — some, though not all, objectors would add — is really not so bad a thing as is imagined).

Some divine-command theories are, we agree, problematic. We certainly would reject a theory holding that God can command anything at all, including cruel or awful or crazy actions, and that the recipients of the commands are thereby bound by the commands. But there are more sophisticated versions of divine-command theories, and it is far from evident that they all fail.

In any event, it is a mistake to think that the only nonsecular or theistic ethical theories available are divine-command theories, accounts of morality that root the rightness or wrongness of an act directly in divine commands. Our own preference would be for what might be called a "divine-ordination theory." On this account, God has structured reality in such a way that there exist rational creatures standing in certain relationships to one another and to their creator, and at least some of what is permissible or impermissible is grounded in this structure, whether or not God adds "do this" or "don't do that" to help inform us of the facts of the matter. True, the divine will or volition shapes the structure of reality; but once that structure is in place, various obligations are thereby in existence. It is possible that an allgood, omnipotent, omniscient God could not create a world like ours without providing for an afterlife in which wrongs are righted, possible that we have a destiny that transcends the natural order. And even if such a God *could* create a world like ours without an afterlife, God did not do so, many theists hold. According to this picture, the standard objection to absolute prohibitions against murder — the objection that adhering to such prohibitions may sometimes have consequences disastrous for humankind — dissolves. For there are no ultimately disastrous consequences, no ultimate catastrophes, if there is a good God who ordains for human beings a supernatural end such as the one promised in major revelatory traditions.

This will not do, the objector may reply. That human beings have absolute rights, such as the right not to be murdered, rests not in the fact that human beings are ordered to God; rather, the key fact is that we are the kind of creatures who *could be* ordered to God.[16] We are creatures with a certain innate dignity, and that dignity roots our absolute rights. That we possess this dignity is a fact determined over our heads, so to speak; but it is a fact about the natural order. No reference to the supernatural is required to explain the fact.

We agree that we are the kinds of creatures who could be ordered to God. We also agree that this is enough to rule out *arbitrary* assaults. But we are calling into question whether any being with this kind of dignity could be assailed by others possessing equal dignity, for the sake of preserving the lives of many who also possess this dignity. It may be *said* that an assault on a person with this dignity is unacceptable even though ultimate catastrophe may result; but it is very difficult to know where the rule is supposed to come from. It's not obvious, and it is doubted by many. We are suggesting that a grounding for the precept is necessary, and that the only adequate ground is theistic. Notice, too, that while it is said that we are "orderable" to God, the deeper point is that we have an intrinsic dignity. Talk of "orderability to God" is just a way of putting this point. It may in one respect be a helpful way of stressing that we have an inherent dignity; but it can carry the misleading suggestion that the existence of God is an essential ingredient of the description of our dignity. Presumably, the person who makes the objection wants to say that even if there were no God, we'd remain what we are. So the position collapses into the second formulation of Kant's categorical imperative: humans must all be respected because of their humanity.

Perhaps, on the account of divine ordination we are envisioning, it is open to God *not* to give a command against suicide and, more generally, intentionally killing the innocent. But we can see something of why God might give the command: there are no ultimate catastrophes in a world created by an all-powerful, all-knowing, and perfectly good deity. God may, in giving the command, make our lives harder than they would have to be, but not

---

16. This objection comes from our colleague John D. Kronen.

without reason, just as parents may make heavy demands on their children — to secure for them great goods. Lesser demands could be made, but the better way involves the greater demands.[17]

Therefore, we reject the first part of the objection presented above. There is, in fact, a non-consequentialist alternative to non-consequentialist secular ethical theories. And this alternative is worth exploring.

Sometimes our argument has occasioned a response such as this: "There must be something wrong with what you're saying, because what you've done is give an argument for consequentialism, and everybody knows consequentialism cannot be right." We have given an argument for consequentialism only if theistic moral theories are ruled out of bounds, of course. But we agree that if that ruling is accepted, the suicide argument is a powerful argument for consequentialism.

And why should this be so surprising, especially to theistic philosophers, who, in our experience, resist the line of argument we've set out every bit as vehemently as do agnostics and atheists? Removing axioms from a mathematical system will curtail what can be derived. (For example, in what is called "neutral geometry," which is Euclid's geometry without the parallel postulate, a good number of Euclid's theses cannot be deduced.) Removal of foundational ideas of theism and Christianity should be expected to limit the moral "theorems" that can be derived. If there is, in fact, a creator who ordains us for a supernatural end, can that really be irrelevant to ethics? As Elizabeth Anscombe has pointed out in her classic discussion of modern moral philosophy, philosophers sometimes unconsciously cling to a nonsecular conception of law even as they kick out the religious underpinnings; but over time, as they detach themselves from the religious traditions, they do come to believe less and less in inalienable rights.[18]

After all, if the foundations of ethics are theological, it does not follow that secular ethics (in other words, philosophical ethics, ethics that refrains

17. Obviously, this notion of divine ordination theory requires explication. We have attempted to explain it a little more fully, and respond to some obvious objections, including objections modeled on standard criticisms of divine command theories, in Menssen and Sullivan, *The Agnostic Inquirer*, chap. 5, secs. 5.4.4 and 5.5.5. But much more work on the idea is needed.

18. G. E. M. Anscombe, "Modern Moral Philosophy," originally published in 1958, reprinted in *The Collected Philosophical Papers of G. E. M. Anscombe*, Vol. III: *Ethics, Religion and Politics* (Minneapolis: University of Minnesota Press, 1981), pp. 26-42.

from appeal to revelation) is anything less than terribly important. Philosophy illuminates problems faced by secular ethical theories such as relativism and at least some forms of utilitarianism. And philosophy clarifies and adjudicates issues in revealed ethics. And, though an absolute prohibition against murder may be indefensible on purely philosophical grounds, much of philosophical ethics may remain in place: the ethical principles Aristotle defends, for instance, and perhaps much of what Kant says about ethics, and perhaps most of natural-law theory as well. Finally, philosophy clarifies its own limits: the argument of this essay is philosophical, though it is an argument for an ethics that extends beyond pure philosophy.

The objection we set out at the beginning of this section forks. Some objectors who see our argument as pointing toward consequentialism find that to be an appalling result; others see consequentialism as unobjectionable. Why think that we must jump to the ship of theism, they ask, to escape the fate of consequentialism? The fate is not so bad. Now this reaction is not an objection to the soundness of the suicide argument itself; rather, it anticipates an argument we have not spelled out here in detail. Or, if you will, it comments on the significance of the conclusion of our suicide argument.

Our sentiments are with those chilled by the prospect of consequentialist ethics. Consequentialism requires radical changes in our worldview. And while some of the philosophers Anscombe had in mind, who have become less and less attached to inalienable rights, may be making the radical changes, many will be resistant. The choice we face here is starkly presented by consequentialist Kai Nielsen, who writes in *Ethics Without God* that, with respect to torturing and killing the innocent in acts of terrorism, "there are circumstances when such violence must be reluctantly assented to or even taken to be something one, morally speaking, must do."[19] In those scenarios, terrorism and murder become not just options but obligations.

Even philosophers who have *argued* for the claim that the absolute prohibition against murder does not hold, that it must be set aside under circumstances in which calamity appears imminent, have difficulty embracing the claim. Consider Michael Perry, who argues at some length that it is not possible to find purely philosophical arguments for the conclusion that there are absolute human rights, but then concludes that "[t]he much more important point is practical, not theoretical: Even if *no* human rights are, as moral rights, absolute, *some* human rights, as international legal rights, should be —

19. Kai Nielsen, *Ethics Without God*, 2nd ed. (Buffalo, NY: Prometheus, 1990), p. 132.

and, happily, are — absolute."[20] Our laws need to protect us from our philosophy. But it is not a stable equilibrium: one side or the other will change.

We are heartened that not all contemporary agnostic and atheistic philosophers opt to discard the absolute prohibition against murder, against intentional killing of the innocent. Thomas Nagel gives a superb beginning explanation of why terrorism is wrong:

> The core moral idea is a prohibition against *aiming* at the death of a harmless person. Everyone is presumed to be inviolable in this way until he himself becomes a danger to others; so we are permitted to kill in self-defense, and to attack enemy combatants in war. But this is an exception to a general and strict requirement of respect for human life. So long as we are not doing any harm, no one may kill us just because it would be useful to do so. This minimal basic respect is owed to *every* individual, and it may not be violated even to achieve valuable long-term goals.[21]

Nagel rejects consequentialism and embraces the exceptionless precept "never murder." The question is, why is every human being owed the basic respect enshrined in the precept? Nagel's answer to the question "what is wrong with terrorism?" is fine as far as it goes — indeed, it is laudable as far as it goes — but it is not complete. Chemists' explanations do not go as far as do physicists' explanations, do not go far enough to give a complete account of reality. Nor do secular explanations of the inalienable right to life go far enough. They are woefully inadequate for supporting exceptionless precepts. Revealed ethics can ground respect for every human being in the structure of a world created by a loving God, who ordains that our own end is intertwined with love of one another and love of God. Such love is inconsistent with murdering each other, even in the most extreme circumstances, where from an earthly vantage point it may appear that, unless we target the innocent, all will be lost. All will not be lost if God is in charge. There are no ultimate catastrophes in a world made by a good God.

---

20. Michael J. Perry, *The Idea of Human Rights: Four Inquiries* (Oxford: Oxford University Press, 1998), p. 106.

21. Thomas Nagel, "What Is Wrong with Terrorism?" in Louis P. Pojman and Lewis Vaughn, eds., *The Moral Life*, 3rd ed. (New York: Oxford University Press, 2007), p. 1004.

Outrageous Evil and the Hope of Healing:
Our Practical Options

Jerry L. Walls

I

One of the most distinctively human things about us is our sense of moral outrage. This sense is rooted in our awareness that there is a profound gap between the way things are and the way they ought to be. The sense of outrage I have in mind goes beyond the fact that we make moral judgments and evaluations. It is a deeply felt conviction that some things, such as the cruel mistreatment of innocent children, are so unspeakably bad that they deserve our severest condemnation. In its most extreme form it can make us feel that the gap between the way things are and the way they ought to be is so wide that reality itself must be indicted.

When moral outrage reaches these proportions, it can intensify the problem of evil to the boiling point, and it can make belief in a God of perfect power and goodness seem utterly implausible for the many who feel the pressure of this problem. If a God with such attributes had created our world, so it is argued, he would not have designed it in such a way that these sorts of outrages could occur. And if, despite all appearances, there is a God responsible for creating our world, our sense of outrage makes clear that our foremost moral obligation is to rebel against him.[1]

---

1. Of course, I have in mind Dostoevsky's character Ivan Karamazov, who focused his argument on the suffering of children.

But often the reaction to horrendous evil goes beyond rebellion to the complete loss of faith. Elie Wiesel no doubt speaks for many who experienced the unspeakable atrocities of the holocaust in these memorable lines.

> Never shall I forget the little faces of the children, whose bodies I saw turned into wreaths of smoke beneath a silent blue sky. Never shall I forget those flames which consumed my faith forever. Never shall I forget that nocturnal silence which deprived me, for all eternity, of the desire to live. Never shall I forget those moments which murdered my God and my soul and turned my dreams to dust.[2]

Wiesel's description of how this experience destroyed his dreams illustrates what Marilyn Adams has recently called "horrendous evils." What makes such evils "so pernicious is their life-ruining potential, their power prima facie to degrade the individual by devouring the possibility of positive personal meaning in one swift gulp."[3]

Moral evil, particularly when it is so brutally heartless and performed at such an overwhelming magnitude as the holocaust, is especially prone to evoke moral outrage. However, natural evil can also seem cruel to the point that it, too, elicits moral protests. The stunning devastation of the 2004 tsunami affected many people that way and provided skeptics with further confirmation of their conviction that our world cannot be the creation of a loving God.[4] Writing in *The New York Times,* David Brooks said that events like this make it clear that we are mere "gnats" in an indifferent universe. "The earth shrugs and 140,000 gnats die, victims of forces far larger and more permanent than themselves."[5] Indeed, the tsunami may well become for this generation the symbol of natural evil that is the counterpart to the holocaust as the symbol of moral evil. The massive scale of these events magnifies the horror of evil and intensifies the outrage toward a world where such things happen.

2. Elie Wiesel, *Night* (New York: Avon, 1969), p. 44.

3. Marilyn Adams, *Horrendous Evils and the Goodness of God* (Ithaca: Cornell University Press, 1999), pp. 27-28.

4. However, Susan Neiman contends that what marks modern consciousness is that the problem of "natural" evil such as the Lisbon earthquake is "utterly different" from moral evil such as the holocaust. See her *Evil in Modern Thought* (Princeton, NJ: Princeton University Press, 2002), pp. 3, 39.

5. Cited in "The Tsunami: Asking the God Question," *The Week* 5 (Jan. 14, 2005), p. 15.

This intense sense that there is something radically wrong with our world, that so many things happen that ought not to happen, is a profound recognition that we and our world are in desperate need of deep healing if our lives are to be fully meaningful. In what follows, I wish to begin by examining more closely the very moral outrage that signals our deep sense that things are askew. For now, I simply want to observe that the legitimacy of moral outrage is often taken for granted by those who deploy evil as a weapon to assault faith in God. That is, it is tacitly assumed that moral outrage has the same significance and meaning regardless of whether or not one believes in a good God, or even whether or not one believes in God at all.

I shall contend that this assumption is far from obvious, and it requires careful scrutiny. To bring this claim into sharper focus, I shall briefly consider four starkly different options with respect to the nature of ultimate reality, and I will then highlight the differences in how each one of these accounts for our sense of moral outrage. To put it another way, we must examine the ontology of outrage in order to assess these matters honestly. To get at this ontology, I want to consider the view that there is no God, the view that God is supremely powerful but not good, the view that God is perfectly good but limited in power, and, finally, the classic view that God is both supremely good and powerful. I shall conclude with some reflections on the distinctive resources that canonical theism offers for addressing horrendous evil and renewing our deepest dreams.[6]

What will emerge is that the meaning and significance of moral outrage varies considerably, depending on our view of ultimate reality, and that the practical implications do as well. We shall see that these beliefs determine not only how seriously we should take our sense of outrage, but also what realistic hopes we have for healing the huge gash that separates the way things are from the way they ought to be. The practical implications I will focus on have to do not only with how we should think about the victims of evil, but also with what realistic hope we have that our efforts to oppose and defeat evil might succeed. A healthy view of evil, I want to suggest, is one that is not only honest in the face of evil but also allows us to retain hope. Denial and despair, by contrast, are unhealthy alternatives to an honest grappling with evil that maintains hope.

---

6. For more on this term, see William J. Abraham, *Canon and Criterion in Christian Theology* (Oxford: Clarendon, 1998).

II

To get a preliminary idea of the argument, reflect on the following statement from C. S. Lewis's spiritual autobiography, which describes his mindset before his conversion. "I was at this time living, like so many Atheists and Antitheists, in a whirl of contradictions. I maintained that God did not exist. I was also angry with God for not existing. I was equally angry with him for creating a world."[7] As this comment suggests, some reactions of anger are profoundly misguided. To be rationally warranted, moral outrage, at least as it is commonly expressed, requires certain beliefs, beliefs that may not in fact be accepted by the one expressing that outrage.

To bring this claim into sharper focus, let us begin with the view that there is no God. The first point to highlight here is that, if this is true, then ultimate reality is amoral. If ultimate reality is matter, energy, and natural laws, and if we — along with our universe — are the products of such impersonal causes, then our moral sentiments have the same origin. Our moral feelings and our tendency to make moral judgments have been produced by a reality that has no such feelings and makes no such judgments. In other words, our moral sensibilities, as well as our other mental and personal faculties, have risen above their source.

Given this shaky pedigree, it is highly doubtful that morality, including our sense of outrage, can have the same status and significance that it has in traditional thought. Naturalists themselves often admit that traditional ideas of moral obligation and objective right and wrong make little sense in a world whose ultimate constituents are matter and energy and whose resources for explanation are physical and biological. For instance, consider the comment of noted naturalist moral philosopher Peter Singer on the implications of explaining our moral principles in such terms: "Far from justifying principles that are shown to be 'natural,' a biological explanation can be a way of debunking what seemed to be eternal moral axioms. When a widely accepted moral principle is given a convincing biological explanation, we need to think again about whether we should accept the principle."[8]

What Singer acknowledges about particular moral judgments and

---

7. C. S. Lewis, *Surprised by Joy* (New York: Harcourt, Brace & World, 1955), p. 115.

8. Peter Singer, "Ethics and Sociobiology," in James E. Huchingson, ed., *Religion and the Natural Sciences: The Range of Engagement* (Fort Worth: Harcourt Brace Jovanovich, 1993), p. 321.

principles applies more broadly to the notion of obligation itself. To whom or to what could we be obligated in a fully naturalistic world? Do we *owe* it to the natural order to behave in a certain way? Does it have the will or the power to hold us accountable if we choose to live selfishly, to deceive and cheat, and moreover, if we have the savvy and resources to avoid getting caught?

Of course, naturalists will insistently remind us that they take morality quite seriously and can account for it in their own terms. A leading spokesman for this view is the Harvard biologist Edward O. Wilson, who believes that the "struggle for men's souls" in this century will be over precisely the issue of the origin of morality. Against the traditional view that morality has a transcendent or supernatural source is the view that morality is a human creation. The essence of this view is that human beings have been genetically disposed over generations of biological evolution to make certain choices: through the process of cultural evolution some of these choices have hardened into laws and obligations. If the predisposition to so choose is strong enough, it is accompanied by the belief that the behavior in question is commanded by God, or in some other fashion required of us in an objective and absolute sense.

It would take us too far afield to pursue the details of this fascinating account of our moral feelings and judgments, but one point is worth emphasizing. According to this account, a crucial factor that gives morality its force over us is the influence of some beliefs that are objectively false, in particular the belief that morality has divine sanctions or some other such objective warrant behind it. In an article written with Michael Ruse, Wilson puts the point quite bluntly: "In an important sense, ethics as we know it is an illusion fobbed off on us by our genes to get us to cooperate."[9] In other words, evolution has wired us to believe morality is objectively binding on us, that we are categorically obligated to take it seriously and to live by its dictates. In reality, there is no such obligation as we are inclined to believe, but the illusion is nevertheless a useful one for it moves us to cooperate and get along with each other.[10] Living by the rules of morality is a mutually ben-

---

9. Michael Ruse and Edward O. Wilson, "The Evolution of Ethics," in Huchingson, *Religion and the Natural Sciences,* p. 310.

10. Of course, not all naturalists would agree that morality is an illusion. Platonists, for instance, and intuitionists would insist that morality is not only objective but self-evident. Utilitarianism is another instance of a naturalist account of objective morality. As Alasdair MacIntyre notes, however, intuitionism and utilitarianism declined into emotivism

eficial thing, generally speaking, and it obviously promotes survival, which is the one sacrosanct value of naturalistic evolution.

The same basic analysis goes for moral outrage for those who accept this account of morality. We have been wired to have this feeling about certain actions, and the disapproval this generates not only discourages such behavior but also moves us to punish it and to empathize with those who are the victims of it. This outrage, it must be emphasized, partakes in the illusory character of ethics that Wilson and Ruse identify. For the outrage stems from the deeply rooted conviction we feel that certain actions are violations in the most profound sense, and that such actions are utterly forbidden on pain of supernatural sanctions.

Next, let us consider the possibility that there is a God who is enormously powerful, powerful enough to create our world, but who is not morally good. Let us assume this God is indifferent to our moral values and judgments, even our most basic ones. Let us assume that such a God does not value our flourishing and happiness and that he is not committed to truth.

Given such a God, it is natural to ask why he would create us to have the moral sensibilities that we do. Here we can only guess. Perhaps God did so because he finds it amusing or takes a certain aesthetic pleasure in our moral expressions. Maybe he has even wired us to believe that he shares our deepest and best moral judgments. God wants us to believe that he values what we call justice, that he is opposed to innocent suffering, and that he can be counted on to support our own efforts in their behalf. But perhaps, in reality, he is indifferent to our idea of justice and is entertained by human misery.

What this points up, I would argue, is that the idea of an amoral God creating humans with the moral sentiments we have is deeply incoherent. A creator who designed us to have such strong feelings about justice and the like, but did not share them himself, would not be amoral, but devious at best. If we were to discover that there actually were such a God, we would be deeply distressed. We would feel deeply deceived and that we were the victims of a perverse delusion. So, given our strong moral valuations, if the one who created us to have them does not share them, the notion that he is morally indifferent is eliminated and we are left with an evil deity.[11]

---

in the twentieth century. See MacIntyre, *After Virtue*, 2nd ed. (Notre Dame, IN: University of Notre Dame Press, 1984), p. 64.

11. It would take us too far afield to argue this in detail here, buy I have done so in "Hume on Divine Amorality," *Religious Studies* 26 (1990): 257-66. The notion of an evil deity

Let us next consider the idea that there is a God of limited power, but who is morally good. He may or may not have created our world, but he does not have sovereignty over it in anything like the traditional sense. Given this view, it is not altogether clear how to describe this God's relationship to the world. If he did not create the world, are God and the world mutually dependent? Did God somehow emerge from the physical world in something like the manner naturalistic evolutionists believe human consciousness emerged? Unlike the previous view, there are variations of this account of God that have been popular in contemporary theology: in some of these variations God is a personal being, but in others it is less clear whether he is or not. Sometimes those who speak of God in these terms seem to think that our human moral sensibilities and inclinations are themselves "God."

For the sake of discussion and in the interest of clarity, let us assume that this God is a personal being who is at least capable of communicating his will to rational creatures such as us humans. Given this assumption, we could describe our moral sensibilities as a reflection of God's own moral nature. That is, our moral intuitions and judgments at their best are a response to what God has proposed to us with the intention of enhancing our lives and the overall beauty of the world. In this sense, we have God's support for our moral efforts and projects to improve the world.

Finally, let us consider the traditional view that there is a God of perfect power and goodness. According to this view, ultimate reality is moral in the strongest sense possible. This world and everything that exists were created and are sustained by a God of perfect love. Humans were created in God's image, and so our moral intuitions and judgments at their best are a reflection of God's very nature. Morality is neither a deceptive delusion wired into us by a devious deity, nor an illusion "fobbed off on us by our genes," but rather one of the best clues we have to understand ultimate reality and the meaning and purpose of our own lives. Morality is as deeply rooted as it could possibly be, for it is grounded in the nature of a being who not only desires that justice and goodness will prevail, but who also has the power and wisdom to ensure that it will.[12]

---

has not often been put forth as a serious option, but one thinker who did so was Marquis de Sade. See Neiman, *Evil in Modern Thought*, pp. 170-96,

12. For a fuller development of this argument, see Jerry L. Walls, *Heaven: The Logic of Eternal Joy* (New York: Oxford University Press, 2002), pp. 161-73, 185-93.

III

The practical ramifications of these various views are perhaps already becoming apparent, so let us turn now to articulate these explicitly. As a preface to this discussion, I want to reflect for a moment on a couple of statements from a writer who challenges the whole enterprise of theodicy. In contrast to the classical attempt to make rational sense of evil, Kenneth Surin urges a "practical theodicy" that seeks to take concrete action to relieve suffering and to do whatever is possible to eliminate it. In contrast to such practical measures, Surin alleges, traditional theodicy may even be immoral, because the attempt to explain how evil is compatible with the existence of God may subtly justify it in a way that makes it seem acceptable. In this sense, the project of theodicy is actually complicit with evil. To emphasize the contrast, Surin cites the view of Johann-Baptist Metz, expressed in this statement: "There can be prayer after Auschwitz because there was prayer in Auschwitz. But, and this is now the crucial question, was there 'theodicy' in Auschwitz? *Could* there have been 'theodicy' in Auschwitz?"[13] Prayer is seen as a practical attempt to cope with evil, whereas theodicy is a theoretical attempt to account for evil in rational terms. In the same vein, Surin quotes Irving Greenberg as follows: "No statement, theological or otherwise, should be made that would not be credible in the presence of the burning children."[14]

Despite Surin's intention, what I think these statements actually show is that it is profoundly misguided to set practical theodicy in opposition to theoretical theodicy. We can see this is in Surin's suggestion that prayer is appropriate after Auschwitz, whereas theodicy is not, which brings to the fore a number of crucial questions. For a start, what must be assumed to make prayer a meaningful activity? Not only must God be a personal being, but God must also be a good being who cares for us. Moreover, God must have the power to help in some way. These are the very claims that the traditional theodicist wants to affirm are compatible with the reality of evil in our world. To deny any of them is to make prayer a profoundly misguided activity, or at best an instinctive visceral utterance or primal cry with no rational content or intention whatever. To appeal to prayer while dismissing these claims as irrelevant is only a pious evasion posing as a higher form of sensitivity to the harsh reality of evil.

---

13. Kenneth Surin, "Taking Suffering Seriously," in Michael L. Peterson, ed., *The Problem of Evil* (Notre Dame, IN: University of Notre Dame Press, 1992), p. 342.

14. "Taking Suffering Seriously," p. 344.

The harsh reality is that all of us have to decide what we shall believe about God in light of the fact that terrible things happen in our world, not only those that are due to horrendous choices by our fellow human beings but also those due to natural forces that are utterly beyond our control. Moreover, what we believe about this most fundamental of all questions has enormous implications for the victims of such tragedies. In particular, what we believe about God determines what kind of hope there may be, if any, that the tragedy that befell them can be rectified. Furthermore, we have to decide what makes the effort to fight against evil worthwhile, and what, if anything, we should do to relieve the suffering of those whose lives have been devastated by tragedies.

What we think about these matters also has significant implications for our own psychological and emotional health. Psychologist Robert A. Emmons notes that there is a rapidly accumulating literature on "stress-induced growth" and that this literature places considerable emphasis on the notion of meaning as crucial for positive change in response to suffering. He notes the irony in the fact that many philosophers have cooled to the topic of the meaning of life, while social scientists have been warming to it and investigating it with fruitful results.

> The scientific and clinical relevance of the personal meaning construct has been demonstrated in the personal well-being literature, in which indicators of meaningfulness predict psychological well-being, while indicators of meaninglessness are regularly associated with psychological distress and pathology. . . . The conclusions that a person reaches regarding matters of ultimate concern — the nature of life and death, and the meaning of suffering and pain — have profound implications for individual well-being.[15]

Emmons goes on to cite psychological studies that support the conclusion that a "religious or spiritual worldview provides an overall orientation to life that lends a framework for interpreting life's challenges and provides a rationale for accepting the challenges posed by suffering, death, tragedy and injustice."[16]

Keeping these points in mind, let us begin by thinking through some

15. Robert A. Emmons, *The Psychology of Ultimate Concerns* (New York: Guilford Press, 1999), p. 145.
16. Emmons, *The Psychology of Ultimate Concerns*, p. 147.

of the implications and practical consequences of the belief that there is no God. First, there is no rational ground to be angry at natural disasters, nor is there any rational target for our outrage. These are merely the product of a natural order that is not only blind but indifferent to the pain and suffering that it causes. Evil in this sense is hardly unexpected in a naturalistic universe, so it does not pose a problem in any sense analogous to the problem it poses for theists. The surprising thing in such a universe is not that there should be extreme pain and destruction, but that creatures should exist who have consciousness and make the sort of moral evaluations we do in response to it. In a naturalist universe there is nothing like God to hear our protests or to care about them. Quarks, gluons, and laws of nature cannot hear our cries of anguish or our expressions of outrage.

Moreover, the amoral nature of ultimate reality is underscored by the naturalistic account of how our universe will likely end. According to most atheistic cosmologists, our universe is destined to expand forever, losing energy and disintegrating as it does until all life is destroyed. Consciousness, love, aesthetic and moral sensibility will be extinguished by the same natural order that accidentally produced them in the first place. According to this view, the sober truth is that all the things that give our lives meaning are temporal, interim products of an order that did not intend them and has no awareness of them and will eventually obliterate them. In the long run, and in the big picture, our efforts on behalf of goodness and justice will vanish without a trace.

Furthermore, our sense of moral outrage about horrendous actions by our fellow human beings is blunted by the claim that morality as it has traditionally been understood is an illusion. I have heard Ruse speak on these matters, and he is often asked how morality can continue to have force if his account of it is true. Isn't it likely that people will see through the illusion, come to recognize their moral feelings as deceptive in some sense, and consequently feel less disposed to respect them and act on them? Ruse dismisses this suggestion as a groundless worry. He replies that our genes are working overtime to keep us in line, so we need not worry that there will be a widespread revolt against morality.

I am much less sanguine than is Ruse about the ability of our genes to keep us in line if it comes to be widely accepted that the deeply ingrained human belief that morality is transcendent is merely an illusion genetically programmed into us by years of biological and cultural evolution. If the only obligation we have to avoid certain behavior is the demand of human law, and if we are not accountable for our choices to a moral source that has transcendent authority, then our whole sense of outrage at those who choose to flout our standards loses much of its edge.

It is an uncomfortable truth that the demands of morality are sometimes at odds with personal gain and even survival. If the dictates of morality are transient sentiments ultimately explained in terms of their survival value for the species, what good reason is there to choose morality over personal advantage for those not inclined to do so? This question is especially urgent in the case of those who gain the power and resources to disdain moral constraints that would protect innocent persons.

Naturalists may try to reason with those who burn children. They may, in their outrage, oppose them with force and may even prevail over them in the battle for survival. But what do they say in the presence of burning and drowning children? Or what do they say later, in the aftermath of such tragedies, to try to make sense of them and to maintain any sort of rational meaning? It is a well-known phenomenon that sometimes people give up their faith in God in response to such unspeakable tragedies. Eventually, however, they must squarely face the implications of this choice. Not only have those who have given up faith in God given up the hope that such evils could ever be rectified to their own satisfaction; they have also consigned those very sufferers to oblivion. To conclude in the presence of a burning or drowning child that there is no God is to conclude that the child has gone up in smoke, or been swept away, never to be heard from again. It is to conclude that the child's death is a monument to the absurdity of life, an emblem of the eventual fate of all who breathe and love and grieve and rage. This conclusion is devastating for the goal of maintaining a positive view of meaning, not to mention the psychological health and well-being to which such meaning is integral.

In short, the practical upshot if there is no God is that moral outrage is in many ways a futile emotion, not only because ultimate reality is indifferent to it, but also because ultimate reality will eventually destroy everything we value most. It makes no sense to be mad at the blind workings of the natural order, and even our revulsion at treacherous human choices is a somewhat illusory product of a system that rewards survival above all.

Now let us consider the practical implications if there is a God of enormous power, who is perverse, if not outright evil. I have in mind here not the dualistic view that there is a good God as well as an evil one battling it out, but instead the view that the only God is an evil one. In this case, it would be altogether understandable to rebel against God. But a moment's reflection makes it clear that such rebellion would be utterly pointless. While we might experience catharsis or personal moral satisfaction from our expressions of rebellion and outrage, such a God would likely view them as amusing rants: the more eloquent and passionate, the better. Maybe he even manipulates our expressions of outrage and our efforts to achieve justice as dramatic fodder in what is for him a dark comedy. Children who are burning or drowning may be fortunate if a more horrific fate does not await them in future worlds. Perhaps the suffering and injustice of this world is merely a warm-up for the torment he has planned for us in future episodes. It is hard to imagine a view of life that could be more demoralizing and meaningless than this. If there is an evil deity who genuinely deserves our rebellion, our lives could not be more tragic and absurd. And our attempts to relieve suffering and promote justice could not be more futile.

Next, let us consider the practical implications of believing in a God who is morally good but limited in power to persuasion and suggestion. In this case, God empathizes with us in our expressions of outrage and supports us morally in our efforts to relieve suffering and promote justice. However, there is no reason to be confident that evil will finally be defeated, nor that the universe can ultimately avoid the fate predicted by naturalistic cosmologists. This God may remember victims of tragic evil, but it is doubtful that there is personal conscious survival beyond the grave. While this view is not as demoralizing as the view that God is evil, it is severely limited in its resources to underwrite hope. This is not to deny that this view has its attractions, not the least of which is that it avoids implicating God in horrendous evil. But in the end it is not clear that this God offers us much more than an optimistic version of naturalism, with its confidence in human creativity and goodwill, can provide.

Finally, let us consider the practical implications of believing the traditional view of classical theism that there is a God who is perfect in power as well as goodness. In the first place, this view assures us that our outrage at evil resonates with the deepest reality of a God who loves us and desires our well-being. Moreover, we can oppose evil and work to relieve suffering and promote justice with the confidence that God not only supports us in our present efforts, but also that he will himself complete the task of defeating evil conclusively and decisively in his coming kingdom. Our efforts, then, are in no way vain or futile, because evil and death are the temporal, transient realities, and love and joy and goodness are the eternal realities that shall forever prevail when death and evil have been destroyed.

In addition to encouraging our moral efforts, this also has profound implications for how we should think about the victims of terrible tragedy. When children are burning at the hands of lawless dictators, it is the worst of all times to silence the claim that there is a God of perfect goodness and power to whom we are all accountable, or to lose confidence in his love for us. Likewise, when children are swept away by the waves of a tsunami, it pays them no honor to conclude that the forces of nature are the ultimate reality, subject to no higher power. To trust that a God of supreme power and love hears the prayers of those who suffer unspeakable horror does, however, honor them. To trust in this way is neither to trivialize nor to show disrespect for their suffering, nor is it in any way to justify the actions of their tormentors. Rather, it is to insist on the continuing significance and dignity of their lives and the power of God to renew and heal them.

This is not to suggest that we know the details of why God allows such horrors to occur, and any theodicy that offers clean-cut answers is likely to seem incredible in the presence of burning or drowning children. In a very real sense, trust in God does not eliminate the problem of evil, but intensifies it. It is precisely because of faith in God's supreme power and goodness that evil seems so out of place in our world. The naturalist, as noted above, has no corresponding reason to find evil surprising or out of place in our universe, nor does anyone who could take seriously the idea of an evil deity. Ironically, however, not to have a problem of evil for these reasons is actually to have a far bigger problem, for in these scenarios evil is normal, if not ultimate in some sense. To a lesser — but still significant — degree, the same is true of those who believe that God is good, but rather limited in power. But for those who believe in a God of perfect love and power, there is indeed something not only profoundly outrageous, but deeply abnormal, about evil and suffering.

The price of "normalizing" evil is a steep one that people should consider carefully. It is to give up the hope of deep healing for ourselves and our universe. Susan Neiman has pointed out this cost for those who come to view events previously understood as evils merely as natural events. "We no longer expect natural objects to be objects of moral judgment, or even to reflect or harmonize with them. For those who refuse to give up moral judgments, the demand that they stop seeking the unity of nature and morality means accepting a conflict in the heart of being that nothing will ever resolve."[17] To accept as irresolvable such a jagged conflict in the heart of being is a heavy cost indeed.

Therefore, trust in a God who can never allow us to normalize evil is a

---

17. Neiman, *Evil in Modern Thought*, p. 268.

two-edged sword. While it intensifies the problem in one sense, it also gives us the most powerful resources to maintain realistic hope in the face of it and to believe the conflict Neiman identifies will be resolved. Such trust gives us reason to take moral outrage utterly seriously as an accurate gauge of the nature of ultimate reality and to believe that the difference between good and evil is profoundly real. We can fight against evil with the confidence that we are not fighting a losing battle against ultimate reality. We can be angry at evil while loving God and trusting in his goodness and love for us.

This fully honest and realistic appraisal of evil is actually a consideration in favor of taking seriously the Christian account of things. For an instance of this, consider William Abraham's autobiographical reflections on how this played a role in his conversion from atheism to Christianity.

> What I found carrying enormous weight was the extent to which Christianity absolutely refused to blunt the reality of evil by denying it, taming it, pushing it to the margins of existence, covering it up cleverly and the like. On the contrary, it took the reality of evil so seriously that evil showed up all over the place when one came to expound and explain its teachings and practices.[18]

Abraham's reference to the "teachings and practices" of Christianity that take seriously the reality of evil points us to the distinctive resources of canonical theism for dealing with this issue. At the heart of these teachings is the claim that Jesus of Nazareth was the incarnation of the Son of God, whose death atoned for our sins. The climax of this story is a stark account of Jesus facing the forces of evil head-on and defeating them at every turn, maintaining love in the face of hatred, forgiveness in the face of treachery and injustice.[19] The brutal nature of Christ's death is an anchor of realism that forever demonstrates that God has encountered evil at its worst and can offer healing for the deepest scars it has inflicted.

Consider the story of Richard Hoard, whose father was a lawyer who was prosecuting a ring of bootleggers. When Hoard was a freshman in high school, he woke one morning to a loud blast that radically altered his life.

---

18. William J. Abraham, "Faraway Fields Are Green," in *God and the Philosophers: The Reconciliation of Faith and Reason* (New York: Oxford University Press, 1994), p. 166.

19. Cf. N. T. Wright, *Evil and the Justice of God* (Downers Grove, IL: InterVarsity Press, 2006), pp. 75-100.

The blast was from a bomb that had been planted in his father's car and instantly killed him when he turned the ignition. Hoard describes how the anger and bitterness from this tragedy contaminated his adolescence and infected all facets of his life. His fragile faith, moreover, was easily destroyed largely because he had a syrupy-sweet picture of Jesus that seemed far removed from the horrors he had experienced. This picture was shattered one evening when he attended a meeting where someone had erected a rough wooden cross with the bark still intact, a vivid contrast to the sanitized brass crosses that often adorn churches. Hoard says: "'A hell of a way to die,' I thought, staring at the tree. 'Nailed up like that.' And suddenly a thought I had never before considered struck me clearly, like a sword piercing my heart: It was real. As real as my own father's murder."[20]

This insight was a crucial turning point for him. He came to see faith in Jesus Christ not as an evasion of the harsh reality of evil, but as an honest way to come to terms with the pain and sickness in his soul that had festered for years. After accepting forgiveness for his own sins, he experienced further emotional and spiritual healing when he was able to forgive his father's murderer and release the anger and bitterness that had crushed his spirit and numbed his soul.[21]

All of this reminds us of the biblical doctrine that we live in a fallen world, a world in which we have significant freedom and where we often fall far short of God's intentions for us. The natural order is implicated in our disobedience and also falls short of what God ultimately intends for his children, when his will shall be done on earth as it is in heaven. In the meantime, as the apostle Paul wrote, the created order groans in anticipation as it awaits the final redemption of its human inhabitants (Rom. 8:18-25).

Paul's emphasis in this text on the redemption of our bodies points up the fact that the Christian hope goes beyond emotional and spiritual healing to embrace the entire cosmos. The ultimate ground of this grand vision of healing, is of course, the resurrection of Jesus.[22] For the Christian, that the

---

20. G. Richard Hoard, *Alone Among the Living* (Athens, GA: University of Georgia Press, 1994), p. 207.

21. For Hoard's account of this, see *Alone Among the Living*, pp. 196-215.

22. In my view, making this claim requires taking seriously the historical evidence for Jesus' resurrection as well as making the relevant philosophical arguments for the supernatural and the possibility of the miraculous. For examples of such argument, see William J. Abraham, *Divine Revelation and the Limits of Historical Criticism* (Oxford: Oxford University Press, 1982); Paul Copan and Ronald K. Tacelli, eds., *Jesus' Resurrection: Fact or Figment?*

man on the cross was the Son of God incarnate is a decisive demonstration not only of the depth of God's love for us, but also that he is intimately with us in our suffering. That he was raised from the dead gives us rational grounds to trust that the worst horrors of this life can be overcome by his creative power and that our hope that life has positive meaning will be fully satisfied. Nicholas Wolterstorff has made this point with passionate eloquence in a comment on the difference it makes in our outlook to believe that Christ was raised from the dead. His words carry a depth of personal conviction: they were written in the context of his own struggles with the problem of evil after the tragic death of his son in a mountain-climbing accident.

> To believe in Christ's rising from the grave is to accept it as a sign of our own rising from our graves. If for each of us it was our destiny to be obliterated, and for all of us together it was our destiny to fade away without a trace, then not Christ's rising but my dear son's early dying would be the logo of our fate.[23]

To take Christ's rising as the logo of our fate is to believe that God has taken decisive action to show us the strength of love. It is to believe that it is there, not in the horrors of natural or human history, that we can best take measure of the reality that is larger and more permanent than ourselves.

Viewing things from this vantage point prevents faith in God's perfect power and love from degenerating into a desperate expedient in the face of not only history's worst horrors but the worst tragedies in our own personal experience. We need not resort to hoping against hope that there is a God greater than evil, or holding on to faith in God because it is the only way to keep our sanity. More than sanity — indeed, psychological and emotional health — is to be found in a view of reality definitively shaped by the doctrines of canonical theism, a view that allows us to face evil not only honestly but in hope that our healing will be complete when the work of redemption has run its full course.[24]

A Debate Between William Lane Craig & Gerd Ludemann (Downers Grove, IL: InterVarsity, 2000); Gary R. Habermas and Antony G. N. Flew, *Resurrected? An Atheist and Theist Dialogue,* ed. John F. Ankerburg (Lanham, MD: Rowman & Littlefield, 2005); Richard Swinburne, *The Resurrection of God Incarnate* (Oxford: Clarendon Press, 2003).

23. Nicholas Wolterstorff, *Lament for a Son* (Grand Rapids: Eerdmans, 1987), p. 92.

24. Thanks to the editors of this volume for helpful comments on an earlier version of this essay.

Bibliography of William J. Abraham's Published Works (1979-2008)

Books

The Divine Inspiration of Holy Scripture. Oxford: Oxford University Press, 1981.

Divine Revelation and the Limits of Historical Criticism. Oxford: Oxford University Press, 1982. Reprint, Oxford Scholarly Classic, 2000.

The Coming Great Revival: Recovering the Full Evangelical Tradition. San Francisco: Harper & Row, 1984.

An Introduction to the Philosophy of Religion. Englewood-Cliffs, NJ: Prentice-Hall, 1985.

The Rationality of Religious Belief: Essays in Honour of Basil Mitchell. Edited with Steven W. Holtzer. Oxford: Clarendon, 1987.

How to Play Theological Ping-Pong: Essays by Basil Mitchell. Edited with Robert Prevost. London: Hodder & Stoughton, 1989.

The Logic of Evangelism. Grand Rapids: Eerdmans; London: Hodder and Stoughton, 1989.

The Art of Evangelism: Evangelism Carefully Crafted into the Life of the Local Church. Sheffield: Cliff College Publishing Company, 1993. Spanish-language edition published in 2000.

Waking from Doctrinal Amnesia. Nashville: Abingdon, 1995.

Unity, Charity and Liberty: Building Bridges Under Icy Waters. Edited with Donald Messer. Nashville: Abingdon, 1996.

Canon and Criterion in Christian Theology: From the Fathers to Feminists.

Oxford: Clarendon Press, 1997. Paperback edition, with new preface, published in 2002.

The Logic of Renewal. London: SPCK; Grand Rapids: Eerdmans, 2003.

John Wesley for Armchair Theologians. Louisville: Westminster/John Knox, 2005.

Crossing the Threshold of Divine Revelation. Grand Rapids: Eerdmans, 2006.

Canonical Theism: A Proposal for Theology and the Church. Edited with Jason E. Vickers and Natalie B. Van Kirk. Grand Rapids: Eerdmans, 2008.

Articles

"Some Trends in Recent Philosophy of Religion," *The Theological Educator* (Spring 1979): 93-103.

"The Concept of Inspiration in Classical Wesleyan Theology." In *Festschrift for Frank Bateman Stanger,* edited by Kenneth Cain Kinghorn, pp. 33-47. Wilmore, KY: Francis Asbury Publishing Company, 1982.

"The Perils of a Wesleyan Systematic Theologian," *Wesleyan Theological Journal* 17 (1982): 23-29.

"Conceptualism," "Episcopacy," and "Monergism." In *Beacon Dictionary of Theology,* pp. 127-128; 186; 344. Kansas City, MO: Beacon Hill Press, 1983.

"Religious Experience and Apologetics," *Journal of The Irish Christian Study Centre* 1 (1983): 84-93.

"Inspiration, Revelation and Divine Action: A Study in Modern Methodist Theology," *Wesleyan Theological Journal* 19 (1984): 38-51.

"Redeeming the Evangelical Experiment," *Theological Students Fellowship Bulletin* 7 (1985): 11-13.

"The Wesleyan Quadrilateral." In *Wesleyan Theology Today: A Bicentennial Theological Consultation,* edited by Ted Runyon, pp. 119-26. Nashville: Kingswood Books, United Methodist Publishing House, 1985.

"Revival and Personal Holiness," *Christian Life* 48 (1985): 24-25.

"On How to Dismantle the Wesleyan Quadrilateral," *Wesleyan Theological Journal* 20 (1985): 34-44.

"Church Growth Theory and the Future of Evangelism," *Journal for the Academy of Evangelism in Theological Education* 2 (1986-87): 20-30.

"Cumulative Case Arguments for Christian Theism." In *The Rationality of Religious Belief: Essays in Honour of Basil Mitchell,* edited with Steven W. Holtzer, pp. 17-38. Oxford: Clarendon Press, 1987.

"Awaiting the Promise." In *Suddenly from Heaven,* edited by Mark Rutland, pp. 4-10. Atlanta: Trinity Foundation, 1988.

"Evangelism, the Language of Zion, and the Human Predicament," *Perkins Journal* 41 (1988): 19-25.

"Intentions and the Logic of Interpretation," *Asbury Theological Journal* 40 (1988): 11-25.

"Predestination and Assurance." In *The Grace of God, the Will of Man,* edited by Clark H. Pinnock, pp. 231-42. Grand Rapids: Zondervan, 1989.

"Oh God! Poor God! The State of Contemporary Theology," *The American Scholar* 57 (1989): 557-63. Also published in *The Reformed Journal* 40 (1990): 18-23.

"Athens, Aldersgate, and SMU: The Place of Evangelism in the Theological Encyclopedia," *Journal for the Academy of Evangelism in Theological Education* 5 (1989-90): 64-75.

"The Epistemological Significance of the Inner Witness of the Holy Spirit," *Faith and Philosophy* 7 (1990): 434-50.

"The State of Christian Theology in North America." In *Great Ideas Today,* pp. 242-86. Chicago: Encyclopedia Britannica, Inc., 1991.

"Is the Language of the Gospel Inherently Sexist?" *Expectations* 1, no. 1 (1992): 4-6.

"The Challenge of the Next Decade of Evangelism: From Assimilation into the Church to Assimilation into the Kingdom," *Expectations* 1, no. 2 (1992): 3-6.

"Renewal in Evangelism: The Anglican Scene in England," *Expectations* 1, no. 3 (1992): 5-7.

"Renewal in Evangelism: The House Church Movement in England," *Expectations* 1, no. 4 (1992): 4-6.

"Epistemology, Religious." In *The Blackwell Encyclopedia of Modern Christian Thought,* edited by Alister E. McGrath, p. 156. Oxford: Blackwell, 1993.

"Faraway Fields Are Green." In *God and the Philosophers,* edited by Thomas V. Morris, pp. 162-72. New York: Oxford University Press, 1994.

"The Theology of Evangelism: The Heart of the Matter," *Interpretation* 48, no. 2 (1994): 117-30.

"The Revitalization of United Methodist Doctrine and the Renewal of Evangelism." In *Theology and Evangelism in the Wesleyan Heritage,* edited by James C. Logan, pp. 35-50. Nashville: Kingswood Books, 1994.

"United Methodists at the End of the Mainline," *First Things* 84 (June/July 1998): 28-33.

"C. S. Lewis and the Conversion of the West," *Perspectives: A Journal of Reformed Thought* 10 (January 1995): 12-17.

"Orthodoxy and Evangelism: Observations and Comments on a Recent Conference in the United States," *Sourozh* 60 (1995): 1-14.

"Doctrinal Confession and the Renewal of the Church: The Confessing Movement in the United Methodist Church." An address given at a national gathering of the Confessing Movement within the United Methodist Church in Atlanta, April 28-29, 1995.

"Confessing Christ: A Quest for Renewal in Contemporary Christianity," *Interpretation* 51, no. 2 (1996): 117-29.

"Scripture and Revelation." In *The Blackwell Companion to Philosophy of Religion,* edited by Philip L. Quinn and Charles Taliaferro, pp. 584-90. Malden, MA: Blackwell, 1997.

"Revelation Reaffirmed." In *Divine Revelation,* edited by Paul Avis, pp. 201-15. Grand Rapids: Eerdmans, 1997.

"Terrorism and Forgiveness." In *Reflections on Forgiveness and Spiritual Growth,* edited by Andrew J. Weaver and Monica Furling, pp. 137-48. Nashville: Abingdon Press, 2000.

"Commitment to Scripture." In *Where Shall My Wond'ring Soul Begin? The Landscape of Evangelical Piety and Thought,* edited by Mark A. Noll and Ronald F. Thiemann, pp. 37-44. Grand Rapids: Eerdmans, 2000.

"The Epistemology of Conversion: Is There Something New?" In *Conversion in the Wesleyan Tradition,* edited by Kenneth Collins and John H. Tyson, pp. 175-94. Nashville: Abingdon, 2001.

"'I Can See People, but They Look like Trees Walking': A Response to Professor Webster," *Scottish Journal of Theology* 54 (2001): 238-43.

"A Response to Stanley Grenz," *Wesleyan Theological Journal* 36, no. 2 (2001): 45-49.

"Loyal Opposition and the Epistemology of Conscience," *Asbury Theological Journal* 56 (2001): 135-147.

"From Revivalism to Socialism: The Impact of the Poor on Harry Ward." In *The Poor and the People Called Methodists 1729-1999,* edited by Richard P. Heitzenrater, pp. 161-80. Nashville: Abingdon, 2002.

"What Should United Methodists Do with the Quadrilateral?" *Quarterly Review* 22 (2002): 85-88.

"On Staying the Course, On Unity, Division and Renewal in the United Methodist Church." In *Ancient and Modern Christianity: Essays in*

Honor of Thomas C. Oden, edited by Kenneth Tanner and Christopher Hall, pp. 170-83. Downers Grove, IL: InterVarsity, 2002.

"The Offense of Divine Revelation," *Harvard Theological Review* 95, no. 3 (2002): 251-264.

"Keith Ward on Religion and Revelation." In *Comparative Theology: Essays for Keith Ward,* edited by T. W. Bartel, pp. 1-11. London: SPCK, 2003.

"Revelation and Natural Theology." In *Alister E. McGrath and Evangelical Theology,* edited by Suun Wook Chung, pp. 264-79. Carlisle: Paternoster, 2003.

"Ecumenism and the Rocky Road to Renewal." In *The Ecumenical Future,* edited by Carl E. Braaten and Robert W. Jenson, pp. 176-87. Grand Rapids: Eerdmans, 2003.

"Afterword," *Didaskalia* 14 (2003): 63-68.

"Saving Souls in the Twenty-first Century: A Missiological Midrash on John Wesley," *Wesleyan Theological Journal* 38, no. 1 (2003): 7-20.

"Loving God with Our Mind," *Zion's Herald* 177, no. 2 (2003): 5-6; 39-44.

"The Future of United Methodism," *Zion's Herald* 177, no. 6 (2003): 17-18.

"Faith, Assurance, and Conviction: An Epistemological Commentary on Hebrews 11:1," *Ex Auditu* 19 (2003): 65-75.

"The End of Wesleyan Theology," *Wesleyan Theological Journal* 40, no. 1 (2005): 7-25.

"Inclusivism, Idolatry, and the Survival of the (Fittest) Faithful." In *The Community of the Word: Toward an Evangelical Ecclesiology,* edited by Mark Husbands and Daniel J. Trier, pp. 131-45. Downers Grove, IL: InterVarsity Press, 2005.

"Education, Social Transformation, and Intellectual Virtue," *Christian Higher Education* 5, no. 1 (2006): 3-19.

"The Existence of God." In *The Oxford Handbook of Systematic Theology,* edited by John Webster, Kathryn Tanner, and Iain Torrance, pp. 19-34. Oxford: Oxford University Press, 2007.

"Introduction," "Canonical Theism: Thirty Theses," "Handing on the Teaching of the Apostles: Canonical Episcopacy," "The Emergence of Canonical Theism," "Canonical Theism and Evangelicalism," "Canonical Theism and the Future of Systematic Theology," and "Canonical Theism and the Life of the Church." In *Canonical Theism,* edited with Jason E. Vickers and Natalie B. Van Kirk. Grand Rapids: Eerdmans, 2008, pp. xii-xix, 1-10, 43-60, 141-55, 256-70, 287-315.

Contributors

Frederick D. Aquino is associate professor of theology and philosophy in the Graduate School of Theology at Abilene Christian University. His recent publications include *Communities of Informed Judgment: Newman's Illative Sense and Accounts of Rationality* (Catholic University of America Press, 2004) and *Unveiling Glory,* coauthored with Jeff Childers (ACU Press, 2004). He has published articles in *Restoration Quarterly, Downside Review, Newman Studies Journal, Christian Higher Education,* and *Louvain Studies.*

Ellen T. Charry is associate professor of theology at Princeton Theological Seminary. She is currently completing *Life Abundant: God and the Art of Happiness* (Eerdmans) and is the author of *Inquiring after God* (Blackwell, 2000) and *By the Renewing of Your Minds* (Oxford University Press, 1997). She is immediate past editor of *Theology Today* and is a general editor for *The Christian Century.* She is the author of numerous essays and articles appearing in journals, encyclopedias, and handbooks of theology.

Paul L. Gavrilyuk is associate professor of historical theology in the department of theology at the University of St. Thomas in St. Paul, Minnesota. His recent publications include two books, *The Suffering of the Impassible God: The Dialectics of Patristic Thought* (Oxford University Press, 2004) and *Histoire du catéchuménat dans l'église ancienne* (Éditions du Cerf, 2007), and articles in the *Journal of Theological Studies, Scottish Journal of Theology, Vigiliae Christianae,* and other scholarly journals.

Douglas M. Koskela is assistant professor of theology at Seattle Pacific University. He is the author of *Ecclesiality and Ecumenism: Yves Congar and the Road to Unity* (Marquette University Press, 2008). He is also the author of a number of articles in scholarly journals.

Sandra Menssen is professor of philosophy and chair of the department of philosophy at the University of St. Thomas in St. Paul, Minnesota. She is past coeditor of *Logos: A Journal of Catholic Thought and Culture,* and coauthor (with Thomas D. Sullivan) of *The Agnostic Inquirer: Revelation from a Philosophical Standpoint* (Eerdmans, 2007). She is the author of numerous articles in the philosophy of religion.

R. R. Reno is professor of theology at Creighton University. His recent publications include *Redemptive Change: Atonement and the Christian Cure of the Soul* (Trinity Press International, 2002), *In the Ruins of the Church* (Brazos, 2002), and *Sanctified Vision: An Introduction to Early Christian Interpretation of the Bible* (Johns Hopkins University Press, 2005), coauthored with John J. O'Keefe. He currently serves as the general editor of the *Brazos Theological Commentary on the Bible* and features editor for the journal *First Things.*

Thomas D. Sullivan is professor of philosophy and Aquinas Chair in Philosophy and Theology at the University of St. Thomas in St. Paul, Minnesota. He is a national award-winning teacher who has published widely in logic, metaphysics, ethics, and the philosophy of religion. His most recent work, coauthored with Sandra Menssen, is *The Agnostic Inquirer: Revelation from a Philosophical Standpoint* (Eerdmans, 2007). His articles on the topic of killing and letting die have been anthologized for over thirty years.

Jason E. Vickers is associate professor of theology and Wesleyan studies at United Theological Seminary, Dayton, Ohio. His books include *Invocation and Assent: The Making and Remaking of Trinitarian Theology* (Eerdmans, 2008), and as coeditor, *Canonical Theism: A Proposal for Theology and the Church* (Eerdmans, 2008) and the forthcoming *Cambridge Companion to John Wesley* (Cambridge).

Geoffrey Wainwright, a minister of the British Methodist Church, is the Cushman Professor of Systematic Theology in the Divinity School of Duke University. He played a leading part in the writing of the "Lima text" of Faith and Order, Baptism, Eucharist and Ministry (1982). Since 1986 he has chaired the World Methodist Council's doctrinal dialogue with the Roman Catholic Church. His latest book is *Embracing Purpose: Essays on God, the World and the Church* (Epworth, 2007).

Robert W. Wall is the Paul T. Walls Professor of Scripture and Wesleyan Studies at Seattle Pacific University. He has authored several books, including *The New Testament as Canon* (with E. E. Lemcio) (Continuum, 1992), *The Community of the Wise: The Letter of James* (Continuum), and *The Acts of the Apostles* in the New Interpreter's Bible Commentary series (Abingdon). He is an editor of the *Library of New Testament Studies* (Continuum) and has published many essays of biblical criticism and theology in journals, dictionaries, Festschriften, and other collections for scholars and clergy.

Jerry L. Walls is professor of philosophy of religion at Asbury Seminary. Among his books are *Hell: The Logic of Damnation* (University of Notre Dame Press, 1992), *Heaven: The Logic of Eternal Joy* (Oxford University Press, 2002), and *The Oxford Handbook of Eschatology* (editor, Oxford University Press, 2008).